PARLIAMENTS AND LEGISLATURES

Janet M. Box-Steffensmeier and David T. Canon, Series Editors

The Presidential Agenda

Sources of Executive Influence in Congress

ROGER T. LAROCCA

THE OHIO STATE UNIVERSITY PRESS
Columbus

Library of Congress Cataloging-in-Publication Data
Larocca, Roger T.
The presidential agenda : sources of executive influence in Congress / Roger T. Larocca.
   p. cm.—(Parliaments and legislatures)
Includes bibliographical references and index.
ISBN 0–8142–1033–3 (cloth : alk. paper)—ISBN 0–8142–9110–4 (cd-rom) 1. Presidents—
United States. 2. Political leadership—United States. 3. Political planning—United States. 4.
Executive power—United States. I. Title. II. Series: Parliaments and legislatures series.
JK516.L254 2006
328.73'07456—dc22
                          2006009444

Cover design by Dan O'Dair.
Text design and typesetting by Jennifer Shoffey Forsythe.
Type set in Times New Roman.
Printed by Thomson-Shore, Inc.

9 8 7 6 5 4 3 2 1

Contents

Illustrations

Figures

Tables

PART I

The Theoretical Problem of Presidential
Agenda Setting in Congress

· 1 ·

An Informational Theory of Presidential Agenda Setting

Introduction

Clinton's Plan for Health Care Reform in the 103rd Congress

In February 1993, President Bill Clinton announced in his first speech before a joint session of Congress that health care reform would be his administration's top priority. Seven months later, in September, Clinton gave a speech before both chambers of Congress calling for a national health insurance program. In the wake of Clinton's September speech, in which he offered a detailed proposal and its potent symbol, the Health Security Card, health care reform dominated the schedules of House legislators more than any single policy issue Congress had faced in more than a decade.

Health care reform was not a new issue. Universal health care legislation had been introduced in the 1930s, 1940s, and 1970s. Michigan Representative John D. Dingell Sr. introduced a national health insurance bill in 1943, and his son, House Commerce Committee chair John D. Dingell Jr., continued to introduce a national health insurance bill in each Congress of his half-century tenure in the House. Despite these tireless efforts by "one of the most powerful and effective committee chairman ever" (Barone, Ujifusa, and Cohen 1997), universal health care legislation never found its way out of Dingell Jr.'s committee in the House, let alone to a floor vote in either chamber (Rovner 1995). Not until a national health care plan became the president's main focus in 1993 did Congress seriously consider it. Largely through his two televised addresses to Congress,

Clinton was able to raise the salience of the health care issue to the point where Congress was impelled to take action. A *Los Angeles Times* poll in June 1993 found that only 9% of survey respondents believed that health care was the "most important problem" facing the country, well behind the percentage who believed that the most important problem was the economy (20%) and also trailing those who mentioned the budget deficit (12%) and unemployment (10%). However, on September 25, only three days after Clinton's address, a similar *Los Angeles Times* poll showed that health care was considered the most important problem by a larger percentage (16%) of survey respondents than any other problem. Clinton had seemingly raised the health care issue to be understood by many as the most important issue facing the country, and Congress responded by scheduling hearings and markups on the issue. Although no health care bill even reached a vote for final passage, Clinton succeeded in dominating the congressional agenda for several months.

Bush's Proposal for Radio Frequency Auctions in the 102nd Congress

In 1991, President George H. W. Bush submitted draft legislation, H.R. 1407, to auction the use of a range of radio transmission frequencies that had been reserved for government use (*CQ Almanac* 1991, 157). Unlike the Clinton health care plan, Bush did not mention radio spectrum auctions in any of his State of the Union addresses. Interest in the auctions was confined largely to industry and economic specialists, and the issue remained unfamiliar to most voters. The House Democratic leadership and the powerful Commerce Committee chair, Dingell Jr., opposed the use of auctions instead of traditional lotteries because of a fear that competition would squeeze out minority-owned and other smaller broadcast companies.[1] In spite of both Democratic opposition and public unfamiliarity, the House Commerce Committee considered spectrum auctions in hearings and the Senate Commerce Committee marked up and reported a bill to the Senate floor that included auctions after Bush submitted his draft legislation.[2]

The argument for the economic efficiency of auctions is complex and would have proven more challenging than Clinton's Health Security Card to explain to the broader public.[3] Economists argued that some entrepreneurs had entered the traditional government lotteries with the sole intent of obtaining licenses and then later selling the licenses privately for a substantial profit, essentially pocketing as private profit what would otherwise have been collected as a public tax. Studies by the National Telecommunications and Information Administration (NTIA) in the Department of Commerce showed that certain types of auctions could reduce the incentives for such profiteering, while delivering more efficient market-like prices for the licenses (e.g., National Telecommunications and Information

4

Administration 1991). Although Reagan and Bush had recommended auctioning the radio spectrum in their budget proposals to previous Congresses, in the 102nd Congress Bush submitted detailed draft legislation to implement the auctions (Allard 1993).[4] Because of the complex and technical nature of spectrum auctions and the lack of public interest in them, it is unlikely that many members of Congress would have come to a full understanding of the benefits of auctions without the expertise provided by the administration's proposal. In fact, once they understood the anticipated effects of auctions, some Democrats began to see that they could be used to add significant revenue for other programs and threw their support behind them. In particular, Dingell Jr., who had actually placed a provision prohibiting spectrum auctions in H.R. 2965 in the 101st Congress, was noted to have "seen the light" and the budgetary advantages of auctions by the end of the 102nd Congress (Mills 1993).

The president's use of executive expertise in the form of draft legislation acts as an alternative mechanism to his major addresses for presidential influence on the congressional agenda and has received far less attention in political science research. Instead of raising public salience, the expertise in the president's draft legislation can provide important new information to members of Congress that can alter their agenda decisions. This expertise is at the president's disposal as the head of the enormous federal bureaucracy and its thousands of policy experts, like those of the NTIA. Through the legislative clearance process, the president has gained control over which departmental proposals are forwarded to Congress as draft legislation, and this has given presidents the opportunity to harness this expertise in order to influence the congressional agenda. In this book, I compare the president's influence on the congressional agenda arising from the policy expertise in his draft legislation (i.e., the legislative clearance process) to the influence arising from the traditionally recognized presidential programming that takes place through his major addresses, and I show that the often-overlooked legislative clearance process frequently offers the president a more persistent and more effective influence on the congressional agenda.

The Puzzle of Presidential Agenda Setting

In the common textbook view, modern presidents are generally understood to be the chief agenda setter in Congress (e.g., Nelson 2002). The president, however, has no formal authority to compel Congress to consider his legislation. Although the Constitution requires the president to report to Congress on the state of the union and to recommend any legislation he finds "necessary and expedient," the Constitution does not require Congress to consider the president's recommendations. The president cannot even introduce a bill in Congress without getting a representative or senator to sponsor it. The only formal legislative power granted to the president by the Constitution, the veto, is exercised at the end of the legislative process, after bills have been passed by both the House and Senate. So how are presidents able to influence the issues that are taken up by Congress at the very beginning of the legislative process? Despite recent scholarly attention to these questions,[5] there is still no convincing argument for why Congress puts aside its own agenda priorities in order to work on the issues considered "necessary and expedient" by the president—particularly when the president and majorities in Congress are from different parties. This book looks for the source of this influence in the modern presidential functions of legislative programming, the promotion of issues in the president's major speeches, and in legislative clearance, the submission of draft bills written by executive agencies to Capitol Hill.

Part I explores the theoretical question of why Congress defers to the president when the president has no formal power over its agenda. My research suggests that the president's agenda-setting influence can arise from two informal powers: (1) the provision of information to voters through public addresses, which influences the way voters evaluate the agenda choices of Congress; and (2) the provision of information to Congress in draft bills from executive agencies regarding the policy consequences of different courses of legislative action. That is, the president is able to set the legislative agenda both because he has a more powerful ability than Congress to communicate information to voters and therefore to inform them of the optimal course of public policy for the nation, as Clinton did on health care policy, and because he has greater control than Congress over the vast policy expertise of executive agencies, like the NTIA expertise Bush employed to promote radio spectrum auctions.

Part II seeks to answer the empirical questions of how, to what extent, and in what stages of the legislative process does the president influence the congressional agenda? A sketch of the main results suggests that the president is able to use public appeals to influence a broad range of issues on the floor stage of agenda setting in the House, but only during the beginning of his term. However, the president is able to use executive policy expertise to influence committee stages (e.g., hearings and markups) in both the House and the Senate agendas throughout his term(s), but only for issues that are technical or relatively noncontroversial.

Defining Agenda Setting

Before developing my informational theory of agenda setting, I must first distinguish the two common meanings for "agenda setting" in the political science literature. Traditionally scholars who claim that the president sets Congress's legislative agenda have meant that he decides the major legislative issues on which Congress works.[6] More recently, formal theorists have defined agenda setting as the process of determining the specific voting order of alternative bills or amendments within a single issue area (Romer and Rosenthal 1978). Though I also take a formal theoretic approach, I return to the traditional definition of agenda control as control over the issues under consideration, rather than control over the voting order of alternative bills on a given issue. By under consideration I mean those issues that are marked up in subcommittee or committee and those that reach the floor. I will also be less concerned with whether the president has influence over what bills ultimately pass than with whether he has influence over which issues Congress considers at these critical stages of the legislative process. This approach represents a departure from studying the effects of an actor with a formal authority to determine the agenda (e.g., Romer and Rosenthal 1978) and toward studying how an actor who has no such formal power still comes to exercise this kind of influence in practice.

Because the president has no specific formal powers over the congressional agenda, the problem of how he is nevertheless able to set the agenda has the potential for broad application to agenda-setting problems beyond those involving the president and Congress. In particular, it applies to situations where an agent has no formal control over an institution's agenda and yet tries to use either outside pressure or expertise to influence the institution's agenda. For example, this basic agenda-setting setup can also be used to model the efforts of interest groups and nongovernmental organizations to use both salience-raising activities and expert policy studies to influence the issues considered by policymaking bodies at the local, national, and international levels.

Theoretical Explanations for Presidential Agenda Setting

My informational theory of presidential agenda setting has been both informed by and developed in response to other influential models of agenda setting, including bounded rationality models and "going-public" models. I will discuss these briefly before presenting my own models.

Bounded Rationality Perspectives on Agenda Setting

The most influential model of congressional agenda setting has been the "garbage can" model that John Kingdon (1984) adapted from the bounded rationality models of organizations of Cohen, March, and Olsen (1972). Kingdon offered the garbage can model as an alternative to the bottom-up models of agenda setting, including rational choice approaches that suggested that agenda items rose to the congressional agenda after they had become salient in the general public. On the contrary, Kingdon finds that some issues, like deregulation, seemed to rise on the agenda without broad public support and with plenty of entrenched opposition. He proposes instead that agenda setting is a mix of three separate processes: problem recognition, solution development, and political opportunity, and—most importantly—that each of these processes operates independently of the others. In other words, government bureaucrats developing policy solutions do not always coordinate their agenda with congressional leaders trying to address policy problems. Moreover, there is also unpredictability in the way these actors come into contact with each other, though they can also be brought together by a policy entrepreneur, who has a unique ability to match solutions with problems. In spite of the actions of policy entrepreneurs, Kingdon argues the agenda-setting process can be disorganized and unpredictable even when all individual actors behave rationally.

Although Kingdon employed the garbage can as an alternative to rational choice explanations, his political entrepreneurs behave similarly to strategic actors modeled by game theorists. These entrepreneurs anticipate conditions and the reactions of others in choosing their own actions to further their goals. It is not clear from Kingdon's model, however, why policy experts and political decision makers in the model do not also behave strategically. In other words, why don't the policy analysts look around for problems to solve, and why don't they anticipate coming problems and try to develop expertise in advance? One could ask a similar question of the political decision makers. Why don't they anticipate coming political conditions and figure out where to find the expertise needed to solve their pressing and future public policy problems? Both of these types of actors seem to behave unusually myopically, especially compared to the policy entrepreneurs.

As an explanation for this myopia, analysts who use the garbage can model and its extensions, like Kingdon (1984), Feldman (1989), and Baumgartner and Jones (1993), point to Herbert Simon's bounded rationality critique of the rational actor model as too demanding of the informational processing capacities of human decision makers (Simon 1982). According to Simon, humans cannot analyze all possible strategies and they cannot even observe all of the information typically modeled in rational choice models. From this perspective, the real difference between Kingdon's entrepreneurs and his other policy actors may be their information-processing capacity. Entrepreneurs may be able to act more strategically because they see more of the "big picture" in a given political situation than any other actor. Although Simon's bounded rationality critique is compelling, it was developed before the advent of incomplete information models (Harsanyi 1973) in game theory, which offer a response to many of the important information limitations of human decision makers that Simon pointed out (Rubinstein 1998). Furthermore, a question remains about why policy entrepreneurs are free from this kind of myopia if bounded rationality is a feature of all human decision makers.

Feldman, in her 1989 study of policy experts, offers another reason why policy experts might look myopic from the perspective of the larger political agenda process. Intentionally or not, Feldman's analysis suggests that much of the seeming myopia of bureaucratic policy analysts may stem from the restrictions of bureaucratic rules and procedures rather than a limitation in the expert's own rational capacity. Her interviews suggest that bureaucrats continue to view their role as solving problems even when that rarely is the end result of their policy reports (Feldman 1989, 114). The frustration that analysts themselves feel when impelled to work in ways that take them away from addressing problems suggests that Kingdon's decoupling of the solution and problem processes may be as much a question of institutional design as of the inherent myopia in policy analysts.[7] Such institutional constraints could also be modeled within a rational choice framework without resort to imposing different levels of bounded rationality on different actors.

The garbage can model is further extended by Bryan D. Jones (1994), who claims that abrupt changes in the salience of issues in U.S. national politics occur because of changes in the issues to which voters give their attention rather than because of changes in voters' actual preferences on those issues. In his model, political elites, like the president, are able to shift the focus of public attention from one issue to another, even if they are able to have little influence over public policy preferences on any given issue. Indeed, Jones shows that aggregate policy preferences are remarkably stable over time, and therefore changing preferences cannot explain more volatile changes in issue salience among the general public.

Jones also claims that voters face an overabundance, rather than a paucity, of information about policy. In his bounded rationality model of political change, a change in the agenda does not come about because of the provision of new information about policy. Instead, political change comes from attention shifts that are not necessarily governed by the laws of rationality. The overabundance of available information results in voters' inability to decide which of this information to use in making their decisions.

Jones sets his model of agenda setting against rational choice models by claiming that attention shifts are governed by the laws of bounded rationality. That is, human beings are limited information processors and are typically only able to process information serially, or one issue at a time. Jones's work, however, mixes elements of rational choice models within a bounded rationality framework. For Jones, once voters are focused on one salient issue area they are able to make policy choices within that issue dimension by the dictates of the spatial models of rational choice. In chapter 3, I present an alternative model of presidential agenda setting which suggests that even shifts in public attentiveness can be understood as a process of rational, albeit imperfect, decision making, and that the president can indeed provide information that influences these shifts.

The chief difference between my approach to agenda setting and garbage can approaches lies in modeling all political actors and voters as potentially strategic agents (i.e., like Kingdon's policy entrepreneurs), who receive messages, whether from the president or mass media, skeptically rather than uncritically. In Jones's model, for instance, voters may care about unemployment simply because it appears repeatedly in the news. A skeptical, rational choice voter, however, would only be concerned about the economy if such messages came from a news program she trusts.

The garbage can models fail to recognize that informational asymmetries can be a source of power if exploited by strategic agents. In the garbage can model, some actors acquire policy information that remains unobserved by others because of built-in human limits on information processing. However, in this model actors do not intentionally acquire such informational asymmetries in order to gain strategic advantages. A rational choice model of the informational asymmetries between policy analysts and policy decision makers can be used to examine whether either side has an interest in acquiring private information in order to exploit the other side's ignorance for its own political advantage.

Gilligan and Krehbiel (1987), for instance, explore how the policy expertise gained by the specialization of congressional committees allows them to get final bills biased in their favor compared to the median voter on the House floor. There is a strategic trade-off whereby the floor gives up some policy concessions to the committee in return for the policy expertise provided by the committee. The part of this that is missed by bounded rationality approaches is that committees actively cultivate informational advantages by specializing in order to gain this influence over the policies that are passed. In chapter 4, I will show that presidents since FDR have strategically cultivated such informational advantages over Congress in order to gain more influence in the policymaking process.

"Going Public" and the Congressional Agenda

Kernell (1993), in a widely influential study, *Going Public: New Strategies of Presidential Leadership,* introduced an alternative model of agenda setting that is more directly aimed at understanding the president's influence on Congress. Kernell argues that modern presidents have been forced to "go public" and lobby legislators indirectly through their constituents because they have lost the ability to bargain with congressional leaders "with promises of goods and services for their constituencies." Instead of such bargaining, "if a large number of votes is needed, the most obvious and direct course is to go on prime-time television to solicit the public's support" (Kernell 1993, 31). Miller (1993) and Canes-Wrone (2001) have brought the "going-public" argument within a more rigorous rational choice framework, arguing that the president's ability to "go public" can lead to his influence over legislative outcomes because the president's speeches can shift the salience of issues and therefore alter the policy preferences of members of Congress. Canes-Wrone (2001) formalizes and enriches this argument in order to explain why the president does not therefore seek to go public on all issues.

Kernell's going-public thesis assumes that the president will be able to stimulate the electorate in the district of the targeted member of Congress (hereafter MC). This either means that he can bring out voters in the district who would not normally vote or that he will provide new information to ordinary voters who will use it to update their beliefs about the ideal policy. Reagan sometimes made such appeals to voters explicit in his televised addresses: "I urge you to contact your Senators and congressmen. Tell them of your support for this bipartisan proposal" (quoted in Kernell 1993, 130). In the case where the president chooses to go public, then, an MC will presumably be forced to alter his legislative behavior to accord with the new ideal policy of the median voter in his district. If the MC does not alter his voting, he might be susceptible to defeat in the next election by a challenger who proposes a policy platform closer to the median constituent's. Gronke, Koch, and Wilson (2003) have recently found evidence that voters' attitudes toward their representatives are indeed shaped by the representative's support for the president. This electoral check provides the going-public thesis with an automatic enforcement mechanism. However, as an agenda-setting technique, going public may be too resource hungry to influence a large number of issues. Kernell (1993), for example, notes that Reagan was refused network television time in 1985 and 1986 after his addresses failed to attract enough viewers. Typically, the president will submit dozens of bills to Congress each session, but it is unlikely that the president can use the going-public strategy for more than a handful of these issues. Instead, Kernell claims, "The president finds the threat to go public frequently more attractive than the act" (Kernell 1993, 37).

There is some internal inconsistency, however, in Kernell's claim that a president's threat to go public is as effective as the act of going public. If the presidential threat is a promise to go public in order to make unresponsive incumbents susceptible to challengers closer to the induced ideal policy, then an MC who goes along with the president thereby insulates himself from such a challenge. However, since the president only threatens to go public in this circumstance, he has not actually induced the threatened changes in the constituency's ideal policy. An MC who responded to the threat by updating his policy is thereby left with a policy that deviates from the unchanged median voter in his district. He has thereby opened himself up for a challenge from a candidate who places himself closer to the median's still-unchanged ideal policy. Because of this, it is never in the interest of an incumbent to respond to the mere threat to go public. Going public is therefore only likely to serve as an agenda-setting tool on a more limited scale, i.e., when the president actually carries out the threat.

Canes-Wrone (2001) produces a more rigorous formalization of Kernell's going-public model and offers an explanation of how the threat to go public may still sometimes be credible. But this model restricts attention to the policy choice on a single issue and does not consider the president's ability to influence which issue is chosen by Congress. Although the choice among policy alternatives on a single issue is the more common meaning of "agenda setting" within the rational choice tradition (Romer and Rosenthal 1978), I seek to explain the more conventional and more fundamental type of agenda setting, the choice of which issues to address.

Like Kernell (1993), Miller (1993), and Canes-Wrone (2001), I adopt a rational choice framework and argue that when the president introduces his agenda items in his public addresses, he is able to raise the salience of issues that hold more potential utility for voters. But I also argue that the president's success in raising the salience of issues is not automatic but depends on his credibility with voters.

An Informational Theory of Agenda Setting

Both the bounded rationality studies and the "going-public" argument present incomplete pictures of the president's agenda-setting influence. Bounded rationality studies fail, for instance, to explain why only policy entrepreneurs seem to act in a strategically rational manner, anticipating the actions and reactions of other actors. It is not clear, for instance, why voters would not be strategic in responding to agenda-setting attempts by the president or the media. The going-public models fail to fully explain how the mere threat to go public can provide the president with influence over the choice of which issues Congress considers. I develop alternative models in which the president is able to influence the issues on the congressional agenda both by providing information to voters that is helpful in evaluating legislative behavior and by controlling information that is useful to Congress in its policymaking decisions. By providing information to voters through public addresses, the president is able to influence the way voters evaluate congressional behavior. By controlling the information of the federal bureaucracy through draft bills submitted to Congress, the president is able to provide expertise about policy consequences of different courses of legislative action and thus influence the issues Congress chooses to work on.

Avenues of Influence

Public addresses include those issues the president identifies as significant enough to include as a part of his legislative program (Cohen 1997; Rudalevige

2002). Issues in executive draft legislation, by contrast, commonly include the issues that must be dealt with as a matter of course in the functioning and adapting of government as well as technical policy innovations proposed by executive departments (Neustadt 1954; Wayne 1978). Issues in the president's public addresses are handled differently from legislative clearance issues because they are more important to the president and are often more contentious.

Public Addresses

When the president is referred to as the foremost agenda-setting influence in Congress, this is usually a claim about the issues raised by the president in his State of the Union addresses or in other key speeches, not by the many technical draft bills that are passed through the White House to Congress without public notice. Although elements of the president's public program are also submitted to Congress in the form of draft legislation, high profile presidential agenda items are primarily promoted through public addresses. Barbara Sinclair's (1995) assessment of Congress's ability to set its own agenda suggests what type of effect the president's speeches might be intended to have: "Agenda setting can be pursued through in-house activities intended to influence the legislative process directly and through external activities aimed at favorably shaping the environment in which legislative decision making takes place" (274–75). If the congressional leadership exercises agenda influence through direct control over the legislative process, then the president, who has little direct control, might exercise agenda influence by favorably shaping the public environment, e.g., influencing the expectations of voters with regard to legislative action. Therefore, the public nature of the president's program is a key part of its influence, because by providing information to voters about the best course of legislative action, the president can influence the way voters evaluate the actions of their members of Congress.

Kernell (1993, 25) claims that the president can use public addresses to ensure passage of his proposals by Congress. Although this claim may overestimate the president's influence because it essentially assumes the voters are automatically responsive to the president's message, it is quite likely that by going public the president can inform voters of the urgency of policy issues he is addressing. To the extent that the voters agree with the president about which policies are pressing concerns, MCs seeking reelection have a greater incentive to consider the president's policy issues, if not his particular proposals on these issues.

It is true that voters are sometimes ill-informed to make voting decisions during congressional elections because they observe the consequences of legislative action only over time and are therefore unsure of whether or not their representatives are making good policy decisions. It was difficult, for example, for voters to determine whether the Medicare catastrophic illness coverage would improve health care at the time it was being considered in 1987 and 1988. It became very clear by 1989, however, that many voters regarded it as unnecessary or bad policy, and it was repealed before the 1990 midterm elections (Himelfarb 1995).

Nonetheless, the president can play a role in informing the voter through his public addresses.[8] Cohen (1997) and Iyengar and Kinder (1987) have shown that the president can have a significant effect on which issues voters consider important. Recent studies (Cover 1985; Simon, Ostrom, and Marra 1991; Atkeson and Partin 1995; Gronke, Koch, and Wilson 2003) have also shown that the voters' views of the president can affect their congressional vote. Attention to the president's agenda thus arises naturally among MCs concerned with reelection.

I develop a formal model in chapter 3 in which the president serves as an agent for voters by providing them information, e.g., issue priorities that voters can then use to evaluate legislative behavior. I argue that the information the president provides to voters can indeed affect the electoral fate of MCs. In chapter 3, I will show that the president can influence the congressional agenda in this way even when he is able to convey only very coarse (i.e., imperfect) information to the voters. Finally, the formal model in chapter 3 suggests that in equilibrium with presidential agenda setting, Congress chooses legislative actions more in accord with national interests than it would choose in the absence of the president's monitoring role. This occurs simply because the president's issues are driven by his national constituency, whereas MCs would otherwise be inclined to turn to the more parochial interests of their individual constituencies.

My proposed model of this presidential influence in the public addresses model can be broken down into five steps:

1. The president observes private information about the most important policy issue for the nation.
2. The president announces to the public and Congress a request for legislation on this issue.
3. Congress hears the presidential message and decides whether to continue with its own priority issue or to work on the issue identified by the president.
4. Voters observe the policy issues considered by Congress and decide whether to reelect their MCs in the midterm election.
5. Voters observe their benefits (in hindsight) from policies proposed by the president and enacted by the first Congress and decide whether to reelect the president.

Again, my concern is with the president's ability to influence the issues considered by Congress rather than the exact policy outcome on these issues. It turns out, however, that these concerns are intertwined. Both the choice of policy issue by Congress and the message sent to voters by the president depend on the policy outcomes that can be passed on each issue. Nevertheless, the concern of the voters in this model is over which issue is made a legislative priority, because I assume that the voters cannot fully observe the benefits and problems of specific policies except in hindsight. The predictions of this model are tested on detailed, issue-level data on legislative activity in Congress in chapters 6 and 7.

Legislative Clearance

The president also exercises informal influence on the congressional agenda through a process called legislative clearance, whereby the White House sifts through legislative proposals of the federal agencies and departments, withholds those which are unimportant or objectionable to the president's policy goals, and sends to Congress proposals that further White House objectives.

Through the legislative clearance process, created by FDR, the White House reviews all of these agency-drafted bills in the White House before they are forwarded to Congress to ensure that the proposals are consistent with White House goals. The clearance process thus allows the White House to control the policy expertise that is relayed from the executive agencies to congressional committees (Wayne 1978). Executive proposals that are approved by the legislative clearance process are sent on to Congress as draft legislation. These proposals incorporate the specialized information acquired by the agency or department. This information is useful to Congress in making its agenda choices, i.e., in its choice of which issue to consider. In chapter 4, I model the process by which the president can use policy expertise he channels from the bureaucracy to influence the congressional agenda.

My model accounts for the fact that Congress understands that the president's policy goals are often different from its own, and observes that the information presented in the draft legislation will be biased in the direction of the president's or executive agency's preferred policy ends. If the president and Congress have identical policy goals, the president's draft legislation can perfectly reveal the executive's policy expertise about the consequences of the bill (Crawford and Sobel 1982). With divergent policy preferences, however, Congress will not know how much of the bill is informative about the likely policy consequences of the legislation and how much is biased by the president's preferences. In these cases, Congress will not be able to fully trust the administration bill as a reliable means of achieving Congress's goals. In response, Congress may hold hearings and markup on bills submitted by executive agencies rather than reporting them directly to the floor, in order to acquire further information about the topics of these bills.

When Congress holds hearings and markup sessions for issues submitted by the president, it can research and amend the legislation it is considering to counterbalance some of the bias in any executive-authored draft. In particular, it may call in executive branch officials and outside experts who are well informed on the issue. Despite these alternative sources of policy expertise, the president's draft legislation may serve an informative role. For example, at the beginning of this chapter, I described how George H. W. Bush was able to use technical expertise in draft bills from the NTIA to put radio spectrum auctions on the agenda of the 102nd Congress. Though there are alternative sources of information, Congress has limited resources and cannot explore the consequences of all possible pieces of legislation. In choosing agenda items, Congress must estimate both the policy preferences of its constituents on an issue and the likely policy consequences of enacting a bill on that issue. The president's drafts will be informative of the likely policy consequences of legislation on an issue, since draft legislation incorporates the expertise of the executive agencies. In the 102nd Congress, MCs began to see the unanticipated benefits of radio spectrum auctions after the submission of Bush's draft bills and the issue was given serious consideration on the congressional agenda, particularly in the Senate. Congress must weigh its more certain understanding of the consequences of the president's issues against the uncertain consequences of working on another issue that is uninformed by such expertise. Since the information contained in the president's draft legislation can be somewhat informative as long as presidential and congressional policy preferences are not too far apart (Crawford and Sobel 1982), the president's submission of draft legislation may have a significant positive effect on the probability that an issue reaches the congressional agenda or beyond.

Information the president provides to Congress can thus shape the value Congress places on different courses of legislative action, because it can reduce the risks involved in taking action on an issue on which Congress was not previously well informed. In chapter 4, I develop a formal model of legislative clearance which generalizes the basic one-dimensional Gilligan and Krehbiel (1987) model of congressional delegation to the multidimensional context of presidential agenda setting. I will show that the president can exercise agenda-setting influence through the legislative clearance process, but that this influence can only be effective on issues where the president either holds a large advantage in expertise, like spectrum auctions, or where the president's preferences are similar to Congress's. Legislative clearance is thus expected to be most influential either on issues that are noncontroversial, generating little disagreement between Congress and the president, or on highly technical issues where the amount of the federal bureaucracy's private information or policy expertise might be quite extensive relative to the difference in policy preferences between the president and Congress.

Since the agenda setting that occurs through the expertise in executive draft legislation is expected to be most effective on noncontroversial or technical issues, it may have its greatest impact on that part of the congressional workload that involves matters of continuing concern or issues arising from previous legislative enactments, rather than on bold new policy initiatives where the president may be as uncertain as Congress. For example, large and complex laws, like the Social Security Act and the Clean Air Act, require constant updating by minor and sometimes major legislative amendments that draw little public attention and are often highly technical. Many of these amendments originate as draft bills in the legislative clearance process where the president can decide which ones to forward to Congress and which to hold back. Since this kind of influence is expected to persist throughout the president's term, and since the "continuing agenda" makes up a large and growing part of the legislative agenda (C. Jones 1994), I argue that the president may ultimately exercise a greater overall influence on public policy through the persistent influence of his draft legislation on this continuing agenda rather than through setting the agenda for a handful of major legislative initiatives.

My proposed model of the legislative clearance process can be broken down into three steps:

1. The president observes the policy expertise gathered by an executive agency on a given policy issue.
2. The president decides whether to submit a draft bill that contains executive expertise on the issue.
3. Congress decides whether to act on its own priority issue with uncertainty about policy outcomes or on the president's issue with more certainty about the final policy outcome.

This model looks like an adaptation of the standard Gilligan and Krehbiel (1987) setup for modeling the informational role of committees in the lawmaking process, but there are two important differences: the model involves the choice among multiple issues, i.e., agenda setting, as well as the choice of policy on one of these issues; and here it is the president who provides policy information, though he enjoys neither the proposal power nor the amendment power that is shared by congressional committees. The equilibrium solution to this model is presented in chapter 4, and it suggests that presidents can indeed harness such expertise to influence the issues under consideration but only under the conditions stated above: for issues that are either highly technical or noncontroversial. These predictions are tested on new issue-level data in chapters 6 and 7.

A New Issue-Level Analysis of Presidential Agenda Setting

Previous studies of presidential agenda setting have analyzed the president's influence on enactments (Chamberlain 1946; Moe and Teel 1970; Goldsmith 1983; C. Jones 1994), proposals (Light 1991; Peterson 1990), bills (Edwards and Barrett 2000; Edwards, Barrett, and Peake 1997; Taylor 1998; Theriault 2002), and hearings (Edwards and Wood 1999; Flemming, Wood, and Bohte 1999). Aside from Light (1991) and Peterson (1990), none of these studies has been conducted at the level of analysis, policy issues, that is most appropriate for studying agenda setting. Issues provide a more suitable unit of analysis for examining agenda setting than bills because many bills cover the same issue and are substitute solutions for the same problem. A hearing on a single policy issue may involve half a dozen bills. And many bills are laid on the table at some stage of the legislative process in favor of a substitute on the same issue that advances further on the agenda. In this case, the issue advances on the agenda, but it is not apparent from looking at the original bill. Furthermore, many bills cover a multitude of issues, some of which may advance further and others which may stall.

Conducting analysis of the congressional agenda at the level of issues instead of bills provides a more accurate understanding of the agenda process, but issues are not as easy to analyze as bills because they are harder to identify and distinguish. As I explain in chapter 5, I employ relational database techniques to exploit the multidimensional nature of most bills and to construct a database of congressional activity with issues as the unit of analysis. This new relational database of congressional issue consideration allows me to directly study the issues as well as the bills on the congressional agenda, while still controlling for the valuable contextual variables associated with individual bills, like the number of sponsors, the main sponsor's ideology, and whether the bill is multiply referred, and many others. What results is a completely new dataset on the legislative activities and characteristics of issues rather than bills, and it provides penetrating insight into the nature of the congressional agenda process.

I explore the implications of my informational models of presidential agenda setting with new highly detailed data on the legislative actions on all bills referred to the House and Senate Commerce Committees over twelve Congresses (1979–2002). My data probe into the inner workings of committees and subcommittees and allow me to construct an unprecedented and detailed examination of the forces shaping each stage of the agenda process from committee consideration to the floor in both the House and the Senate.

I also take into account the roles of important actors who are sometimes neglected in studies of presidential and congressional agenda setting and law making, like committee leaders and the Senate. And I analyze the effect of influential stages of the legislative agenda process that are sometimes overlooked, such as "requests for executive comment" and floor consideration under "suspension of the rules."

Finally, I use path-analytic statistical techniques to pinpoint the president's direct effect on each distinct stage of the agenda process, as well as the indirect effects he exercises on these stages through his influence on other actors such as committee chairs and the other chamber. This means that I can separate the president's direct influence on each agenda stage from any indirect influence that he exercises by working through important committee leaders or from the indirect influence he exercises in one chamber by setting the agenda of the other chamber.

Altogether, I construct a detailed and complex portrait of the president's influence on the congressional agenda, including the methods of influence that are effective, what kinds of issues these methods influence, what stages of the agenda process the president influences, and at what points in his presidency these influences are effective.

Plan of the Book

As the subsequent chapters will demonstrate, much of the president's influence over the congressional agenda arises from the role he plays in acquiring and providing information about the optimal direction of national public policy both to voters and to Congress.

Chapter 2 introduces the conceptual and technical tools of rational choice methodology that will be used to model the president's agenda-setting influence. In particular, I introduce a two-dimensional spatial model that provides a very general representation of the problem of issue-level agenda setting. Chapter 3, "Public Addresses and the Legislative Programming Process," develops a formal model of the president's agenda-setting influence that arises from providing the voters with information about the most urgent policy issues facing the country. The president can exercise influence through this process even when the policy preferences of the president and Congress are opposed, but this influence is expected to disappear after the president's first Congress.

Chapter 4, "Draft Bills and the Legislative Clearance Process," develops a formal model of the presidential agenda-setting influence that arises from executive policy expertise. Executive policy expertise lends the president influence over the congressional agenda only when the executive has a large advantage in expertise or when the president and Congress share somewhat similar policy preferences, but the president can exercise this power throughout his term. Chapter 5, "Redefining Congressional Agenda Setting," discusses the inadequacies of studying bills to understand agenda setting and describes the advantages and disadvantages of the novel approach of studying the congressional agenda at the level of policy issues. Chapter 5 also describes the complex legislative process and the difficulty of determining when an issue is "on the agenda." I analyze issue-level data to identify the three most important agenda stages in the agenda process in the House: hearings, markup, and floor. Chapter 6, "Presidential Agenda Setting in the House," presents tests of the predictions of the formal models presented in chapters 3 and 4 using new data on the pre-floor action on all issues referred in the House Energy and Commerce Committee from 1979 through 2002. Chapter 7, "Presidential Agenda Setting in the Senate," presents a model of the role of the Senate in presidential agenda setting and tests the predictions of this model using new data on the pre-floor action on all issues referred in the Senate Commerce Committee from 1979 through 2002. Chapter 8, "Information and Presidential Agenda Setting," reviews the findings of the book, considers extensions of the argument, and discusses the political implications of the president's agenda-setting power.

· 2 ·

Game Theory and Presidential Agenda Setting

As the government shifted portions of the radio-broadcasting spectrum from military to commercial use in the late 1980s, the increasing value of the radio spectrum led economists to question the government's policy of using a lottery to provide exclusive licenses nearly free of cost. In return for free use of the spectrum, broadcasters were expected to provide emergency broadcasting and other public services, but some license recipients who had acquired licenses then sold them at a high profit (Mills 1990). When the George H. W. Bush administration offered a draft bill proposing that the Federal Communications Commission implement a sophisticated method of auctioning these spectrum licenses in order to introduce market mechanisms for their distribution, the Democratic leadership in the 102nd Congress complained that this would price the spectrum out of the reach of minority broadcasters and others who received licenses for a nominal fee in the lottery. In face of both Democratic opposition and public unfamiliarity with the issue, both the House and Senate still devoted a share of their crowded agendas to Bush's spectrum auctions. The House Commerce Committee considered spectrum auctions in hearings and the Senate Commerce Committee marked up and reported a bill to the Senate floor that included auctions after Bush submitted his draft legislation proposing auctions. In this chapter, I will use the spectrum auction issue in the 102nd Congress to illustrate a simple game-theoretic model of the agenda-setting process that I will then elaborate in chapters 3 and 4 in order to explore the president's influence on the agenda.

First, I use the example of spectrum auctions in the 102nd Congress to introduce spatial models and the median voter theorem, a fundamental result that greatly simplifies modeling the policymaking process. I then generalize the basic one-dimensional spatial model to a two-dimensional model in order to provide a general characterization of the agenda-setting process. This basic agenda-setting model has the potential for broad application to agenda-setting problems beyond those involving the president and Congress. In particular, it applies to situations where an agent has no formal control over an institution's agenda and yet tries to use either outside pressure or expertise to influence the institution's agenda. For example, this basic agenda-setting setup can also be used to model the efforts of interest groups and nongovernmental organizations to influence the issues considered by policymaking bodies at the local, national, and international levels. I develop this basic agenda-setting model to illustrate how the president's sole formal legislative power, the veto, offers very limited influence in congressional agenda setting. This is in marked contrast to policy making on a single issue, where the veto is understood to wield considerable influence (e.g., Cameron 2000). In the next two chapters, I apply the general agenda-setting model to the processes of presidential programming (public addresses) and legislative clearance (draft bills), and I derive the conditions under which these processes can yield influence on the congressional agenda.

Issue-Level and Bill-Level Agenda Setting

For political scientists, "agenda setting" can refer to two very different processes: (1) determining the voting order among alternative bills; or (2) determining the issues under active consideration. As an example of the first, bill-level type of agenda setting, consider the spectrum allocation bills introduced in the 102nd Congress, including the administration proposal for auctions, H.R. 1407, sponsored by Rep. Don Ritter; and the Democratic proposal, H.R. 531, which proposed traditional lotteries to allocate the spectrum. Amendments were also suggested that would add user fees to the licenses and that would tax the total revenue from use of the spectrum. As represented in figure 2.1, these proposals can be arranged from lowest to highest on a single dimension according to the

FIGURE 2.1 Spatial representation of policies on spectrum allocation in 102nd Congress

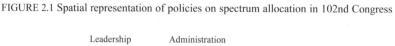
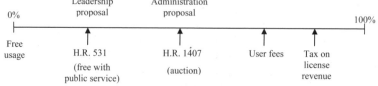

amount that is charged for use of the spectrum: lotteries, auctions, user fees, and taxes on total revenue.

After bills are reported or discharged from committee, the House Rules Committee can report "special rules" that govern the order in which these alternative bills and amendments will be voted—if the special rule is adopted by the House. An actor, like the House Rules Committee, which has the ability to determine the voting order of such alternatives is denoted a "monopoly agenda setter" in this literature, and the effects of such control are known to be potentially extensive (Romer and Rosenthal 1978). The most powerful influence arises from the use of modified or closed rules that prohibit some or all amendments from being considered at all. In the extreme case, a monopoly agenda setter can offer take-it-or-leave-it offers to those making policy decisions. Committee chairs can also act as monopoly agenda setters in scheduling bills for hearings and markup.

Rather than looking at this monopoly agenda-setting power, however, I focus on the informal power to influence the issues under consideration. This issue-level, agenda-setting power has received less attention in formal analysis, but I argue that it can often be more important for policy outcomes than direct control over the voting order among alternative bills (bill-level agenda setting). For example, in the 102nd Congress, there were many issues of potential importance for the Democratic majority that did not reach committee or floor consideration. The question for issue-level agenda setting is what influences led to the consideration of radio spectrum auctions rather than many other possible issue priorities that never received consideration by the committee or floor. It is thus a question of the broader issues under consideration rather than just the alternative bills under consideration on a given issue. In this chapter, I provide a formal way of modeling such issue-level agenda decisions.

For the study of presidential agenda setting in Congress, only the broader issue-level agenda setting is relevant, because the president has no formal authority to schedule the voting order of bills in Congress. In fact, the president cannot even introduce a bill into Congress without a member of Congress sponsoring his legislation. Furthermore, whereas the bill-level agenda setting is usually exercised as an explicit formal power, e.g., in the power of the Rules Committee to report rules that structure the voting on bills and amendments, issue-level agenda setting is usually exercised through the president's informal powers, like persuasion and bargaining. The president's sole formal legislative power, the veto, is exercised at the end of the legislative process. The veto can therefore influence the agenda setting that occurs at the beginning of the legislative process only indirectly, e.g., in the form of a threat. A veto threat may persuade Congress not to work on a given issue, but the threat does not allow the president to determine what issue Congress will turn to instead.

Since the president has no direct formal powers over the legislative agenda, the problem I study is quite general. For example, the agenda-setting model I develop may help explain how legislatures, committees, and other organizations come to be led or influenced by certain members inside or outside of the organization who have no formal leadership role in the organization. How does an agent who has little or no formal power over a group of decision makers nevertheless come to exercise informal influence over the set of issues that will be considered by these decision makers? In this chapter, I develop a formal model to represent this canonical issue-level, agenda-setting problem. In the next two chapters, I will explore the source and extent of these informal powers in the context of the president's influence over the congressional agenda.

First, I introduce the median voter theorem, a fundamental result that permits a legislature to be modeled as a single agent under some rather general conditions. Then I propose a two-issue model of agenda setting that captures a wide range of political processes. In the next two chapters, I use this basic agenda-setting model to formally explore the impact of the president's legislative programming and clearance powers on the congressional agenda.

The Median Voter Theorem

The median voter theorem is a fundamental building block of many game-theoretic models of policy making, including the two models I construct in chapters 3 and 4. In many cases it greatly simplifies the analysis of complex and otherwise intractable strategic situations. In the discussion that follows and throughout the rest of the book, I make a formal distinction between an issue and a policy or bill. By an issue I mean a whole spectrum of possible policy solutions to a given problem. For example, the problem of radio frequency allocations may suggest a spectrum of legislative remedies, each of which can be represented by a separate bill. A spatial model assumes that each issue can be represented by an infinite variety of legislative responses that can be arrayed along a single line in some sensible ordering. In figure 2.1, I order several of the proposed spectrum allocation solutions from the 102nd Congress in order from less to more taxation from left to right.

Ordering all policies on a single-issue dimension allows the assignment of a unique numerical measure to each policy and more importantly the ability to measure the policy distance between the bills so that the utility of different policies can be measured as a function of the policy's distance from an actor's ideal policy. I assume that each of the policy alternatives yields spectrum prices that range from 0% to 100% of the revenue value of the license. The utility function, u_c, of the median legislator in the House then can be represented as the negative-squared distance between his ideal point, c, and the enacted policy, b. This means that the median's utility is maximized at his ideal policy, c, where it is equal to 0, i.e., $u_c(c) = 0$. Squared distance is typically used to measure disutility because this leads to a symmetric "single-peaked" utility function where policies the same distance to the left or to the right of the voter's ideal point are equally distasteful.

Technically, the negative quadratic utility functions and one-dimensional issue space imply a complete and transitive ordering of the median legislator's preferences over all possible policy outcomes. Complete preferences occur when an actor is able to compare all possible policy alternatives on the issue and indicate either that she prefers one or the other or finds them equivalent. Transitive preferences imply that whenever, for instance, an actor prefers H.R. 531 to H.R. 1407 and prefers H.R. 1407 to user fees, then she must prefer H.R. 531 to user fees. Preference orderings that are both complete and transitive constitute a minimum condition for game-theoretic modeling. Without such "coherent" preferences, agents cannot necessarily be considered rational because they make inconsistent choices. Rational agents are thus defined simply as decision makers with coherent preferences who choose actions that they believe will lead to outcomes they prefer.

If a group of legislators has single-peaked utility functions on a single-dimensional policy issue, then the median voter theorem insures that the ideal policy of the median legislator will defeat any alternative policy in pairwise voting (Downs 1957). The median legislator's policy can defeat any alternative because the median is the middle legislator. Thus, if someone proposed a policy to the left of the median's ideal policy, the half of the legislators located to the right of the median would prefer to vote for the median's policy. And if someone proposed moving policy to the right of the median, then the majority of legislators to the left would prefer to vote for the median's position. Thus, a majoritarian legislature like the House is often represented in models simply by its median legislator, who is assumed to propose and pass his ideal policy on each issue under consideration.[1] I make use of this simplification in this chapter and in the next two chapters, but I will consider a generalization of this median voter model in chapter 7 on the Senate, which—because of the filibuster—does not seem to act as a majoritarian institution (e.g., Brady and Volden 1997; Krehbiel 1998).

A General Model of Policy Making

The basic model of the issues considered in agenda setting throughout the book is represented in figure 2.2. While a large number of issues may be considered by any Congress, I argue that the basic process involved in issue-level agenda setting can be captured using a model with just two issues (dimensions). For example, in figure 2.2 Congress faces the issues of acid rain and radio frequency auctions. Without loss of generality, the prevailing policy, or status quo, is located at 0 on both issues. Since utility is measured as negative-squared distance, the president has more potential utility to gain from policy change on issue two, where his ideal policy p_2 is far from the status quo, than from policy change on issue 1, where his ideal policy p_1 is already close to the status quo. Congress has more potential utility to gain on issue 1, where its ideal point c_1 is further from the status quo. An agenda-setting problem in this model arises only when Congress and the president are limited to changing policy on only one issue. If Congress could work on all possible issues, it would not have to face a choice of which issues to put on the agenda and which to leave off. While Congress certainly works on more than one issue per session, this abstraction is intended to capture the fact that each Congress is restricted by time and resources in the number of issues it can consider. Thus, each Congress must make agenda choices that force it to ignore some issues it may regard as important.

I first consider a general policymaking game where (1) the president signals to Congress his desired agenda issue, through either a policy proposal on this issue or a veto threat against the other issue; (2) Congress then chooses an issue and passes a bill on the chosen issue that may or may not be different from the status quo; and (3) the president signs or vetoes the bill. Here I examine the conditions under which the president's veto power can lead to influence over the issue chosen by Congress. In the next two chapters I examine the president's informal influences over the agenda using the same two-issue model. Formal development of the game proceeds as follows: First, I propose utility functions that reflect the policy preferences of the president and the median legislator (making use of the median voter theorem to represent the legislature by its median member). I

FIGURE 2.2 Spatial representation of ideal points on two issue dimensions

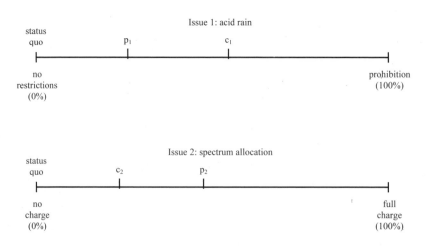

consider only one legislative chamber in this game as well as in chapters 3 and 4, but I bring in bicameral concerns in chapter 7. Then, I specify the choices that are available to the president and Congress and the order in which they occur. Next, I define a strategy for each player and propose an equilibrium solution concept that will be used to solve the game. Finally, I specify a set of strategies that satisfies this solution concept. These equilibrium strategies provide the model's predictions about presidential and congressional policymaking behavior.

Utility, u_i, for each actor i is calculated as the sum of the negative squared distance from the actor's ideal point to the enacted policy. Let $i = p$ for the president and $i = c$ for Congress, so that the total utility u_i for a policy $\{x_1, x_2\}$ is:

$$u_p = -(p_1 - x_1)^2 - (p_2 - x_2)^2$$
$$u_c = -(c_1 - x_1)^2 - (c_2 - x_2)^2$$

A utility function serves essentially as an abstract model of an actor's preferences in the policymaking game. As such, it serves as a guide in determining the actor's optimal strategy given the choices available to him and the strategies of the other actor. By specifying each actor's utility as a simple sum of the negative-squared distances on both issues, I am assuming that the actor's preferences across these issues are additively separable. This means that the policy enacted on one issue has no bearing on the actor's preferences on the other issue. This abstraction is likely to fail whenever issues are related in some way, such as through balanced-budget constraints. For example, the more money spent in one policy area may reduce an actor's assessment of the ideal amount to be spent in other areas. Unfortunately, consideration of such issue nonseparability within formal models leads to complex games, which do not yield general solutions. In the simple models of agenda setting that I consider, I thus assume that the two issues under consideration are additively separable, while recognizing that this assumption may fail in some cases.[2]

The basic agenda-setting game begins with the president's choice of issue 1 or 2. The president sends a message to Congress indicating which issue he would prefer Congress to address. In practice, this message may take the form of a mention in his State of the Union address, draft legislation submitted to Congress, or even a veto threat. Next, Congress chooses to consider either issue 1 or 2 and then chooses a policy on the chosen issue. Finally, the president either signs or vetoes this bill. The president and Congress then realize their net utility from the chosen issue and policy.

A strategy for the president in the policymaking game consists of both a choice of issue to signal and a sign/veto decision for each possible bill Congress may pass. Congress's strategy specifies an issue and policy for each message that the president may send. This strategic situation requires a "dynamic" rather than a "simultaneous-move" game, because Congress acts after observing the president's message choice, and the president signs or vetoes after observing Congress's policy choice. Dynamic games with no hidden information are commonly solved using an equilibrium solution concept known as "subgame perfect" equilibrium. Subgame perfection is a refinement of Nash equilibrium that requires that the actors' strategies form a Nash equilibrium in each subgame. A pair of strategies form a Nash equilibrium whenever neither actor can improve his utility by unilaterally changing to a different strategy. In other words, both actors choose strategies that are optimal given the other actor's strategy. In this way, a Nash equilibrium is meant to represent behavior that is self-reinforcing, i.e., in equilibrium. A subgame consists of both an actor's decision at some point in the game and all possible subsequent decisions of all actors. In the agenda-setting game, there are an infinite number of subgames because Congress can pass any law on the two policy dimensions. All of the possible sign/veto decisions that the president may face for each possible congressional bill form separate subgames. In addition, all actors with moves in a given subgame already know all of the actions that have occurred before that subgame is reached in the game. Subgame perfection thus requires that actors with choices in subgames will not want to change their Nash equilibrium strategy after seeing what the other actor has already done. Subgame perfection therefore eliminates the possibility of an equilibrium that includes a strategy supported by an incredible threat, like the presidential threat of vetoing a policy that he actually prefers to the status quo. The subgame perfect equilibrium concept simply specifies that if the president is going to hurt himself more by carrying out this veto threat than by signing it, then it is not rational for him to carry it out if Congress does pass such a bill. If Congress is aware that the president will hurt himself by carrying out the veto threat, then it can ignore such veto threats as bluffs and force the president's hand. One of the advantages of adopting subgame perfect as the solution concept is that solutions that are supported by such incredible threats are ruled out, even though they may form a Nash equilibrium in the overall game. In the next two chapters I will utilize a further refinement of Nash equilibrium, perfect Bayesian equilibrium, which insures that actors update their beliefs rationally about hidden information that they do not fully observe.

Subgame perfect equilibria are often solved by backwards induction, where one determines the optimal strategies in the terminal subgames of the game and then solves progressively earlier stages based on knowledge of how that game is expected to play out in later stages. Thus, in the last move of the game the president's sign/veto strategy must constitute a Nash equilibrium; i.e., it must be the president's best response to the policy passed by Congress. Thus, the president signs an acid rain bill, $b = \{x_1, 0\}$, if it is closer to his ideal acid rain policy than the status quo on that issue, $0 < x_1 \leq 2p_1$. The president also signs a spectrum auction bill, $b = \{0, x_2\}$, if it is closer to his ideal spectrum auction policy than the status quo on that issue, $0 < x_2 < 2p_2$. This means that the president will sign any bill that he prefers to the status quo, even if he threatened to veto such a bill.[3] In figure 2.3, I illustrate the policies vetoed by the president on the air pollution and spectrum auction issues with crosshatched intervals.

Given that the president will sign any bill that he prefers to the status quo, we can proceed with backwards induction to determine Congress's optimal issue and policy choice. As long as the agenda-setting conditions, $c_1 > c_2$ and $p_1 < p_2$, hold, Congress prefers to enact its ideal policy c_1 on the acid rain issue, and the president prefers to change policy on the spectrum auction issue. Since the president's veto strategy dictates when Congress can successfully enact his bill, the equilibrium strategy of Congress is to choose its ideal acid rain policy, $b = \{c_1, 0\}$, whenever this is acceptable to the president, $0 < c_1 \le 2p_1$. As illustrated in figure 2.3, if $c_1 > 2p_1$ the president would veto c_1, and Congress, anticipating this, would instead pass a more moderate acid rain bill, $b = \{2p_1, 0\}$, if this bill offers it more utility than its best possible bill on spectrum auctions. If $c_2 > c_1$, Congress chooses its ideal policy on the spectrum auction issue, $b = \{0, c_2\}$, as long as the president will not veto it. If $c_2 > 2p_2$, the president would veto c_2, so Congress adjusts its policy to the policy closest to its ideal point that is still acceptable to the president, i.e., $b = \{0, 2p_2\}$, if this is better than the best policy it can obtain on acid rain. Notice that Congress's optimal decision does not depend at all on the president's signal but only on his veto strategy. This occurs because Congress can determine when the president will or will not veto a bill from his sign/veto strategy, which it can deduce from the president's ideal policies on both issues. A different dynamic would arise if Congress did not know the president's exact ideal policy, in which case the veto may play a broader role.

FIGURE 2.3 Example of policy effects of veto in subgame perfect equilibrium

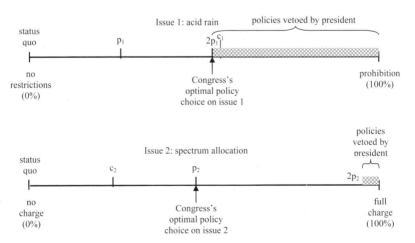

29

Proceeding with backwards induction, the president's message strategy must be optimal given Congress's policy strategy. However, since Congress's policy choice does not depend at all on the president's message, the president can send any message in equilibrium. Such messages, whether they are veto threats or policy proposals, will have no influence on the congressional agenda in this simple policymaking model. Thus, in the general policymaking game, there is not a unique subgame perfect equilibrium because the president's messages can be ignored with impunity by Congress, and therefore it does not matter what the president says in his messages. The president's messages, by themselves, have no credible agenda-setting influence in this model.

The president's veto has a very limited agenda-setting role because Congress can often modify its policy on its own preferred issue so that it is acceptable to the president rather than changing to the president's preferred issue. For example, in the example given in figure 2.3, although Congress is not able to enact its ideal policy on issue 1, c_1, it is able to find a policy acceptable to the president, $2p_1$, that it prefers to any policy on issue two. The veto does, however, prohibit Congress from enacting extreme policies, $x_i > 2p_i$, on either issue. In the models of presidential agenda setting in chapters 3 and 4, I explore how the president's influence over the agenda can arise from other informal influences. In particular, the president's messages become influential when they contain private information held by the president that is transmitted to either Congress or voters and that may alter their policy or voting decisions. In these cases, what the president says in his message may indeed matter.

The solution of this simple agenda-setting model suggests that the veto has very limited agenda-setting influence in Congress. If Congress knows the president's range of acceptable policies, the veto can only be used to prevent the enactment of policies where Congress holds policy interests that are very different from the president. For example, if the president wants to increase the cost of spectrum licenses, while Congress wants to decrease the cost, then the veto effectively acts to block consideration of that issue. When there are two issues where the preferences are not diametrically opposed, then the effect of the veto is very limited. Although I do not consider this case, if Congress is uncertain of the range of policies acceptable to the president, the veto may be more effective. Congress may, for example, avoid working on an issue priority because of uncertainty about whether the president will sign or veto the final bill. Nevertheless, even in this case the veto is likely to exercise minimal influence because it only keeps Congress from working on a specific issue without otherwise affecting the alternative issue that is taken up by Congress. In the next two chapters I consider presidential agenda powers that allow the president to specify the issue taken up by Congress rather than just specifying the issues that are off-limits.

In this chapter, I have shown how game-theoretic models of the policy process can utilize the median voter theorem to construct simple models of the policymaking and agenda-setting processes. I have also introduced the basic elements of game-theoretic models, including utility functions, subgames, strategies, and equilibrium solution concepts that will be employed more extensively in chapters 3 and 4. I developed a simple model of the agenda-setting process that predicted that veto threats could have only limited influence over the agenda choices of Congress. In the next two chapters I examine the president's ability to influence the congressional agenda through his major speeches (legislative programming) and through draft legislation (legislative clearance). To characterize these processes, I use the same two-issue agenda-setting framework I introduced in this chapter. The predictions of these models are then tested using new data on the congressional agenda-setting process in chapters 6 and 7.

· 3 ·

Public Addresses and the Legislative Programming Process

In his first address to a joint session of Congress in 1981, President Ronald Reagan asked Congress to "put a cap on how much the Federal Government will contribute" to state Medicaid expenses (Reagan 1981). Medicaid had often been a polarizing issue that united Democrats in its defense and Republicans in opposition. Reagan's Medicaid cap issue was so contentious that the House Commerce Committee could not reach agreement and reported two contrasting Medicaid bills to the floor. Reagan's Medicaid cap was ultimately rejected by Congress in favor of a less drastic spending cut in Medicaid, but not before it was given serious consideration in both the House and the Senate. What is remarkable, however, is that a Democrat-controlled House let this largely Republican issue arise on the agenda when it could have been easily squelched by House committee and party leaders. In this chapter I explore how the president is able to use his State of the Union addresses and other major addresses to place such issues on the congressional agenda—even when the issue is unfavorable to the majority party.

In his address to Congress, Reagan had highlighted the Medicaid cap as a prime example of the ways the government could save money. Although health care costs had been rising at around 15% per year, Budget Director David Stockman proposed a 5% cap on the increase in expeditures for Medicaid in 1982 (*CQ Almanac* 1981, 577). This seemed a draconian limit to some members of the Democratic House majority, but Reagan had brought a Republican majority to the Senate after his 1980 election victory, and a group of Southern Democrats in the House sided with Reagan frequently on critical policy questions. Neither chamber gave Reagan the 5% spending cap he desired. The Senate passed a cap at 9%, and the House rejected the spending cap in favor of a less drastic cost control. Ironically, a key supporter of the House proposal was Democrat Henry Waxman, chair of the Health subcommittee of Energy and Commerce. Waxman was a staunch defender of Medicaid, and as Health subcommittee chair, was ideally placed to block the administration's downsizing of Medicaid. Formally, Waxman had far more control over the congressional health care agenda than Reagan because Medicaid bills had to go through his subcommittee where he could unilaterally schedule hearings and markups.[1] Politically, Waxman was opposed to the administration plan, claiming that it "may well have more tragic consequences than any other administration [budget] proposal" (*CQ Almanac* 1981, 479). In this chapter I will explore why such a powerful subcommittee chair would yield control of the agenda to a presidential policy issue he opposed. I argue that the president's major public addresses, particularly those delivered to a joint session of Congress, give him an unrivaled chance to shape what issues voters consider most important. I argue that it is this constituent concern for the president's policy agenda that shapes congressional interest in the policies included in the president's State of the Union addresses.

Congressional party leaders provide signals that are informative in this regard only when they can speak authoritatively for their partisans in Congress, i.e., only when they can credibly deliver the policies. It is more often the case that the majority party's interests are not so homogeneous. As Sundquist (1981) and C. Jones (1994) claim, Congress is sometimes forced to turn outside to the president for leadership because it faces a difficult coordination problem. The reason the Speaker cannot often serve in this capacity is that the majority party is often too heterogeneous to agree on a unified agenda (Rohde 1991). In rare circumstances, such as James Wright in 1987 and Newt Gingrich in 1995, the Speaker may be able to wrest control of the congressional agenda from the president. A Speaker without a unified majority party, however, does not enjoy enough effectiveness to draw significant public attention to his proposals. The president, as the sole nationally elected representative, can provide this salience single-handedly. Whereas congressional leaders appear on the evening news and in newspapers infrequently, the president is featured in the news almost daily— even when he is on vacation! This gives the president a considerable advantage over congressional leaders in shaping the public salience of issues.

The formal model of legislative programming developed in this chapter generates the prediction that the president's major speeches can set the congressional agenda on major national issues, but the effectiveness of this type of agenda setting declines rapidly over time during the president's tenure. This declining political capital is a direct result of the fact that voters are less able to hold the president accountable for the effects of his policies as the end of his tenure approaches.

The Origins of Legislative Programming

Article II, Section 3 of the U.S. Constitution instructs the president to "from time to time give to the Congress information of the state of the union, and recommend to their consideration such Measures as he shall judge necessary and expedient." Since FDR, all presidents have used the State of the Union address as an opportunity to make a major public appeal for their policy proposals to Congress (Light 1991). In the 1921 Budget and Accounting Act, Congress added the requirement that the president also submit an annual budget, and in the Employment Act of 1946, Congress extended this request for presidential reports to the area of unemployment. Later, Congress would also require regular presidential reports on the state of national security, the environment, and housing and urban growth (Sundquist 1981, 144).

Through these required presidential reports, Congress has, in effect, institutionalized the president as national policy leader. Although the president was granted no additional legislative power, the Employment Act of 1946 requires the president to prepare "a program for carrying out policy" in the yearly Economic Report (Sundquist 1981). Thus, the president's economic program joined the State of the Union as a required annual report to Congress on suggested policy proposals, the former mandated by the Constitution and the latter by statute. Only infrequently delivered in person, presidents have sometimes used the economic address to deliver their policy proposals in an address before Congress in their first year, since the incumbent administration is charged with delivering the State of the Union after a new president is elected but before he takes office.

Truman's budget director, James E. Webb, took the final step in institutionalizing presidential agenda setting by establishing presidential programming as an annual process, an institution which all of the postwar presidents have maintained. A few days after the 1948 election, Truman called for all agencies to submit their legislative proposals for the next Congress. Budget Circular A-19, "Legislative Coordination and Clearance," set out guidelines for coordination of the president's legislative program, as well as the clearance process (Rudalevige 2002). The Budget Bureau, and later organizations closer to the president within the White House, would identify important proposals for inclusion in the president's program, e.g., items for inclusion in the State of the Union address or other annual messages.

Issues mentioned in the president's State of the Union address are given special consideration, above issues mentioned in the president's other public addresses, and form what is often called the president's "legislative program." Light (1991), for instance, chose State of the Union messages as the most important indicator of presidential agenda items based on interviews with 126 staff members from five presidential administrations: "Most of the staff members interviewed suggested that we turn to the State of the Union address for the agenda items. Though the message often includes a 'laundry list' of presidential requests, it is viewed by the Washington community as the vehicle for the President's agenda. According to the staffs, the President's top priorities will always appear in the message at some point during the term" (6). Further, as Light (1991), Kessel (2001), and Cohen (1997) argue, because State of the Union addresses are rare events, there is considerable debate and competition in the administration for the policy issues that appear there.

Interestingly, both the Truman and Eisenhower administrations still publicly denied drafting many of their legislative proposals when they were introduced into Congress, typically by committee chairmen (Neustadt 1954). These presidents tried to make a distinction between making policy proposals to Congress, which was their clear constitutional duty, and submitting draft legislation, which might be seen as infringing on congressional prerogative. In the White House, a separate process emerged for draft bills that the White House submitted to Congress, and these draft bills offered a different kind of influence on Congress than the president's major addresses, as I will discuss in the next chapter. First, I turn to a formal examination of the potential influence of presidential addresses on the congressional agenda.

An Informational Model of Presidential Programming

In previous attempts to explain the president's agenda-setting power through his public speeches, Kernell (1993) and Miller (1993) argue that the president's ability to "go public" can lead to his influence over legislative outcomes, because the president's speeches can shift the salience of issues and therefore alter the policy preferences of members of Congress. Canes-Wrone (2001) formalizes and enriches this argument in order to explain why the president does not therefore seek to go public on all issues.

Like Kernell (1993), Miller (1993), and Canes-Wrone (2001), I argue that when the president uses the legislative programming track to deliver his agenda items in his public addresses, he is able to raise the salience of issues that hold more potential utility for voters. However, I argue that the president's success in raising the salience of issues is not automatic but depends on his credibility with voters. For instance, I will show that presidents can send more credible policy information to voters at the beginning of their term than at the end of their term. Particularly in their first Congresses, presidents can play an important role in domestic policy making by providing policy information to voters. Voters, who may ordinarily be inattentive to the issues considered by Congress, can thereby punish Congress by not reelecting representatives whenever Congress fails to deal with what the president considers the nation's most pressing problems.

Since 1939 the Gallup Poll has asked Americans to identify "the most important problem facing the country" in its frequent surveys of public opinion in the United States. Aggregate responses indicate that only about seven items were likely to be mentioned by a significant portion of the electorate at a single time (McCombs and Zhu 1995; Miller 1956; Shaw and McCombs 1977; Zhu 1992). To researchers, these "salient" issues comprised the public agenda, usually dominated by economic (e.g., inflation or unemployment) or foreign policy concerns (e.g., wars) or both.

In order to model the dynamic relationship between the public agenda, as influenced by the president, and the congressional agenda, I provide a more formal definition of salience that captures its meaning in both journalistic usage and its usage in the public opinion literature. I argue that salience consists of two components—the identification of a particular issue area or problem and a realization that this problem is more pressing than other potential problems. Salience thus necessarily involves the prioritization of problems: salient issues causing either more disutility or more potential utility gains than nonsalient issues.[2]

As in chapter 2, I consider a policy world in which there exist only two issues, e.g., the economy and defense. Each of these issues can be represented on independent spatial dimensions by assuming that each voter holds coherent and separable preferences across different outcomes located on these spatial dimensions.[3] With only two issues, I define the salient issue as that issue where the voter believes she can gain more potential utility. Technically, issue i is salient to the voter v if and only if $Eu_v(b_i = v_i) \geq Eu_v(b_j = v_j)$ for all issues $j \neq i$. Here v_i represents the ideal policy of the voter on issue i, and b_i represents the policy outcome (bill) on that issue. Eu_v is a function representing the expected utility of a policy to the voter and is measured as a function of the distance from the policy outcome to the voter's ideal point on an issue. I assume that actors' utility is separable across the two issues i and j so that an actor's ideal policy on one issue does not depend on the policy outcome on another issue. The two issues I consider in this chapter, illegal drugs and the Medicaid cap, would not be independent, for instance, if higher illegal drug use affected how high an actor was willing to set the Medicaid cap.

Voter Uncertainty about Optimal Policies

Using the median voter results that are reviewed in chapter 2, I will consider a single median voter who represents the national electorate. By definition this median voter will always have a salient issue, i.e., an issue where she believes her policy preferences differ most from the status quo. On all other issues, I assume that voter has some uncertainty about the best course of policy action;

i.e., the voter may not realize the full effects of a given Medicaid cap on the number of practices willing to accept Medicaid patients, the budget deficit, or on the cost of health care to non-Medicaid users. If the voter could understand all of these effects, then she would be in a better position to identify the ideal policy on this issue. Because of their greater policy expertise, I assume that the president and Congress become better informed than the voter about policy effects of different levels of Medicaid caps. Access to this policy expertise could help voters better evaluate the policy choices made by the president and Congress. I will argue, however, that the voter needs only very crude information that allows her to assess the most important problem in order to be able to evaluate Congress's agenda choices. It is this information about the most important problem that the president is well suited to provide through his public speeches.

Figure 3.1 represents the canonical agenda-setting problem. There are two issues and three actors: the voter, v; the president, p; and Congress, c. On one issue, illegal drug use, the voter has complete information about the effects of implemented policy so that the voter observes her exact ideal policy to be v_1. This issue may be thought of as the salient issue indicated by the "most important problem" question on the Gallup Poll of national public opinion. Complete information is assumed because voters are more likely to be informed on this issue than on less salient issues for a variety of reasons, including media attention to the problem and the voters' concern for the problem. When Congress focuses its attention on this issue, it is following public opinion. Nontrivial agenda setting arises only if the president is able to divert Congress's attention to another nonsalient issue. The only reason voters would be interested in having Congress work on an issue other than the issue they consider the most important problem

FIGURE 3.1 Configuration of ideal points and uncertainty on two issues in legislative programming

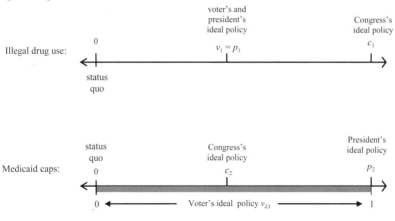

is if there is a another issue where they do not have a full understanding of the effects of implementing different policies. In figure 3.1 the possibility of such an issue is represented by issue 2, the Medicaid cap.

From figure 3.1, it is clear that Congress considers illegal drug use a more important problem because it finds the status quo further from its ideal point on illegal drug use. Similarly, the president finds the Medicaid cap more pressing. I will assume, however, that the voter is unsure whether her ideal point on issue 2 in each period t is at the status quo, $v_{2,t} = 0$, in which case she would find illegal drug use more important, or at $v_{2,t} = 1$, in which case she would find the Medicaid cap more pressing. The voter's relative uncertainty about her ideal policy may arise because she does not know the implementation effects of each policy as well as Congress and the president. The ideal policies of Congress and the president are not indexed by the period t, because they are assumed to be fixed in each period. I will also assume that the voter knows that there is an equal probability of her ideal point on issue 2 being either 0 or 1. In each period, then, the voter faces a completely new issue (issue 2), about which she is uncertain of the implementation effects of any policy. I assume that on each of these new issues and in each period t, she believes her ideal policy is distributed in the same way, i.e., at $v_{2,t} = $ is equally likely to be 0 or 1 in each period t.

Utility is derived as a function of the distance from the player's ideal point to the bill passed by Congress. The only uncertainty is about the voter's ideal policy on the nonsalient issue 2 in each period because of her uncertainty about the implementation effects of different policies on this issue. The policy (bill) enacted by Congress in each period t is represented as $b_t = \{b_{1,2}, b_{2,t}\}$. The preferred policy of each actor a on an issue i is represented as a_i. The utility or welfare of each actor on an issue i in each period t or legislative session is a function of the squared distance between the enacted policy b_t and the actor's ideal policy.

I set up a policymaking game that is repeated over and over in order to model the incentives of actors in repeated interaction. In order to avoid infinitely valued payoffs for some repeated policy choices, payoffs each period are discounted at the rate, δ^{t-1}, where δ represents a common discount factor, and $0 < \delta < 1$. A common discount factor between 0 and 1 means that all actors value future policy benefits less than they do current policy benefits.[4] Actors with lower discount factors are myopic and prefer to choose actions that provide immediate benefits rather than actions that have delayed benefits, even when those delayed benefits are greater. In each period t, an actor a's expected utility from the policy b_t is:

$$\text{voter: } Eu_{v,t} = (\Sigma_i - (v_{i,t} - b_{i,t})^2 - k)\delta^{t-1}$$
$$\text{Congress: } Eu_{c,t} = (\Sigma_i - (c_{i,t} - b_{i,t})^2 + k)\delta^{t-1}$$
$$\text{president: } Eu_{p,t} = (\Sigma_i - (p_{i,t} - b_{i,t})^2 + k)\delta^{t-1}$$

Because of separable preferences, each actor's utility is thus derived as the sum of the actor's utility from the separate issues. Notice that the voter's utility function has the wage term $-k$ and Congress and the president have the wage term k, because the voter must pay a wage to the representative and president in each period in order to make them prefer to deliver the voter's ideal policy in each period in exchange for being reelected.

"Are You Better Off Today Than You Were Four Years Ago?"

When the game begins, nature reveals $v_{2,t}$, the voter's ideal point on issue 2 to the president and Congress but not to the voter. In other words, Congress and the president observe whether there is another issue that could potentially benefit the voter more than the issue the voter considers salient. If $v_{2,t} = 0$, then there is no such issue. If $v_{2,t} = 1$, then issue 2 offers more potential voter utility. The president then sends a message to voters and Congress that may or may not reveal which issue and bill offers the voter the most potential utility. Congress subsequently chooses a policy, choosing both an issue and a specific bill on that issue. It is in limiting Congress to deal with one problem at a time that an agenda problem arises in the first place. If Congress could work on all possible issues at once, delivering perhaps an omnibus policy, then there would be no need to decide which issue is most important. Congress has neither the time nor organizational ability to dispatch policy in such a comprehensive fashion. Its approach is necessarily piecemeal.

The voter observes her previous period utility, the president's message and the policy issues chosen by Congress, and decides whether to reelect the president and Congress. In measuring agenda setting, the concern is with whether the president's message can affect the issue chosen by Congress. If the president does have such an influence, it operates indirectly through his influence on the voter's reelection strategies.

I make a further distinction between major policy issues and minor policy issues. Instead of hinging on the amount of utility available to actors from an issue, like issue salience, major issues are simply defined as those whose policy effects cannot be judged immediately, but only over time. Thus, while different actors can view different issues as salient, I assume that all agree which issues are major vs. minor issues. Examples of major issues include Jimmy Carter's 1979 energy plan, Bill Clinton's 1993 health care plan, and George W. Bush's 2001 homeland security plan. So I distinguish minor issues as those issues whose effects can be known to voters within the same legislative session. These might include disaster relief bills, extending unemployment benefits, and tax rebates.

Alternatively, Congress could concern itself with issues such as pork barrel spending that reveal more immediate benefits to their voters. Since I assume the separability of issues, the only way such short-sighted behavior hurts the long-term interests of the voter is by ignoring more important issues with delayed benefits. In the real world, short-sighted policies like pork barrel spending may affect the voter's long-term interests more directly by, for example, raising the national debt and thus interest rates. In the model below, both issue 1 and issue 2 are assumed to be major issues; i.e., the effects of policies on these issues are not observed before the next congressional election. That the standards for measuring the success or failure of policies often extends beyond a single Congress is suggested by the familiar presidential reelection refrain: "Are you better off today than you were *four years ago?*" used by Reagan in his 1980 election campaign.

Figure 3.2 traces the chronology of the legislative programming stage game for major issues. Notice that the effects, $u_{v,t,}$ of the policy b_t in period t are not realized until after the midterm election $r_{m,t}$. The voter must therefore decide whether to reelect members of Congress before she knows whether Congress has pursued policies that will benefit her. The president can send a message m_t before the midterm election that helps voters evaluate whether Congress has pursued her interests. In the policy space described in figure 3.1, the president can indicate to the voter whether or not the voter's ideal point on issue 2 is further from the status quo than her ideal point on issue 1, in other words, whether issue 2 is more important than issue 1.

After observing the president's message and the policy issue subject to congressional action, the voter must make a midterm reelection decision that can be contingent on the message sent by the president and the policy chosen by Congress, but not on the utility she gains from that policy. After all, she doesn't realize the full effects of the president's major policy proposals until near the end of the presidential term. After the midterm election, the voter observes her actual utility $u_{v,t}$ from the previous legislative action b_t. The president sends another message and Congress chooses another policy b_{t+1} in the second Congress. The voter must make reelection decisions $r_{p,t+1}$ for both the president and Congress in the presidential election year. The stage game is repeated indefinitely whenever

FIGURE 3.2 Chronology of the legislative programming stage game

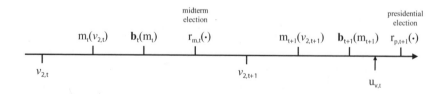

there are no term limits and once when the president is allowed to serve two consecutive terms.

The Dynamics of Presidential Agenda Setting

Since the voter has incomplete information in each period, she is unsure whether her ideal policy on issue 2 will yield her more or less utility than her ideal policy on issue 1. If the voter never acquired information about her preferred policy on issue 2, she could use her knowledge of issue 1 to demand that Congress provide a policy located at her ideal point, v_1, on that issue. The voter gains utility from this policy, but she could do even better if Congress delivered her ideal point on issue 2, v_2, whenever it yields a value higher than v_1. Congress knows when $v_2 = 1$, but is reluctant to choose a policy at the voter's ideal point on this issue because Congress gains lower utility from this policy. Without policy information, then, the voter is not able to efficiently monitor the behavior of her representative. If, however, the voter elects another representative with different interests than Congress, such as the president, he might be able to signal to the voter whenever $v_2 = 1$. This information enables the voter to hold Congress to the higher standard in these cases. The president may have different interests even from a Congress controlled by his party, since he is elected by a different constituency than any member of Congress.

The president's attention to an issue in his State of the Union address or in some other major speech carries an inherent claim that his issue is of overriding importance. As discussed earlier, this is by nature a claim that voters can accrue the greatest benefits if Congress is able to solve this policy problem. In the words of the model developed here, the president is claiming that issue 2, Medicaid caps, has a voter ideal policy located at 1 rather than 0. If the voter were able to elect a president whose interests mirrored hers perfectly, the president would be able to convey this information perfectly to the voter (Crawford and Sobel 1982).

Congress could also make claims about the most important problem facing the country, but voters are aware that individual members of Congress may have interests at odds with the good of the country as a whole. When all members vote for the revealed preferences of their districts, for instance, the aggregate policy result may make all of the voters worse off than some other coordinated policy. Congressional parties also play some role in keeping Congress focused on national concerns. Indeed, in two recent Congresses, the 100th and 104th, the House was able to generate and pass an endogenous national legislative program. But, ultimately, parties have little power to keep representatives from voting their districts. The rewards the party offers in leadership positions and other inducements are secondary to the reelection concerns of incumbents.

41

TABLE 3.1 Legislative programming equilibrium strategies

Actor	Action	First Congress	Later Congresses
president	m_t	signals voter's interests faithfully	signals his own preferred issue
Congress	b_t	chooses voter's preferred policy on issue indicated by president	chooses voter's preferred policy on Congress's preferred issue
voter	$c_{m,t}$, $c_{p,t}$, k	reelects Congress (and pays wage k) if Congress follows president's program	reelects Congress and president (and pays wage k) if she realizes her utility expectations

If the president has ideal points as represented in figure 3.1, then there exists an equilibrium in the repeated game where the president is able to signal information to the voter that allows her to efficiently monitor congressional behavior. This would not be the case if the president's policy interests coincided perfectly with those of Congress, in which case Congress and the president would have an interest in colluding to deceive the voter. The president can essentially signal which issue offers more potential utility, and the voter can use knowledge of this issue to make reelection decisions regarding Congress. I list the strategies that constitute a perfect Bayesian equilibrium in the legislative programming game in table 3.1. A formal statement and proof of equilibrium are given in Appendix A.

The voter must design her strategy regarding the reelection of Congress in a way that makes choosing a policy at her ideal point in each case attractive, or incentive compatible, to Congress. Notice, for example, that Congress always does best policywise in any given term by choosing a policy located at its ideal point on issue 1, c_1. The voter, therefore, has to make reelection contingent on Congress choosing a different policy in order to make Congress comply. This leads to an incentive constraint that must always be satisfied in equilibrium. Congress must always prefer its expected net present value of delivering the voter's preferred policy to defecting and choosing its own preferred policy in the current period, which might lead to it being thrown out of office. In particular the incentive constraint requires that Congress prefer to choose the policy v_1 when $v_2 = 0$ and the policy v_2 whenever $v_2 = 1$.

The voter is also concerned that the president sends the proper messages regarding the value of v_2, i.e., information about the most important problem facing the country. As I noted earlier, if the president and the voter share the same interests, the president will always follow the voter's interests without the need for monitoring. Voters, however, rarely elect such trustworthy leaders. In the game I have modeled, the president always prefers a policy $b_2 = 1$ regardless of the value of the voter's ideal point. We might expect the president to always tell the voter that her ideal policy is at the same location on issue 2. But the voter can monitor utility she experiences from legislative action and thereby sometimes observes whether the president has been truthful. For example, if v_2 = 0, the voter can achieve $u_{v,t}$ = 0 but not if v_2 = 1. A presidential signal to set expectations higher than those available from the status quo policy can never be satisfied by Congress. Thus, the voter can monitor the president's honesty in signaling by requiring future utility to equal the expectations set by the president in order for the voter to reelect the president as well as Congress. Moreover, since Congress knows that it will not be reelected when the president sets expectations that cannot be met, it defects in such cases and chooses a policy at its own ideal point—a policy that offers the president less utility than he could have secured from an honest signal. The president thus finds an incentive to signal honestly independent of the voter's reelection strategy for him. I will discuss why this is not generally the case in presidential agenda setting in the next section. For now I want to establish the significant role played by a president who can send informative signals to voters. The chief role of the president in the game is educating the voter about the most important problem so that the voter can more efficiently monitor Congress's agenda choices. This distinguishes this model from the Gilligan and Krehbiel (1987) model of information transmission, which I use to model legislative clearance in the following chapter. In the Gilligan and Krehbiel model, the amount of information that can be conveyed between two actors is determined by the similarity of their preferences, and perfect information can only be transmitted between actors who have identical interests. My model of legislative programming is novel because it shows how introducing an elected third party, the president, can lead to full information revelation to the voter and thus to fully efficient representation—even when actors do not have identical preferences. The key difference from the Gilligan and Krehbiel setup is that additional agenda-setting agents, like the president, can be employed for the sole purpose of acquiring and revealing hidden information, which the voter could not have credibly acquired from the Congress. The principal role of the president in his major addresses is, I contend, exactly the provision of this type of policy information to voters in order to influence the issues on the congressional agenda.

Table 3.1 specifies a separating equilibrium in the legislative programming game in which the voter gets her optimal legislative issue and bill in the first term and in which the president's message influences both the issue and bill chosen by Congress. A separating equilibrium is defined as a behavioral prediction where the president sends different messages depending on his private information about the implementation effects of the policy, so that the voter can separate issues where her ideal policy is low from issues when her ideal policy is high. A formal specification of equilibrium strategies is presented in Appendix A.

FIGURE 3.3 Presidential preferences with respect to congressional preferences for Legislative Programming Equilibrium for $\delta = 3/4$ and $k = 1/4$.

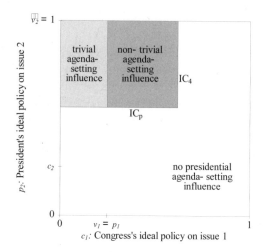

Nontrivial agenda setting occurs even though the president plays no direct role in the legislative process in the model. The president's agenda-setting influence is nontrivial when Congress chooses an issue other than that which it would have chosen without presidential signaling.

In figure 3.3, I arbitrarily set v_1, v_2, p_1, and c_2 and plot in gray the values of c_1 and p_2 for which presidential agenda setting occurs in equilibrium. The president's ability to use the legislative programming process to set the congressional agenda depends on the relationship between the ideal policies of the president, Congress, and the median voter. Incentive constraint IC_p indicates that the president will only be willing to send informative messages to the voter when the president's ideal policy on issue 2 is sufficiently far from the status quo that he prefers to work on issue 2 rather than Congress's priority, issue 1. Incentive constraint IC_4 indicates that Congress will only be willing to respond to the president's agenda-setting messages when the preferences of Congress and the voter are not too far apart on issue 1. In the light gray area marked "trivial agenda setting," both the president and Congress prefer to work on issue 2. When c_1 falls to the right of IC_4, it is very large compared to c_2, and Congress prefers to work on issue 1 regardless of the president's message. Although the range of ideal policies where non-trivial agenda setting occurs is restricted in figure 3.3, it is also clear that the preferences of the president, Congress, and voter do not have to be identical for perfect communication to occur. When non-trivial presidential agenda setting does occur, i.e., in the light gray area in figure 3.3, its results can be dramatic because the voter gets her ideal policy on her most important issue in some periods.

The Consequences of Legislative Programming

The equilibrium strategies in table 3.1 lead to several predictions about the presidential agenda-setting power that derives from public addresses. First, the president only exercises this agenda-setting influence during his first Congress. The second Congress still delivers the voter's ideal policy, but on Congress's preferred issue rather than on the issue indicated in the president's message. Second, Congress is reelected in each period, even though it ignores the president's messages after the first period. Finally, the president and Congress do not have to have identical preferences for the president to exercise this type of agenda influence.

If one thinks of the interest of the members of Congress as coincident with those of special interest groups or those who provide campaign contributions, then the role of the president is fundamental in keeping the actions of Congress geared towards the national constituency rather than such special interests. If the interests of Congress are understood instead as the particularistic interests of each congressional district, then the president's role here can be understood as turning Congress to collective goods legislation. With this interpretation it is easy to see that without presidential agenda setting collective goods legislation would be worked on less frequently by Congress.

The Plausibility of Presidential Mandates

The predictions of the public address model of presidential agenda setting are consistent with the idea of "presidential mandates" because both stress the president's effectiveness at the beginning of his term. It is often argued in journalistic coverage of politics that presidents can translate an electoral mandate, if they secure one, into policy success in Congress. Technically, a mandate is a set of instructions from the voter that tell the politician how to vote (Pitkin 1967). A president who secures a mandate in an election might see himself as instructed and empowered by voters to enact the policy proposals he emphasized in his electoral campaign. However, the idea that mandates occur in presidential elections has been disparaged by political scientists (e.g., Dahl 1990; Edwards 1989; Kelley 1983), who see the electorate as too ill-informed and candidates as too vague in their policy positions for a clear mandate to exist. Still, talk of mandates is heard from both politicians and journalists, and Conley (2001) points out that both Reagan and Clinton claimed mandates from the voters. Conley discards the traditional view of mandates and interprets them instead as inferences that members of Congress make about the level of public support for the president's program. Her understanding of a mandate is very close to what Paul

45

Light (1991) calls "presidential capital," congressional and popular support that presidents can use in support of major policy changes. Conley's model offers a helpful way of understanding presidential policy making, because she shows how futile it is for presidents like Clinton to try to claim a mandate when they do not have the congressional and public support for major policy change. In other words, she dispels Dahl's fear that the "myth" of a mandate "elevates the president to an exalted position at the expense of Congress" (Dahl 1990, quoted in Conley 2001), and concludes that presidents cannot use mandate claims alone to dominate policy making.

To simply say, "I have a mandate for change," does not offer the president any additional leverage over Congress, in the way that Dahl had feared. Generally, presidents claim they have mandates when they also have congressional and voter support for major policy change. What matters is not whether the president claims a mandate—since the claim by itself has no effect on Congress—but only whether the president initiates major policy change when political conditions are ripe for that change. Saying "I have a mandate" and introducing major legislation are, in fact, indistinguishable actions in Conley's model. But in rationalizing mandates, Conley also defines a way that they might serve as a unique explanation of presidential agenda setting. Her mandates do not serve as specific instructions from voters but only as imperfect signals of the political conditions for major policy changes. However, Conley's model is also about bill passage rather than agenda setting as I define it, because the president actually serves as a monopoly agenda setter for Congress in her model. Congress either passes the president's bills or it passes nothing at all. I ask instead why Congress would consider the president's legislation when it can alternatively consider any legislation of its own devising. This, as I see it, is the central question in determining the president's effect on the congressional agenda.

While my model of legislative programming produces a prediction similar to mandate theory, i.e., that presidents will be able to influence the congressional agenda with their policy program most effectively at the beginning of their term, the source I identify of this declining influence is quite different. Rather than arising from instructions from voters from the recent election, as in the conventional view, or from inferences about public support for the president, as in Conley's model, I model this influence as arising from the credibility of the policy information the president provides to voters that depends on the president's accountability in the next election. It is at the beginning of the presidential term that such messages have the most credibility, because the term limits imposed on the president by the 22nd Amendment reduce his electoral accountability as his tenure progresses.

·4·

Draft Bills and the Legislative Clearance Process

Central legislative clearance in the executive branch is widely regarded as one of the most powerful tools of the president. Under the aegis of the Office of Management and Budget the hundreds of legislative proposals generated by federal departments, bureaus, and independent agencies are coordinated and reviewed to assess their acceptability as component parts of the president's program. Here, many would argue, the substance of the congressional agenda is determined.

—Robert S. Gilmour, 1971

In February 1983, President Ronald Reagan sent Congress a proposal to further the deregulation of natural gas that had been initiated under President Jimmy Carter in 1978. Carter's deregulation had preserved price controls on gas that was flowing before April 20, 1977, at $1.25 per thousand cubic feet, well below market value. Reagan's draft legislation would remove this price control on any new contracts for this "old" gas. At the time, however, there was considerable consumer concern because natural gas prices were rising rather than falling despite Carter's deregulation (*CQ Almanac* 1983, 366). The most immediate effect of Reagan's proposed decontrol of old natural gas would be to raise prices on the more abundant old gas, though this was expected by the administration to eventually bring down the price of the previously deregulated new gas. The argument that deregulation would bring down prices was complex and depended on a number of uncertain factors.

Public sentiment was running against further deregulation because of rising prices in the face of abundant natural gas. House Commerce chair John D. Dingell Jr. claimed that deregulation of old natural gas would take place "over my dead body" (*CQ Almanac* 1983, 369) and introduced a bill that would re-regulate prices for "new" gas. In this environment, it seems unlikely that the issue of natural gas deregulation would have been given serious consideration without the strong public support of President Reagan. Reagan never mentioned the deregulation of natural gas in his State of the Union and economic addresses before or after submitting his draft legislation. Nevertheless, after Reagan's proposal was introduced, both the House and the Senate took up the issue of natural gas deregulation in committee hearings and markups, and the Senate brought the issue to a floor vote.[1] In this chapter I provide a model to explain how Reagan's draft legislation was able to move natural gas regulation to active consideration in Congress without raising the public salience of the issue.

The policy issue of natural gas deregulation is significant because of its complexity and the resulting uncertainty about any given policy solution: "Predictions were difficult to make because of the impossibility of predicting the "mix of old and new gas pipelines would carry and sell" (*CQ Almanac* 1983, 366). The administration proposal had two features that responded to this uncertainty: it prevented producers from passing along price increases that were greater than the inflation rate, and it allowed pipeline companies to break and renegotiate contracts with gas producers. In short, Reagan's draft legislation drew on technical expertise from the federal bureaucracy that members of Congress found useful because it altered their perception of the problems of natural gas regulation and deregulation. In the end, the 98th Congress failed to pass legislation deregulating natural gas, but it had put aside other important business to give serious consideration to the problem, even though the issue never achieved high salience with the general public. I develop a model to explain how technical expertise can be used by the president to influence the issues on the congressional agenda, and to examine the conditions under which this agenda-setting power is effective.

Miller (1994) and Peterson (1995) argue that there are two types of uncertainty that can plague lawmakers in determining public policy: political uncertainty and programmatic uncertainty. Political uncertainty involves both the state of public support for a policy and the question of who will benefit or suffer from the proposed policies. Programmatic uncertainty involves more technical and objective concerns about what policy will achieve the most effective results. It is in reducing programmatic uncertainty in particular that the president's draft legislation may be useful to Congress. Legislators can rely on personal experience, lobbyists, and opinion surveys as well as major public addresses to try to overcome political uncertainty. Opinion surveys and the like, however, are not helpful in addressing the more technical programmatic uncertainty on complex issues like natural gas deregulation, air pollution, and electromagnetic spectrum auctions. The most important congressional institutions for reducing programmatic uncertainty in technical issues are each member's staff and the committee and subcommittee systems in the House and Senate. While lobbyists and interest groups can also provide valuable technical information, other institutions have also arisen to address the increasingly complex programmatic uncertainty in lawmaking, including executive agencies, think tanks, and congressional agencies like the Congressional Budget Office (Peterson 1995).

The president, by contrast, has a much greater arsenal of technical policy expertise at his disposal. The legislative clearance process, as it has developed, has put him in control of much of the policy expertise emanating from the federal bureaucracy.[2] These resources put the president in a position to have tremendous influence on law making on technical issues. In this chapter I examine how the president can use that informational advantage to shape both what issues are considered by Congress and the policies enacted on those issues.

The Development of the Legislative Clearance Process

In 1921 under President Warren G. Harding, Congress created the Bureau of the Budget and required the president to submit an annual budget for the federal government. Agencies would no longer send their budget requests directly to Congress but would have to have them cleared through the newly created bureau (Neustadt 1954).

Six months after signing the Budget and Accounting Act, the new Budget Director Charles G. Dawes introduced Budget Circular 49 in response to a request by the chairman of the House Appropriations Committee that the Budget Bureau review legislation that diverted appropriated funds to other purposes. The budget circular, which was cleared by the House Appropriations Committee, required that all proposed legislation that would affect the public treasury would be cleared through the Budget Bureau. While the circular allows the bureau to withhold draft legislation that conflicts with the president's fiscal goals, it does not forbid agencies from responding to requests for executive comment on legislation.[3] Instead, such agency comments were to "include a statement of the advice received from the Budget Bureau" (Neustadt 1954). Dawes and the Harding administration, however, met resistance to Circular 49, and it was not implemented until the Coolidge administration. Under Calvin Coolidge the clearance process was used only on bills that required appropriations, and the Budget Bureau commented only on the fiscal matters in the legislation, not on the policy.

Hoover exempted private bills from legislative clearance, and he exempted negative comments on public bills from the necessity of including the Budget Bureau's advice (Neustadt 1954). Private bills, such as bills granting permanent residency to an individual, typically have only a small fiscal or public policy component and are thus of little interest to the Budget Bureau. They are, however, a very important means of constituency service to members of Congress. The president saw no need to attach advice to negative comments produced by agencies because the role of the clearance process at this point was economy.

If that economy was established by the agency acting alone, by recommending against spending entailed in a bill, then the bureau did not have to oversee that agency's actions.

In 1935, FDR issued Circular 336, which established clearance of non-appropriations legislation through the president's Emergency Council as well as appropriations legislation through the Budget Bureau, because he had been "quite horrified—not once but half a dozen times—by reading in the paper that some department or agency was after this, that, or the other without my knowledge" (quoted in Neustadt 1954). Agency bills, comments, and even oral testimony before congressional committees were to include a statement indicating whether it was "in accord with the president's program."

FDR distinguished three types of administration bills he sought to identify: (1) legislation the administration sees as mandatory; (2) legislation that the administration has no objections to; and (3) legislation that the administration opposes. Thus, he identifies the distinction between legislative programming, the first type; legislative clearance, the second type; and the enrolled bill process, which determines whether the president should sign bills passed by both chambers (Neustadt 1954). By 1937, a new Budget Circular 344 placed all clearance functions in the Budget Bureau (later renamed Office of Management and Budget), where they remain today.

Part of Roosevelt's purpose was to separate the landmark legislation from the more routine requests developed in due course by executive agencies. However, if routine legislation is understood as the drafting of amendments to make corrections to current laws, this activity would grow in importance as the size, scope, and number of legislative enactments increased, so that today the "national government has an agenda that is continuous because much of it is generated from existing programs" (C. Jones 1994, 164). In FDR's presidency such routine legislation would indeed seem insignificant compared to the new programs introduced as a part of the New Deal. By the post-reform Congress, however, technical amendments to comprehensive environmental legislation, like the Clean Air Act and the Clean Water Act, could by themselves constitute major legislation.

Despite the use of task forces and vastly differing legislative temperaments of presidents since Harry Truman, Gilmour (1971) reports that the legislative clearance process remained largely unchanged until Richard Nixon. During Nixon's administration, the Bureau of the Budget was brought under tighter presidential control and renamed the Office of Management and Budget (OMB). The OMB is still charged with carrying out the clearance and programming functions under Circular A-19. In addition, Nixon's Reorganization Plan No. 2 of 1970 established the Domestic Council, an inner White House organization that routinely identified items in the legislative clearance process of special importance in order to make them a part of the president's program. Nixon also further politicized the OMB by adding four political appointees at the associate director level so that the review of legislation came more directly under the political appointees rather than the career bureaucrats (Spitzer 1993).

Since Nixon, there have been repeated attempts to centralize the legislative clearance process by reorganizing and creating new offices within the White House, but it is the congressional and presidential environments in which these processes operate that have changed more dramatically (Rudalevige 2002). These changes included the decentralization of Congress after organizational reforms in the 1970s, the rapid growth in the use of party primaries in the selection of presidential candidates after the 1968 Democratic convention and subsequent McGovern-Fraser Commission reforms, and the rise of budgetary politics with the growth of deficit spending in the 1980s. In this environment I will examine, in part II of this book, the president's influence on the congressional agenda arising from both his legislative programming and clearance functions.

An Informational Model of Legislative Clearance

Executive proposals that are approved through the legislative clearance process are sent on to Congress as draft legislation. These proposals incorporate the specialized information acquired by the agency or department about the likely policy consequences of legislative action on the issue. For example, Reagan's natural gas deregulation plan included both a plan to deny pipelines the power to pass through price increases that rose faster than the rate of inflation and a plan to allow pipelines to break old contracts with gas producers that included unfair "take or pay" provisions that forced them to pay for most of the gas ordered even if it was not needed by the time it was delivered. However, because Congress realizes that the president's policy goals are often different from its own, it observes that the draft legislation will also be biased in the direction of the president's or executive agency's preferred policy ends. For example, many members of Congress may have believed that the president was committed to deregulation even if it would lead to higher natural gas prices. If the president and Congress have identical policy goals, Congress can trust the president's draft legislation to perfectly reveal the president's private information about the consequences of the bill. With divergent policy preferences, Congress will not know how much of the bill is informative about the likely policy consequences of the legislation and how much is biased by the president's preferences. Because of this, and the fact that the president cannot easily leverage voters on these less visible and more complex issues, Congress will not always fully trust the administration bill as a reliable means of achieving Congress's own policy goals.

Despite its potential bias, the president's draft legislation may serve an informative role. Congress has limited resources and time and cannot explore the consequences of all possible pieces of legislation.[4] In choosing agenda items, Congress must estimate both the policy preferences of its constituents on an issue, i.e., political uncertainty, and the likely policy consequences of enacting a bill, i.e., programmatic uncertainty. The president's drafts can be informative of the likely policy consequences of legislation on an issue because draft legislation incorporates the expertise of the executive agencies.

I build on the "cheap-talk" communication model of Crawford and Sobel (1982), who model costless communication between two parties with different interests.[5] In one of the first applications of the Crawford and Sobel model to political science, Gilligan and Krehbiel (1987) argued that congressional committees gained more information about the policy effects of different proposals by acquiring expertise in areas where they specialize and then using this expertise in crafting legislative proposals for the floor. In their model, the floor, i.e., the entire House, benefits from this policy expertise by deferring to the committee's proposal rather than re-crafting it to serve the less informed interests of the broader chamber. Gilligan and Krehbiel proposed that restrictive rules governing debate and amendment served to facilitate this deference to more informed committee proposals. In a similar way, I argue, through the legislative clearance process, the president's administration coordinates the wide-ranging expertise of the executive bureaucracy, and this gives it an informational advantage over Congress when legislating on complex and technical issues. As in the Gilligan and Krehbiel committee model, this informational advantage can be used to bring policy closer to the president's ideal on a given issue, but I focus instead on how the president uses this informational advantage to determine what issues are considered by Congress.

I examine the agenda-setting influence that the president wields through bureaucratic expertise with the simple two-dimensional model of the policy-making process developed in chapter 2. The two issues under consideration are the issue considered most important by Congress and the issue considered most important by the president. As an example, I assume that Congress is concerned above all with the air pollution and that the president is concerned above all with the deregulation of natural gas. It is worth reiterating that because of its time and resource constraints, I assume that Congress cannot legislate on both issues. Although this is an unrealistic abstraction, it serves merely to focus the model on the fact that Congress cannot work on all possible issues at once. It is the fact that something has to be left off of the agenda that is the critical part of the assumption. Without such a restriction in the number of actions, there is no agenda-setting problem because Congress can act on all issues that require attention.[6] I assume under this agenda constraint that Congress would therefore prefer to legislate on air pollution, but the president may try to persuade it that natural gas deregulation is a more pressing priority. In the model in this chapter I will also set aside the president's ability to raise the public salience of issues in order to isolate instead his ability to provide expertise to Congress that alters its agenda. In practice, however, the president may employ both techniques of agenda setting on the same issue. I present a formal model to explain whether and how the clearance process gives the president agenda-setting power, and then I use the model to generate predictions about when and where this agenda influence will be effective.

As explained in chapter 2, I define an agenda-setting problem as a choice of which issue to legislate on rather than a choice of the exact policy on a given issue. Concern for the exact policies chosen on each issue will, however, shape which issue is chosen, because both the president and Congress will want to work on the issue where they can bring the status quo further towards their ideal policy.

In the formal model of legislative clearance, two actors, Congress and the president, play a "signaling" game in which the president tries to influence the issue and policy chosen by Congress by providing signals that inform Congress of the unforeseen consequences of legislation. The president observes private information about the possible policy consequences of action on an issue by reviewing executive draft legislation and then he may try to signal this information to Congress in a way that encourages Congress to choose to act on an issue preferred by the president. Any policy chosen by Congress is also subject to a presidential veto. Whenever the president is able to persuade Congress to work on an issue that it would not have considered in the absence of the president's signal, the president is said to exercise nontrivial agenda-setting influence over Congress. In cases of trivial agenda setting, the president's message indicates the issue that would have been chosen by Congress even without presidential agenda setting.

Modeling agenda setting requires measuring Congress's choice of issue dimension as well as its choice of a particular bill within each issue dimension. The agenda choice faced by Congress can be understood as a choice between the issue it ex ante prefers and any other issue on which the president would rather have Congress take action. Congress's ex ante preferences are those it holds before it observes any private information that the president may communicate to Congress in the legislative clearance process. Congress will ex ante prefer the issue on which its ideal policy gives it the most expected utility given its initial beliefs about policy consequences on both issues.

I assume that any given issue that Congress may consider entails some programmatic uncertainty, i.e., either uncertainty about the conditions necessitating policy change or uncertainty about effects of implementing any policy on the issue. The programmatic uncertainty on each issue i is represented as the probability that a positive shift, $\omega_i = \varpi_i$ occurs in the ideal policy of each actor. Initially, on each issue i, the president observes two equally likely ideal policies, p_i and $p_i + \varpi_i$, but he does not know which one applies on each issue because of uncertainty about the value of ω_i. Similarly, Congress has two equally likely ideal policies, c_i and $c_i + \overline{\omega}_i$, but it does not know which one applies on each issue. In the model, the president is able to gain information about whether the policy shift, $\omega_2 = \overline{\omega}_2$, occurs on issue 2 because he obtains draft legislation and other reports created by the Department of Energy or another federal agency. In figure 4.1, I further assume that the president and Congress are equally uncertain on both of the issues under consideration, air pollution and natural gas regulation. This equal uncertainty is represented by the fact that both the president and Congress have a pair of equidistant ideal policies for each issue, representing a similar range of uncertainty spanned by the light and dark grey bands, respectively. Later I will relax the assumption that there is equal uncertainty on both issues in order to analyze what happens to the president's agenda-setting influence when there is more uncertainty on one issue than the other. The president's potential agenda-setting influence arises here because Congress does not observe information about the policy shift on issue 2 and yet this policy shift affects Congress's ideal point in exactly the same way that it affects the president's. It is only because the president and Congress share a common interest in understanding the policy shift, ω_2, that communication of policy information is possible between them. As will become clearer later, if policy shifts affect the president and Congress unequally, less information can be conveyed, all else being equal. And if the policy shift affects the president and Congress in opposite ways, no communication would be possible.[7]

Agenda setting occurs when the president is able to communicate to Congress that a policy shift occurs on issue 2, and this persuades Congress to work on issue 2 where it can deliver its ideal policy rather than on issue 1 where it is still uncertain of its ideal policy. This simple communication problem, however, becomes enormously complicated because the president may prefer that Con-

FIGURE 4.1 Configuration of ideal points on two issues in legislative clearance game

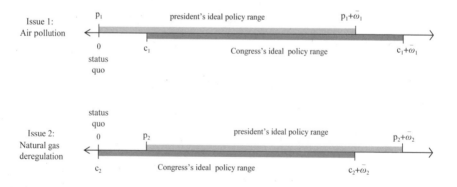

gress work on policy 2 even when there is not a policy shift on that issue. This means that the president will sometimes have an incentive to lie about whether the policy shift has occurred on issue 2. In game-theoretic modeling, however, actors try to anticipate the behaviors of other actors. In this case, Congress can anticipate conditions when the president has an incentive to lie about the policy shift on issue 2, and it will not believe the president under these conditions. This strategic anticipation on Congress's part thus puts limits on the conditions under which communication, and thus agenda setting, is possible. Next I explore those conditions informally, and they are treated formally in Appendix B.

Because of the possibility of policy shifts affecting the implementation of policy on either issue, neither the president nor Congress knows their exact ideal policy initially. I assume that the president and Congress share common knowledge about the high and low values of this uncertain knowledge, indicated by shaded bands in figure 4.1, and that both possible values within that range are equally likely. Thus, instead of a unique ideal policy, the president and Congress each observe two possibilities on each issue: a "low" policy and a "high" policy. Before he observes whether a policy shift has occurred on either issue, the president has a preference for dealing with issue 2, natural gas regulation, where his ideal policy is on average further from the status quo. This can be seen in figure 4.1, where the Congress's ideal policies fall further away from the status quo on the air pollution issue, and the president's preferences fall further from the status quo on the natural gas issue.

I next assume that the president is able to use the expertise of the federal bureaucracy to reduce his uncertainty about the effects of any policy enacted on issue 2. I model the president's acquisition of this private knowledge about the policy shift on issue 2 by assuming that he observes the value of ω_2 at the beginning of the game. Congressional committee staffs may have conducted their own analysis of rising natural gas prices, but they are usually outmatched in technical resources by the executive agencies that are channeled through the legislative clearance process. Lobbyists and policy experts also provide information to Congress, but such information can also only be credibly conveyed when lobbyists and members of Congress share similar policy preferences. This further suggests that the president may not find all bureaucratic expertise equally credible, but I assume that internal policy differences in the executive branch are less disparate than those between the executive and legislature because of the president's appointment and management functions within the executive branch.

Suppose, for instance, that there is uncertainty about why natural gas prices are rising in spite of deregulation and abundant supplies. If Department of Energy analysts discover that many natural gas producers are shifting from production of regulated "old gas" to exploring for "new gas" that can be sold at higher prices because of Carter's deregulation laws, this may imply a need for a policy shift towards more deregulation. Because of its control over the clearance process, the White House can then decide whether or not to forward such draft legislation to Congress.

The president is able to influence Congress's choice of issue with his policy expertise because the uncertain element, ω_2, on issue 2 influences the ideal policies of the president and the Congress in the same way. When ω_2 calls for a high policy from the president, it also calls for a high policy from Congress. Both therefore confront a higher urgency for dealing with issue 2 when ω_2 is high, i.e., when there has been a larger than expected amount of "old gas" producers who have switched to exploring for new gas. Presidential agenda setting can occur when the president is able to convey this information to Congress and persuade Congress to legislate on issue 2 rather than on issue 1. But as I noted earlier, a difficulty arises because if Congress believes whatever the president says, then the president has an incentive to sometimes indicate issue 2 is a priority even when Congress would do better to work on issue 1.

Equilibrium Predictions of the Legislative Clearance Model

In general, there are often many equilibria in cheap-talk games. For instance, a "babbling" equilibrium always exists where the president always sends the same message regardless of ω_2, which is therefore completely uninformative, and Congress chooses an issue and bill based on its unchanged prior belief $E(\omega_2) = \varpi_2/2$. In such a babbling equilibrium, no information is conveyed from the president to Congress, and he exercises no nontrivial agenda influence.

More important for agenda setting is a two-partition equilibrium in which the president sends two different messages depending on the state of ω_2. In nontrivial agenda setting, each message can be understood as signaling which issue and bill Congress should choose. When the preferences of the president and Congress are close enough relative to the amount of uncertainty on issues 1 and 2, an equilibrium exists that satisfies both the conditions for a Perfect Bayesian equilibrium, which is defined in Appendix B, and the conditions for nontrivial agenda setting. Thus, the president is sometimes able to influence the congressional agenda because of the transmission of private information he holds regarding the consequences of different courses of legislative action. The strategies and beliefs listed in table 4.1 constitute a Perfect Bayesian equilibrium of the legislative clearance game for preferences close enough, i.e., when the following four conditions hold:

President's low-message incentive constraint (ICL): $\varpi_2 < p_2 + (\frac{1}{2})[4(p_2)^2 + 4(c_1)^2 - \varpi_1{}^2]^{\frac{1}{2}}$

TABLE 4.1: Agenda-setting equilibrium messages, beliefs, and policies

State of the World $\Omega = (\omega_1, \omega_2)$	President's Equilibrium Messages $m^*(\omega_2)$	Congress's Equilibrium Beliefs $\mu^*(m)$	Congress's Equilibrium Policies $b^*(m\mid\mu^*(m))$
$(0, 0)$			
	$m = 0$	$\mu(0) = 0$	$b = \{c_1 + \overline{\omega}_1/2,\ 0\}$
$(\varpi_1 = 0)$			
$(0, \varpi_2)$			
	$m = \omega_2$	$\mu(\omega_2) = \omega_2$	$b = \{0,\ \omega_2\}$
$(\varpi_1 = \varpi_2)$			

President's high-message incentive constraint (ICH): $\varpi_2 < -p_2 + (\tfrac{1}{2})[4(p_2)^2 - 4(c_1)^2 - \varpi_1{}^2]^{\frac{1}{2}}$

Congress's participation constraint (PC): $\varpi_2 > (\tfrac{1}{2})(2c_1 + \varpi_1)$
President's veto constraint (v): $\varpi_1 > 2c_1$

In equilibrium the president's message is sometimes able to persuade Congress to work on issue 2, $b = \{c_1 + \varpi_1/2, 0\}$, the president's preferred issue, if ϖ_2 is relatively high, i.e., where the constraints ICH and PC are satisfied. This occurs because both the president and Congress suffer greater disutility from ignoring issue 2 when $\omega_2 = \varpi_2$ and is high. In this equilibrium the president is able to reveal his private information so that Congress's beliefs μ are determined by the message m sent by the president. In a two-partition equilibrium, then, the president's signals serve only to indicate whether $\omega_2 = \varpi_2$, in which case Congress prefers to take action on issue 2, or $\omega_2 = 0$, in which case Congress prefers acting on issue 1. In the next section I examine more carefully the conditions under which such agenda setting can occur.

Presidential Agenda Influence through Legislative Clearance

In figure 4.2, the size of the possible policy shift on each issue is held fixed at the same level, $\varpi_1 = \varpi_2 = 1$, and I examine how the president's agenda-setting influence depends on the similarity of the president's and Congress's ex ante ideal policies. Presidential agenda setting is possible when ideal policies of the president and Congress are not identical, but as their preferences diverge the possibility of agenda setting diminishes. In figure 4.3, the incentive constraint, ICL, is one boundary above which agenda setting breaks down. Holding $\varpi_1 = \varpi_2 = 1$, when p_2 is above the incentive constraint, ICL, the president prefers to lie and send the message $m = \omega_2$ even when $\omega_2 = 0$. Congress's participation constraint, PC, indicates the boundary to the right of which Congress will work only on issue 1. Holding $\varpi_1 = \varpi_2 = 1$, when c_1 is greater than $\varpi_1/2$, then Congress will always work on issue 1 because issue 2 never offers greater expected utility.

The question naturally arises whether the president can gain additional influence over the agenda if he is able to acquire private information on issue 1 as well. Surprisingly, when the president is informed on both issues, the range of conditions under which he can reveal full information about the policy shift on issue 2 is reduced. This occurs because a new incentive arises, when the president has private information on both issues, to sometimes divert Congress to issue 2 by falsely signaling that there is no policy shift on issue 1. Congress, aware of the president's incentive to divert, will trust the messages of the president in fewer conditions than is the case when he is informed only on issue 2. This incentive to divert is explored formally in Larocca (2004).

FIGURE 4.2 Conditions on c_1 and p_2 for existence of separating equilibrium when $\varpi_1 = \varpi_2 = 1$

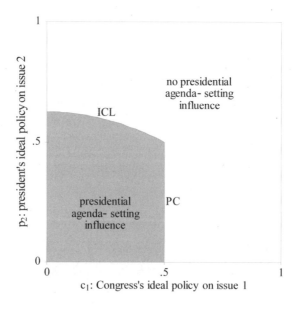

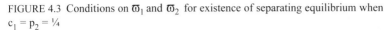

FIGURE 4.3 Conditions on ϖ_1 and ϖ_2 for existence of separating equilibrium when $c_1 = p_2 = \frac{1}{4}$

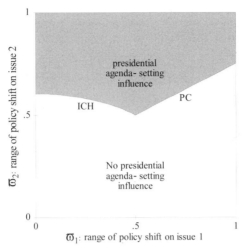

In figure 4.3, I fix the president's and Congress's ideal policies in order to explore how changing the size of the policy shift on each issue influences presidential agenda setting. Here a different picture emerges. Because of the assumptions of the model, this can roughly be interpreted as varying the amount of uncertainty on each issue, while holding the policy preferences constant. The size of the policy shift on issue 2 is more important in determining whether agenda setting occurs. Agenda setting is possible for all positive values of, but only for $\varpi_2 > 2c_1$. When ϖ_2 falls below the incentive constraint, ICH, communication breaks down because the president prefers to send message m = 0, even when $\omega_2 = \varpi_2$, in order to get Congress to deliver policy change on issue 1. Although I do not portray the role of the veto in figure 4.3, it would play an active role in agenda-setting equilibria for $\varpi_1 > 2c_1$, because the president will veto Congress's ideal policy on issue 1 under these conditions. When ω_2 falls below the participation constraint, PC, then Congress prefers to legislate on issue 1 regardless of the occurrence of any size policy shift on issue 2.

Together, the agenda-setting equilibrium conditions displayed in figures 4.2 and 4.3 reveal the conditions under which the president influences the congressional agenda through legislative clearance, i.e., when he has more policy expertise than Congress. The main results are that the president can exercise such influence only when either his policy preferences are quite similar to Congress's, as shown in figure 4.2, or when he has a large informational advantage over Congress on issue 2, as shown in figure 4.3.

The role of the president's informational advantage displayed in figure 4.2 also allows speculation about where in the congressional process the president's draft legislation is likely to have the largest effect on the agenda. Since the president's draft legislation can influence the agenda mainly by providing expertise that reduces programmatic uncertainty on an issue, it is likely to be most effective at stages where expertise plays a more prominent role than political concerns and other considerations. As I will argue in chapter 5, more detailed consideration of bills is given in subcommittee and full committee hearings and markups than on the floor. After bills are considered in subcommittee or committee, Congress is likely to have acquired more information about the issue from these committee activities. Committee consideration is therefore likely to put Congress on a more level playing field with the executive in terms of expertise on the issue. The president's greatest informational advantage therefore is for issues that have not yet been considered in committee stages. Therefore, I expect expertise to play a more prominent role in prompting consideration at these earlier stages, and it is here that I expect draft legislation to have its strongest impact. Thus, the submission of draft legislation on an issue should exert a direct positive influence on whether that issue is considered in committee or subcommittee but less direct influence on floor consideration of the issue.

It is also useful to consider how the president's agenda-setting influence varies throughout his term or throughout the congressional calendar. It should be noted that the expertise of the federal bureaucracy does not necessarily diminish with usage in the way the president's political capital is often said to (e.g., C. Jones 1994; Light 1991). As a result, there should be no necessary decline in the effectiveness of this agenda-setting power throughout the president's term. Thus, the model of legislative clearance yields four predictions about the president's agenda-setting influence: (1) legislative clearance only influences the agenda if the president and Congress are not far apart, e.g., noncontroversial issues; or (2) if the president has a large advantage in policy expertise, i.e., complex or technical issues; (3) this agenda influence is strongest at the committee and subcommittee stages of the legislative process; and (4) this agenda influence is relatively constant throughout the president's term. In the next chapter I argue for the testing of these predictions of the president's influence on issue-level data rather than the more traditional bill-level data on the legislative process.

PART II

An Empirical Study of Presidential Agenda
Setting in Congress

·5·

Redefining Congressional Agenda Setting

In his first address before a joint session of Congress and in a special address in the fall of 1993, President Bill Clinton called for "bold steps to reform our health care system." In the wake of Clinton's speeches, health care reform dominated the schedules of House legislators more than any single policy issue Congress had faced in more than a decade. In addition to numerous public hearings, there were less visible committee markups (in Education and Labor and Ways and Means in the House[1]) and behind-the-scenes bill writing by party and committee leaders. Twenty health care reform bills were introduced in Congress between the time Clinton first called for health care reform and when his bill, H.R. 3600, was introduced (Rovner 1995). In the 103rd Congress, alternative health care reform proposals from Representatives Jim McDermott (H.R. 1200) and Jim Cooper (H.R. 3200) acquired many sponsors and also received hearings. In spite of all of this activity, however, the House leadership failed to bring any version of health care reform to a floor vote.

The fate of Clinton's health care reform highlights two questions that I will address in this chapter. First, to examine only the fate of the *bills* submitted by the president is to miss the president's potential influence in cases where his draft legislation is dropped in favor of one or more alternative bills. For example, if we merely studied the fate of Clinton's H.R. 3600, we would overlook the fact that his focus on the issue of health care reform provoked multiple alternative health care reform bills and that some of these received agenda consideration also. In this chapter, I turn to an examination of how the congressional agenda is influenced by the *issues* raised by the president's proposals, rather than just examining whether the president's *bills* receive agenda consideration. This will allow me to more accurately assess the president's overall influence on the congressional agenda because even if the president's proposal is declared "dead on arrival," it may bring to life other more passable bills that have been initiated by others. Many observers have noted that this might have indeed occurred during the Clinton health reform effort had Clinton not threatened to veto any bill that did not provide "universal coverage" (*CQ Almanac* 1994; Johnson and Broder 1996; Rovner 1995; Schick 1995). Issue-level analysis of presidential agenda setting, however, will require developing a new way of measuring what issues are on the congressional agenda and in presidential proposals. In the first part of this chapter, I develop a new framework for analyzing such issues.

The second question, which arises out of the example of Clinton's health care reform agenda, is how to assess the president's influence on agenda actions that occur before a bill reaches a floor vote. In the case of health care reform, if we were to examine merely floor votes it would seem that Clinton's health care proposal had no influence on the congressional agenda during the 103rd Congress. This is misleading because Clinton's health care reform actually dominated every stage of the congressional agenda except the floor. Even when committee-level agenda setting is fruitless in the sense that it fails to produce enacted laws, it is still important because it crowds out the consideration of other potentially important issues. In this chapter, I explore committee and floor agenda setting in the House in order to determine which stages are most crucial for presidential influence on the agenda.

I begin by explaining how the "units of analysis" previous researchers have used to identify items on the congressional agenda are sometimes misleading, and I then explore the problems and advantages of conducting agenda analysis at the issue level. Next, I identify the most important stages in the House committee and floor agenda process using both bill-level and issue-level analysis, and show how the proposed issue-level analysis leads to a more accurate understanding of the president's influence on the congressional agenda process than the traditional bill-level analysis. I end the chapter by analyzing the relationship between the House and Senate agendas at both the bill and issue level.

An Agenda of Bills or Issues?

Previous studies of presidential agenda setting have analyzed the president's influence on enactments (Chamberlain 1946; Moe and Teel 1970; Goldsmith 1983; C. Jones 1994), proposals (Peterson 1990; Light 1991), bills (Edwards, Barrett, and Peake 1997; Taylor 1998; Edwards and Barrett 2000; Theriault 2002), hearings (Edwards and Wood 1998; Flemming, Wood, and Bohte 1999) and budget requests (Canes-Wrone 2001; Canes-Wrone, Herron, and Shotts 2001). Aside from Light

(1991) and Peterson (1990), none of these studies has been conducted as the level of analysis that I argue is most appropriate for studying agenda setting: policy issues. Issues provide a more suitable unit of analysis for examining agenda setting than bills because several bills cover the same issue and are substitute solutions for the same problem. A hearing on a single policy issue may involve half a dozen bills. And many bills are laid on the table at some stage of the legislative process in favor of a substitute on the same issue that advances further on the agenda. In this case, the issue advances on the agenda, but it is not apparent from looking at the original bill. Furthermore, many bills cover a multitude of issues, some of which may advance further and others that may stall.

Although Light and Peterson study the presidential agenda at the level of issues (proposals), they look only at presidentially initiated proposals. They do not directly address the question of how congressional issues are affected by presidential agenda setting because they do not compare presidentially initated proposals to congressionally initiated proposals. Neither study therefore tests whether the president has a significant independent influence on the congressional agenda.

Using time-series data, Edwards and Wood (1998) and Flemming, Wood, and Bohte (1999) analyze the influence of presidential speeches on congressional hearings over time and find more conflicting results. However, these studies are incomplete in the sense that they do not take into account the numerous bills and issues on the legislative agenda that never receive a hearing. As I will show, many important legislative issues advance on the legislative agenda without receiving hearings. To the degree that such issues are systematically (uniformly) different from the set of issues that receives hearings, the president's influence on hearings may yield a biased estimate of the president's influence on the overall agenda. To mitigate this bias in the analysis of chapters 6 and 7, I measure the president's influence on hearings while simultaneously assessing (controlling for) his influence on other stages of the agenda process. Thus, while hearings cannot be ignored they can at best tell only part of the story of the president's influence on the agenda.

Rather than studying the president's influence on policy initiatives, Canes-Wrone (2001; Canes-Wrone, Herron, and Shotts 2001) analyzes the president's ability to influence the budget allocations of agencies and programs and finds that the president can influence appropriations by making specific appeals in his public speeches. Because of the centrality of the budget process in congressional lawmaking,[2] this level of analysis is very important, but it departs from the conventional concern of the presidential agenda-setting literature, i.e., determining whether and how the president can determine the policy issues for new legislation. My focus lies in this more traditional concern of the presidential agenda-setting literature, and therefore I consider the president's impact on policy issues rather than bills, hearings, or budget allocations.

TABLE 5.1 Ratio of scope (number of bills) of presidential issues to scope of non-presidential issues, for both the State of the Union (SOTU) and presidential draft (draft) legislation

Congress	Issues in State of the Union (SOTU) Address			Issues in Presidential Draft Legislation		
	Average Number of Bills on Non-SOTU Issues	Average Number of Bills on SOTU Issues	Ratio of SOTU to Non-SOTU Bills	Average Number of Bills on Non-Draft Issues	Average Number of Bills on Draft Issues	Ratio of Draft to Non-Draft Bills
96	4.91	11.02	2.24	3.79	5.24	1.38
97	3.56	15.38	4.32	3.43	5.24	1.53
98	4.12	7.24	1.76	3.54	15.09	4.27
99	4.44	15.18	3.42	3.95	16.72	4.24
100	5.45	6.85	1.26	4.23	21.31	5.03
101	5.09	22.07	4.34	4.21	24.25	5.76
102	6.68	19.42	2.91	4.07	21.60	5.31
103	8.34	23.65	2.84	5.18	22.78	4.40
104	9.91	26.27	2.65	3.96	29.23	7.39
105	9.33	15.73	1.69	5.35	41.63	7.79
106	11.28	16.15	1.43	6.25	61.51	9.85
107	10.57	20.00	1.89	5.24	38.53	7.36
Average	6.97	16.58	2.56	4.43	25.26	5.36

Bills (including enacted bills) have been by far the most common unit of analysis in studies of agenda setting. Though bills are convenient units of analysis—they are both easily recognizable and traceable through the legislative process—they can also be misleading indicators of the agenda. As the Clinton health care example demonstrates, many bills are alternative solutions for the same problem and therefore cover the same or similar issues. In order to accurately assess the impact of presidential initiatives, bills that cover roughly the same policy issue must be identified. If this is possible, it is a simple matter then to assess whether the agenda consideration of a bill is affected by its covering the same issue as a presidential initiative. If the president calls for national health care reform, as Clinton did in the 103rd Congress, but not improved drug enforcement, then one would expect to see increased congressional consideration of bills that cover health care reform but not necessarily of bills that cover drug enforcement, all else being equal. But consider the following scenario: (1) The president introduces a policy initiative on national health care reform; and (2) members of Congress deduce that national health care reform will be salient to voters and therefore introduce many alternatives to the president's plan, seeking to gain credit for introducing a salient issue and perhaps even for sponsoring enacted legislation. As a result, there would be more bills on average—all else being equal—on the president's issues than on issues not initiated by the president. As I showed in the beginning of this chapter, this is exactly what happened on health care reform in the 103rd Congress. As long as the analysis is conducted at the bill level, this influx of alternative proposals may either exaggerate or underestimate the influence the president has on the agenda, depending on the stage of the agenda process one considers. To examine this problem, in table 5.1, I list the number of bills and issues covered by the president's State of the Union addresses and presidential draft legislation for the 96th through 107th Congresses.

Table 5.1 shows that on average there are likely to be both more bills introduced on the issues mentioned in the president's State of the Union address and on issues on which the president submits draft legislation. This presents at least two difficulties for studying the president's influence on the agenda consideration of bills: (1) An alternative bill on the same issue may be considered by Congress instead of the president's proposal, making it look like the president did not have an influence on the agenda—even if it was the president's influence that led to consideration of the alternative; and (2) it is also difficult to distinguish whether the president is causing an increase in the number of bills introduced on these issues or whether the president is choosing issues that are already salient in Congress. It is therefore necessary to adjust for the number of bills covered by an issue to avoid mistaking such spurious association for the president's actual effect on the agenda consideration of an issue. To assess the president's influence, then, one needs to identify whether any bill covering the same issue as the presidential initiative receives consideration, and to control for the number of other bills that cover the same issue.

The analysis of issues at the bill level becomes more problematic if each bill can cover more than one issue, as nearly all of the bills I consider do, because one must then decide whether to be concerned with (1) whether any of the issues covered by the bill receives agenda consideration, (2) whether all of the issues covered by the bill receive consideration, or (3) whether some critical proportion of the issues covered by the bill receives consideration. It is more convenient to move the units of analysis from bills to issues, where one can study directly the president's influence on the policy *issues* on the congressional agenda.

The trade-off here is between the precise information available on the agenda actions on individual bills, which are poor proxies for issues, and the more difficult to define and measure information on the agenda actions on issues themselves. I take the second route here in order to more clearly analyze the president's influence on the fate of individual issues on the congressional agenda, which I believe is really the implicit goal of most attempts to analyze agenda setting.

Complications of Using Issues as the Unit of Analysis

Political scientists have developed several available indexes for coding bills into issue areas. Poole and Rosenthal (1997) code roll call votes into one of 99 policy areas. Baumgartner and Jones (1993) code congressional hearings, public laws, and *Congressional Quarterly Almanac* stories into more than 200 topics. Both of these coding schemes succeed in classifying votes or hearings into a single dominant issue area, even though complex bills often cover many issue areas. The ability to identify a single issue for each bill is enormously helpful in subsequent statistical analysis. Issues can become a unit of analysis because the resulting set of issues is mutually exclusive, i.e., bills do not get assigned to two or more issues, and exhaustive, i.e., every bill gets assigned to an issue. A set of mutually exclusive and exhaustive issues helps eliminate the problem arising from the president's inadvertent tendency to promote the introduction of many alternative bills, which I discussed in the previous section, because alternative bills on the same issue are no longer treated separately.

But the increased parsimony from considering issues rather than bills comes at a cost. The use of a limited number of categories forces the grouping together of bills that can be strikingly different. And many bills seem to defy classification into a single area. As an illustration of the first point, note for example that Baumgartner and Jones (1993) do not include a separate category for abortion, but instead code hearings that address abortion rights under their "freedom of speech" topic, combining what are more naturally thought of as quite different issues. The determination of any coding scheme cannot avoid this problem entirely because there is no definitive, mutually exclusive, and exhaustive set of issues. Yet, the set of possible issue categories identified should resonate with what are commonly considered issues on the congressional or presidential agenda. Kingdon (1995) suggests that this means identifying issues at a high level of precision, but this is not possible in the limited Poole and Rosenthal or Baumgartner and Jones taxonomies.

Another serious problem for any issue-coding scheme is the undeniable multidimensional nature of many bills. For example, the economic regulation of airlines concerns both the airline industry and regulatory reform, two separate issues. When a bill is forced into a single mutually exclusive issue, the coder must decide on a dominant topic, a very difficult task for many complex bills. Because of such multidimensional classification problems, I use the Congressional Research Service's Legislative Indexing Vocabulary (CRS-LIV), which codes each bill into multiple topics in addition to using more detailed issue coding than either Poole and Rosenthal (1997) or Baumgartner and Jones (1993). The CRS-LIV has added relevance because it is the database that is actually used by members of Congress and their staffs to find bills that cover a particular topic.

In fact, that is exactly the purpose for which the Congressional Research Service created its taxonomy of issues.

The use of the CRS-LIV index as the basis for analysis presents a new set of problems for statistical analysis. First, the set of CRS-LIV issues changes continuously with the addition of new issues of the congressional agenda and with the refining of the database by CRS. Second, the issues in the CRS-LIV are not mutually exclusive and therefore overlap with some issues being more general than others (unlike the Poole and Rosenthal and Baumgartner and Jones indexes). Moreover, there is a hierarchy of issues from the very specific, like hospital costs, to the very general, like health care, and it is difficult to determine the level of generality at which the president's influence on the agenda should be studied.

Given the breadth and the multifaceted nature of legislative issues and the complex interrelationships among issues, a set of mutually exclusive and exhaustive issues is impossible to establish. As a visual illustration of the problem, consider figure 5.1, which represents the CRS-LIV hierarchical coding of abortion-related issues so that the height of the issue identifies its "scope," or how broad the issue is. Nested issues are linked in figure 5.1 so that the broader issue is above the narrower issue. It is clear, however, that even side-by-side issues that are at the same level of the hierarchy are not identical in scope (e.g., the issue of "health care" is broader in scope than "counseling"). And issues at any given level of scope are likely to overlap, as is the case for the four abortion issues—Abortion, Abortion Procedures, Abortion Policy, and Abortion Counseling—that are located at the same level of scope in figure 5.1.

FIGURE 5.1 The hierarchy and scope of CRS-LIV abortion-related issues in the 107th Congress

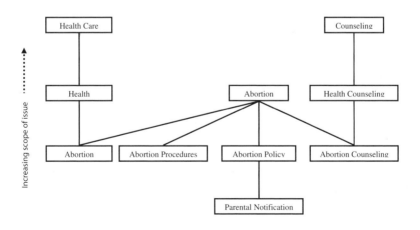

TABLE 5.2 Misleading scenarios resulting from analysis of issues with different scopes

Scenario 1: Presidential Influence Underestimated (real correlation hidden)	**Scenario 2:** Presidential Influence Overestimated (spurious correlation observed)
a. **At any given level of scope, presidential issues are more likely to be on the congressional agenda than non-presidential issues.**	a. **At any given level of scope, presidential issues are no more likely to be on the congressional agenda** than non-presidential issues.
b. **Broad scope issues are more likely to be on the congressional agenda than** narrow-scope issues.	b. **Broad scope issues are more likely to be on the congressional agenda than** narrow-scope issues.
c. **The presidential agenda includes more narrow-scope issues** than broad-scope issues.	c. **The presidential agenda includes more broad-scope issues** than narrow-scope issues.

Rather than searching in vain for a privileged level or scope where the issues are mutually exclusive and exhaustive, I introduce a measure of issue scope as a control variable in the statistical analyses of agenda setting of chapters 6 and 7. Control variables essentially extract the influence of potentially confounding effects, like issue scope. That is, I acknowledge that the president's influence on the agenda consideration of an issue may depend on the scope of the issue under consideration, and I try to avoid the problem of having the scope confound the president's influence on the agenda by explicitly measuring and extracting the influence of the scope of each agenda issue.[3]

Considering CRS-LIV issues rather than bills as the units of analysis, however, opens up the possibility of an ecological inference problem (Achen and Shively 1995). An ecological inference problem is a potential bias that can occur when making inferences about individual-level behavior from aggregate-level data, when the aggregation rule is unknown. Consider the two scenarios shown in table 5.2. Both of the scenarios produce misleading results when one analyzes the president's effect on the congressional agenda using the set of all issues without controlling for issue scope. Two types of mistakes can occur: In scenario 1, one might not observe the president's influence even when it exists if the presidential agenda includes mostly narrow-scope issues, simply because Congress is more likely to act on broad-scope issues. And, in scenario 2, one might think that the president actually has influence if the presidential agenda is more likely to include broad-scope issues, and broad-scope issues are also more likely to appear on the congressional agenda. In other words, the president's actual influence on the congressional agenda can be hidden by the president and Congress focusing

FIGURE 5.2 The complexity of bills and scope of issues as represented in the relationships between tables of a relational database

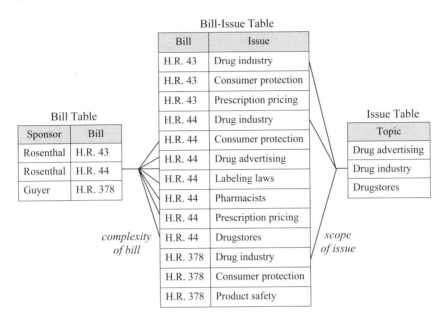

on either broad or narrow issues.

Differing issue scopes do not necessarily mean different sets of issues. A different issue scope might also represent the same issue seen from a different level of aggregation, like the difference between "Abortion" and "Abortion Policy" in figure 5.1. So a correlation of agendas rooted solely in the scope of the issues pursued by the president and Congress is indeed an ecological fallacy. Fortunately, I can measure the number of bills covering each issue, and include this estimate of the scope of the issue as a control variable to mitigate this ecological fallacy.

In figure 5.2, I show the relationship between a table of bills and a table of issues from the 96th Congress as they are represented in a relational database, and table 5.3 lists the titles of the 96th Congress bills in figure 5.2. A relational database contains several interrelated tables of data and links them so that complex relationships between the variables in different tables can be analyzed. For example, my issue-level database contains separate tables that contain information about bills, committees, members of Congress, and issues. These tables can be linked through "queries" in order to produce data that involve data from multiple tables. Because of the multidimensional nature of bills, any given bill might cover several different issues. For instance, H.R. 44 covers seven different issues: the drug industry, consumer protection, drug advertising, labeling laws,

TABLE 5.3 The titles of 96th Congress bills from figure 5.2

- **H.R. 43:** A bill to permit the advertising of drug prices and to require retailers of prescription drugs to post the prices of certain commonly prescribed drugs.

- **H.R. 44:** A bill to amend the Federal Food, Drug, and Cosmetic Act so as to require that in the labeling and advertising of drugs sold by prescription the "established name" of such drug must appear each time their proprietary name is used, and for other purposes.

- **H.R. 378:** A bill to expand the medical freedom of choice of consumers by amending the Federal Food, Drug, and Cosmetic Act to provide that drugs will be regulated under that Act solely to assure their safety.

---

pharmacists, prescription pricing, and drugstores. Because bills that cover more issues are more likely to be more complex, I define a measure I call "complexity" for each bill, which is simply the number of issues covered by the bill, as coded by the CRS-LIV.

Likewise, each issue might be covered by more than one bill. For instance, the drug industry is covered by bills H.R. 43, H.R. 44, and H.R. 378. In general, the more bills covering an issue, the broader is the scope of the issue. For instance, the narrower topic of drugstores is covered by only one of these bills, H.R. 44. The correspondence between number of bills and scope of an issue is not as precise as that between the complexity of a bill and the number of issues it covers, because an issue might be connected to a large number of bills simply because the issue is salient and many members of Congress introduce alternative bills. Nevertheless, the number of bills per issue makes the most convenient measure of an issue's scope that can be used for each of the Congresses I study. Both complexity and scope are used as control variables in later analyses of agenda setting in order to mitigate the variation that occurs in both the scope and degree of overlap in the CRS-LIV issues. In this way I hope to minimize the ecological inference problem that arises in trying to study issues with a hierarchical set of overlapping issues.

In table 5.4, I provide a correspondence between the number of bills (in parentheses) and the number of issues in different stages of the legislative process. Note that while the number of bills receiving hearings is generally higher than the number of bills that pass, the number of issues that receive hearings is almost always less than the number of issues that are passed. Much of this discrepancy occurs because there are typically many substitute bills, which cover largely the same issues, that receive hearings together. When bills are used as a direct measure of issues, the occurrence of these substitutes will tend to overestimate the number of issues under consideration in hearings, because many bills

TABLE 5.4 The number of CRS-LIV issues in different stages of the legislative process among bills referred to the House Commerce Committee (number of bills in parentheses)

Congress	Introduction	Hearing	Markup	Floor	Pass
97	1167	415	289	380	308
	(806)	(111)	(42)	(57)	(42)
98	1376	594	619	654	589
	(812)	(179)	(110)	(82)	(62)
99	1898	551	580	1011	936
	(871)	(124)	(68)	(92)	(61)
100	2471	1138	1090	1547	1474
	(939)	(150)	(91)	(126)	(104)
101	2254	822	668	1010	946
	(1030)	(139)	(69)	(98)	(81)
102	2616	1034	1008	1356	1215
	(1046)	(95)	(67)	(90)	(65)
103	2872	1060	866	1737	1501
	(851)	(62)	(49)	(76)	(57)
104	3264	1284	885	1559	1431
	(799)	(71)	(64)	(95)	(70)
105	2887	1014	821	1323	981
	(850)	(54)	(44)	(81)	(59)
106	3198	1096	991	1552	1215
	(1118)	(76)	(50)	(100)	(67)

Sources: House Commerce Committee Calendars, 1981–99, and THOMAS legislative information system, Library of Congress.

that concern the same topic are likely to be considered in the same hearing. But only one of a given set of substitute bills will be passed by the House, so at the passage stage there is much less overlap, and a smaller number of bills covers a broad range of issues. This suggests a problem of interpreting the meaning of legislative action at early stages of the agenda process with analysis at the bill level. It is also surprising that more bills reach the floor than appear in markup sessions. This occurs because many bills find a way around committee consideration, as I will discuss in the next section.

In chapters 6 and 7, I analyze the president's influence on policy issues covered by all bills submitted to House and Senate Commerce Committees from 1979 to 2002. First, in the next section, I determine the most important stages in the legislative process for presidential agenda setting.[4]

Critical Stages of the House Agenda Process

My analysis of the critical stages of the House agenda process derives from the formal legislative process for bills. Though the study of presidential agenda setting ultimately demands analysis of issues rather than bills, the fact remains that issues are conveyed through most stages of the legislative process by bills and amendments. In the House, issues that have not been introduced by a bill can only be discussed in hearings and in debate, but not included in markup or amendment, because of the House's prohibition against nongermane amendments. In every stage of the House legislative process where the text of a bill can be changed, the nongermane amendment rule applies.[5] Therefore, the formal rules and stages that affect the movement of bills through the legislative process also govern the movement of issues as well. The framework for the analysis that follows, then, will look familiar, since it derives from the traditional legislative process for bills. First, I provide a detailed analysis of how bills pass through that process and then compare it to a detailed analysis of how issues flow through the process. A comparison of the two further demonstrates the problems of using bills rather than issues to analyze the legislative agenda.

There are three distinct institutions through which most bills pass in the House legislative process: (1) subcommittee; (2) full committee; and (3) the floor. In table 5.5, I report the number and percentage of House Commerce bills and issues that are processed through these stages of the House agenda. First consider the pattern for bills. From the 96th through 107th Congresses less than 10%

TABLE 5.5   Percentage of all House Commerce bills and issues in major agenda stages, 1979–2002

	Major Agenda Actions	Total bills	Percent of Bills	Total Issues	Percent of Issues
	Introduction	11,379	100.0	28,804	100.0
Subcommittee:	Executive comment	810	7.1	11,903	41.3
	Subcommittee hearing*	1,126	10.0	9,435	32.8
	Subcommittee markup	696	6.1	8,592	29.8
Full Committee:	Subcommittee report	625	5.5	7,942	27.6
	Full committee markup	731	6.4	9,884	34.3
Floor:	Full committee report	726	6.4	9,701	33.7
	Committee discharged	161	1.4	5,171	18.0
	Suspension of rules	494	4.3	6,090	21.1
	Special Rule	152	1.3	7,233	25.1
	Total floor	990	8.7	13,916	48.3

* Hearings are held in full committee as well, but these are relatively rare in House Commerce, accounting for a total of 28 hearings from 1979–2002.

(990 of 11,391) of bills referred to the House Commerce Committee eventually made it to the floor. Although it is not reported in table 5.5, nearly all bills introduced in the House are referred to a committee. Except in very rare cases when bills are summoned directly to the floor before referral, House procedure requires the Speaker or Parliamentarian to refer all bills introduced in the House to the committee(s) with the proper jurisdiction (Deschler and Brown 1984, 16.3.1). Committee chairs are typically required by committee rules to refer all legislation to the subcommittee with the appropriate jurisdiction within two weeks. This means that almost all legislation routinely reaches the subcommittee stage.

The subcommittees and committees are largely responsible for determining the bills that reach the floor agenda because getting out of committee is the biggest hurdle in the legislative consideration of bills. Once in the subcommittee stage, only a small percentage of bills (5.5%) are ever reported out. But those bills that are reported by subcommittees almost always go on to full committee markup and are reported to the House floor. A higher percentage of bills (6.9%) is reported from full committee than from subcommittee (5.5%) because some bills circumvent the subcommittee stage. In turn, most bills that are reported from committee are granted a floor vote of some kind.

Consider figure 5.3, which offers a more detailed look at the agenda paths of bills by tracing the major paths of all House bills referred to House Commerce from 1979 to 2002.[6] Each arrow in figure 5.3 indicates the proportion of bills that proceed from one stage to another by the percentage indicated next to the arrow and by the relative thickness of the arrow. Subcommittee, full committee, and floor stages of the legislative process are circumscribed by dashed boxes, and more advanced stages of the legislative process generally occur as bills move across from left to right and from top to bottom in the diagram. Since only a very small proportion of bills progress to stages beyond subcommittee markup without going through subcommittee markup, these markups are a critical stage in the House agenda process. By contrast, many more bills go around subcommittee hearings or requests for executive comment, marking them as less essential agenda stages. By this standard, full-committee markup also appears to be essential because only a small portion of bills reach the floor without first being marked up in full committee.[7] But full committee markup is less selective than subcommittee markup because most bills that are reported to the full committee are scheduled for a full-committee markup, whereas only a small proportion of those bills that reach earlier subcommittee stages are scheduled for subcommittee markup.

Figure 5.3 shows that the textbook legislative procedure is a vast simplification of the House legislative process and that there are many routes to floor consideration.[8] Indeed, there are even more routes than shown in figure 5.3, but I have excluded paths that at least 0.2% of bills did not follow in order to keep the figure simple enough for visual interpretation. A 1975 House Administration Committee report identified more than 100 different possible stages in the consid-

FIGURE 5.3 Paths of House bills referred to House Commerce, 1979–2002

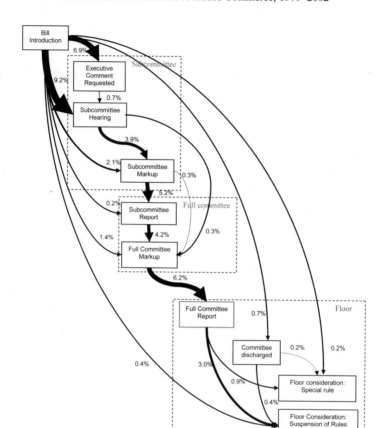

eration of a bill (quoted in Oleszek 2001, 20). The most important stages in terms of the percentage of bills they process are: (1) request for executive comment; (2) subcommittee hearing; (3) subcommittee markup and report; (4) full committee markup and report; and (5) consideration under suspension of the rules or by unanimous consent. The first and last stages are missing from the typical textbook process. All textbook authors, even the otherwise meticulous Oleszek (2001),[9] ignore the first stage—requests for executive comment. Requests for executive comment are formal requests sent to executive agencies for their views on pending legislation. And most textbooks, though not Oleszek in this case, emphasize the granting of a special rule and consideration under these special rules, rather than suspension of the rules. However, most laws—including many on Mayhew's (1991) list of significant enactments—are created from bills that are passed in the House under suspension of the rules because most public bills that reach a floor

FIGURE 5.4 Paths of issues covered by House bills referred to House Commerce, 1979–2002

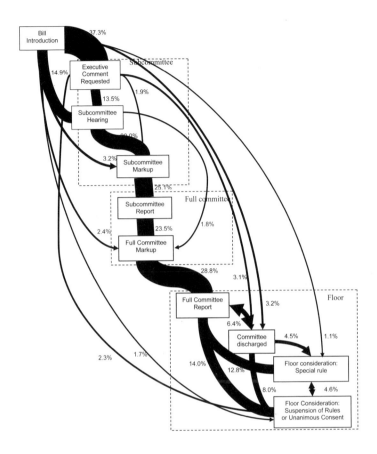

vote pass without significant opposition. Special rules typically limit debate and amendments and can be used to expedite floor consideration and to prevent hostile debate or amendment tactics from undermining a bill. Suspension of the rules and unanimous consent are supermajoritarian procedures that expedite voting on non-controversial, but not necessarily unimportant, legislation.

Returning to table 5.5, a different pattern emerges when one considers issues rather than bills. Nearly 50% of the CRS-LIV issues covered by bills submitted to House Commerce make it to the floor, whereas less than 10% of bills make it to the floor. And although 38.2% of issues receive either subcommittee markup or hearing, a considerable percentage (10.1%) of issues arrive at the floor without receiving these main subcommittee actions. By contrast, a much smaller percentage of bills arrive on the floor without receiving either subcommittee markup or hearings.

Figure 5.4 traces issues rather than bills through House agenda stages. An issue is considered to have advanced from one stage to another if at least one bill covering the issue advances between the given stages, even if there are many other bills on the same issue that do not advance. In comparing figures 5.3 and 5.4, at least four important differences are apparent: (1) There is a much greater percentage of issues than bills that receive attention in the textbook stages of the legislative process. (2) While most bills take a single path through the legislative process portrayed in figure 5.3, a single issue can be both reported by a committee and discharged from the same committee (although through different bills), and a single issue can be considered both under a special rule and by suspension of the rules or unanimous consent (again through different bills). (3) The set of issues under consideration does not narrow as dramatically as the set of bills in later stages of the legislative process. (4) A greater percentage of issues receive requests for executive comment than hearings. It is thus apparent that analysis of agenda influence at the issue level may yield a different, and I argue more accurate, picture of the congressional agenda-setting process.

The first difference between figure 5.3 and figure 5.4 is also the most dramatic. Whereas 38.7% of House-originated issues receive either hearings or request for executive comment and 48.3% of House-originated issues receive floor consideration, only 15.4% of all House bills receive either hearings or request for executive comment and only 8.7% of House bills receive floor consideration. It is often stated that the committees are the graveyards of most bills, or that the committees exercise enormous gatekeeping power, because very few bills ever make it out of committee. Figure 5.4 suggests that much of this graveyard effect may be exaggerated due to the fact that many bills are alternates that cover the same issues. The committees are much less restrictive when the analysis is considered at the issue level. The House Commerce Committee, at least, is not as restrictive in bottling up issues as one would be led to believe by looking at the aggregate fate of its bills.

The above analysis suggests that three pre-floor legislative stages are particularly important in the agenda process for issues: requests for executive comment, subcommittee hearings, and subcommittee markup. I will discuss each of these important agenda stages in turn.

Requests for Executive Comment

As noted earlier, requests for executive comment are formal requests sent to executive agencies for their views on pending legislation. Since 1934, responses to these requests have been channeled through the White House for administration approval before being sent to Congress. The executive comments that are approved by the White House and forwarded to Congress can thus indicate both whether the president will support the legislation and the agency's expert opinion on the issue. Congressional committees will request such information either when they are seeking to obtain valuable expertise held by an executive agency on a given issue or when they desire to know whether the president approves of the policy changes proposed by a given bill.

A committee uses both requests for executive comment and hearings to gather information about a bill or issue. Figures 5.3 and 5.4 show that they seem to be used for different types of bills and issues (16.1% of all House bills receive a request for either executive comment or hearings whereas only 0.7% receive both, and 52% of issues receive a request for either executive comment or hearing whereas only 13.5% receive both). This non-overlapping nature of requests for executive comment and hearings also holds for Senate bills considered in the House and for House and Senate bills considered in the Senate. It is therefore likely that requests for executive comment are used by committees to gather information for different kinds of issues than hearings are. Requests for executive comment seem to be useful where there is either congressional uncertainty about whether a bill is acceptable to the president or where there is congressional uncertainty about the policy effects of a bill. Hearings can also provide the expertise of executive agencies, but in hearings this information is often supplemented by the testimony of outside experts. Hearings thus allow committees to gather information on issues where committees do not trust the information in executive comments, perhaps because of the administration's supervision of this process. And while hearings may also play a role in raising the publicity of an issue, perhaps in order to promote further legislative success, requests for executive comment offer no direct way to raise the publicity of a bill or issue.

Thus, requests for executive comment are likely to occur on issues where either (1) Congress is uncertain about whether the president will veto a given bill or (2) the policy preferences of the committee and administration are not too far apart and where the executive agency has a large advantage in expertise over the committee.[10] I argue that the latter case is most likely to occur on non-controversial or technical issues. On controversial issues, e.g., where the committee's and administration's policy preferences are far apart, the agency's executive comment is likely to be distrusted, and hearings may instead be used to invite testimony from experts whose policy preferences make them more trustworthy to the committee.[11]

Subcommittee Hearings

According to former House Parliamentarian William H. Brown, there are three main types of hearings: "(1) legislative hearings, which are held to consider the enactment of a measure into law, and which provide a forum where information and opinions on the measure can be presented; (2) investigative hearings, designed to inform the House as to activities which may call for legislation; and (3) oversight hearings, which are inquiries that invoke the investigative powers of the House as overseer of federal programs and operations" (Brown and Johnson 1996, 253). Legislative hearings play a direct role in agenda setting, but oversight and investigative hearings can also play a preliminary role by providing a forum for determining whether legislation is needed on a given issue. Such hearings necessarily lie outside of our study because they cannot be easily connected with bills and issues that are later introduced as a result of these hearings. To the degree, then, that such investigative and oversight hearings play a role in setting the later legislative agenda, I underestimate the influence of hearings. I suspect that this influence is small compared to the direct agenda-setting role played by the legislative hearings that I do study.

Many previous scholars have defined hearings as synonymous with the legislative agenda (Baumgartner and Jones 1993; Edwards and Wood 1999; Edwards, Barrett, and Peake 1997; Edwards and Barrett 2000; and Flemming, Wood, and Bohte 1999). The path of a large proportion of bills and issues through the House legislative process without hearings, which is apparent in figures 5.3 and 5.4, calls into question this definition of the agenda. While 28.9% of issues receive hearings and then proceed to further stages of the legislative process, 21.3% of issues proceed to further stages without hearings. This pattern is also reflected at the bill level, where only 4.3% of bills that receive hearings go on to further agenda stages, while 6.1% of bills that do not receive hearings still go on to further stages of the agenda. In chapter 6, I not only will explore the president's influence on the issues covered in hearings but will also examine the effect that hearings may have on later stages of the agenda process. In my analysis, hearings are shown to be an important stage in the agenda process, but not the most important stage in determining which issues reach the floor.

Studies of the president's ability to set the agenda of congressional hearings have found mixed results (Edwards and Wood 1999; Edwards, Barrett, and Peake 1997; Edwards and Barrett 2000; and Flemming, Wood, and Bohte 1999). These studies, however, have not differentiated legislative, investigative, and oversight hearings. The president might have different levels of influence on each of these different types of hearings. As table 5.6 shows, legislative hearings make up less than half of the total hearings held by House Commerce in each Congress from 1979 to 2002. It is also evident from the last column in table 5.6 that many legislative hearings cover more than one bill because the average number of bills in a legislative hearing is greater than one for each Congress from the 96th through the 107th. Many of the bills that are considered in a single hearing are likely to be alternates, so that the number of bills that receive hearings in a single Congress is likely to be a misleading measure of the number of issues under consideration

TABLE 5.6   Average number of bills per legislative hearing in House Commerce, 1979–2002

Congress	Total Hearings	Total Legislative Hearings	% of Total Hearings Legislative	Average Number of Bills per Legislative Hearing
96th	235	104	44.2	2.21
97th	275	89	32.4	1.52
98th	231	113	48.9	1.83
99th	251	81	32.3	1.80
100th	294	124	42.2	1.48
101st	236	108	45.8	1.47
102nd	187	72	38.9	1.76
103rd	197	81	41.1	1.17
104th	116	48	41.4	1.52
105th	150	42	28.0	1.29
106th	187	60	32.1	1.40
107th	152	19	12.5	1.37
96th–107th	2,511	941	37.5	1.61

Source: House Commerce Final Calendars, 1980–2002.

in that Congress's hearings. Thus, by moving the analysis to the level of issues covered by legislative hearings, I avoid the overcounting of items under consideration in hearings that afflicts bill-level analysis.

Subcommittee Markup

As shown in figure 5.3, only a fraction of the bills that receive hearings are also subject to subcommittee markup. Figure 5.4 shows that this is not the case for issues, where nearly the same percentage of issues receive markup (25.1%) as receive hearings (28.4%). This difference can partly be explained by the difference between these types of committee actions. As table 5.6 shows, several bills may be considered in the same hearing, as long as they cover similar topics, but rarely will more than one bill be marked up at a time. Unlike hearings, which can serve many functions, markups are usually used to rewrite and advance legislation. In markup sessions a single bill is considered line by line so that amendments may be offered, including alternative language for different parts of the bill. These committee amendments are presented to the floor as recommendations when the bill is reported. Markups attract less public attention than hearings, but they are more central to the process of reporting bills to the floor because they directly influence the language of the bill, and they are usually followed by the reporting of the bill to the next agenda stage. Bills almost never receive subcommittee hearings after receiving subcommittee markup.

Nearly every bill (98.8% from 1979 to 2002) that House Commerce marks up in full committee receives a favorable vote for report to the floor. In other words, full committee markup and full committee report are nearly synonymous for House Commerce. This is not so clearly the case with subcommittee markup and report, where 85.3% of markups are favorably reported to the full committee, and this difference suggests that subcommittee markup plays a more important gatekeeping role in the agenda process. In other words, whereas the full committee markup stage passes along almost everything it receives, the subcommittee markup stage is more selective in what bills and issues it passes along. This is probably because more detailed consideration is given to issues in subcommittee markup than in full committee markup, where the full committee can rely on the work done by the subcommittee. It is also easier to distinguish statistically the subcommittee markup stage from floor consideration than it is to distinguish full committee markup from floor consideration. For these reasons I define the markup stage of the House agenda process by the occurrence of subcommittee markups alone, rather than combining subcommittee and full committee markups, as I did in the case of hearings.

No previous study of presidential agenda setting has isolated the president's influence on the decision to markup a bill in committee or subcommittee, and yet this is empirically and theoretically one of the most important stages in the congressional agenda process. Because markup involves changing the language of the bill and plays a central agenda-setting role, it is a key place to look for the president's influence. An argument could be made that subcommittee markups are, in fact, the most important single stage in the agenda process, since most bills that are reported from subcommittee pass without amendment on the floor. The difficulty until now has been the inaccessibility of information on subcommittee and committee markups. Until the advent of the THOMAS legislative database, such information was most easily accessible in the legislative calendars of the individual committees, which vary in the amount of legislative information printed depending on the committee. The legislative calendars for the House and Senate Commerce Committees do provide detailed information about subcommittee markups.

The Floor

All bills reported from committee are placed on one of five House calendars: (1) Union, (2) House, (3) Private, (4) Corrections,[12] or (5) Discharge. The great majority of bills, and their corresponding issues, are put on the House or Union Calendars after being reported from full committee. The Union Calendar is used for revenue bills or for bills that authorize expenditures. The House Calendar receives most policy legislation. The Discharge Calendar holds bills that are discharged from committee. Bills are placed on each of these calendars in chronological order, and they are theoretically to be considered from the calendars in that same order. However, almost all bills that are considered on the floor are done so out of order through procedures like suspension of the rules or the granting of a special rule.

Most bills reach the floor by being reported from a committee, in which case the bill is accompanied by a report that "describes the purposes and scope of the bill, explains the committee revisions, notes proposed changes in existing law, and usually, includes the views of the executive branch agencies consulted" (Oleszek 2001, 102). A much smaller number of bills, but a significant proportion of issues, are placed on the Discharge Calendar by being discharged from a committee or on the Corrections Calendar. Although a discharge petition can be used to force a bill out of a committee that refuses to report it, in practice, most discharges occur with the approval of the committee. Bills can also reach the floor without first being placed on a calendar. In particular, bills at any stage of the agenda process can be brought to a floor vote by a vote to suspend the rules or by unanimous consent, even in some cases before they are referred to a committee.

The Bicameral Agenda

Because bills must pass in both chambers before they can be presented to the president for enactment, it is also important to consider the agenda dynamics of the Senate. In figure 5.5, I plot the paths of all 7,879 bills introduced in the 103rd Congress (rather than just those referred to House Commerce) through important stages of both House and Senate consideration. Here again, the thickness of the lines indicates the relative percentage of bills that pass from one stage to another. Besides including all bills from the 103rd Congress, this diagram is different from figure 5.3 in two important ways: (1) I have included the stages of Senate consideration so that I can trace the paths of bills sequentially through one chamber and then the next. (2) Furthermore, I have separated House and Senate bills by different gray lines in the diagrams. As indicated by the light gray lines, the pattern of House consideration for House bills is similar to that for the House Commerce bills plotted in figure 5.3, suggesting that consideration of the bills referred to the House Commerce Committee may be representative of the consideration of bills in the broader House. A more precise assessment of the relationship between House Commerce issues and the issues considered in other com-

FIGURE 5.5 Legislative paths of all 7,879 bills introduced in the 103rd House and Senate

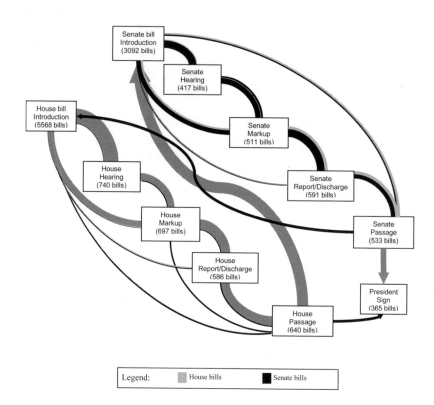

mittees in the 103rd Congress is offered in table C.1 in Appendix C, where the characteristics of bills and issues considered in all committees are compared.

Figure 5.5 also allows me to trace the typical pattern of House bills through the Senate after they pass in the House. House bills tend to follow a different pattern through the Senate than do Senate bills, and House bills are more likely than Senate bills to be considered directly on the floor without intervening committee actions like hearings and markups. It is also clear from the thickness of the light gray lines in the Senate stages in figure 5.5 that the House is a powerful agenda-setting force in the Senate at the bill level. Senate bills are also more likely to be considered directly on the House floor than House bills, but these make up a much smaller proportion of the House agenda than do House bills in the Senate, as seen by the thinner black lines in the House stages. Next I examine these bicameral dynamics at the issue level.

In figure 5.6, I plot the paths of the 7,468 issues that were covered by all 7,879 bills introduced in the 103rd Congress. As was the case for the issues considered by House Commerce alone in figure 5.4, the overall House agenda is

FIGURE 5.6 Legislative paths of all 7,468 issues covered by bills introduced in the 103rd House and Senate

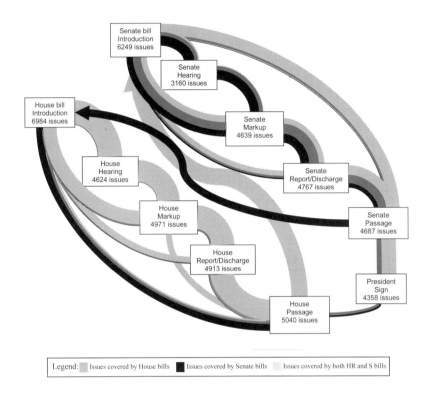

much less restrictive in terms of issues than one would be led to believe by the analysis of bills alone in figure 5.5. I use light gray lines to indicate the paths of issues covered exclusively by House bills, black lines to indicate the paths of issues covered exclusively by Senate bills, and dark gray lines to indicate the issues covered by both House and Senate bills. One of the advantages of using issue-level rather than bill-level analysis is that it permits a visualization of the overlap (dark gray lines) in House and Senate legislation and its role in the agenda process. It is clear from figure 5.6, for instance, that the Senate is far more likely than the House to have both House and Senate bills at a given legislative stage that cover the same issue. The visualization of overlapping issues also reveals more clearly than the bill-level diagram of figure 5.5 the extent of the House's influence over later stages of the Senate agenda. Indeed more House issues (light gray) passed in the Senate than Senate issues (black) and shared issues (dark gray) combined.

It seems, then, that an issue may stand a greater chance of advancing on the Senate agenda if it is introduced in a House-passed bill. This is not surprising both because any House-passed bill will be informed by the policy expertise acquired during House consideration and because the Senate faces less political uncertainty about issues that have already passed in the House. Other considerations being held equal, House-passed measures stand a better chance of being enacted than other bills in the Senate because the crowded House agenda has already been navigated. Issues originating in Senate bills face a similar advantage in the House agenda process, but they make up a much smaller share of the bills introduced in the House and must contend with a more crowded House agenda. Because of this greater House "presence" in the Senate, I will take special care in analyzing the influence of the House on the Senate agenda in chapter 7. I will consider, for instance, whether the president may be able to exercise influence on the Senate agenda indirectly by controlling the House agenda.

Conclusion

In this chapter I have laid out a new framework for studying congressional agenda setting at the issue level rather than at the bill level, while still taking into account the valuable multidimensional nature of bills. The study of issues provides a more intuitive and accurate grasp of the kind of agenda setting that is often associated with the president, i.e., an informal influence over the issue topics considered by Congress. When studying such hierarchical and overlapping issues I have shown that it is necessary to take into account both the scope (number of bills) of issues and the complexity (number of issues) of the bills with which they are associated.

The agenda process of such issues looks in several ways quite different from the pattern of the consideration of bills in the House. A much higher percentage of issues than bills proceed to floor consideration. Issues also figure more prominently at the request for executive comment, discharge, and special rule stages. The most important stages in the agenda consideration of issues are requests for executive comment, subcommittee hearings and markup, and the various forms of floor consideration. I have also shown that House and Senate can exert influence over the issues on each other's agendas, and the House in particular cannot be ignored in looking at influences on the Senate agenda. In the next chapter I examine the president's influence on the consideration of issues in these most important stages of the House agenda process. In chapter 7, I examine the president's influence on the consideration of issues in the most important stages of the Senate agenda process.

·6·

Presidential Agenda Setting in the House

In chapters 3 and 4, I argued that the president's ability to influence the congressional agenda can arise from at least two processes: (1) through public appeals in his speeches that raise the salience of an issue; and (2) through draft legislation that channels the policy expertise of the federal bureaucracy. In this chapter I will examine how the president has been able to use both of these processes to advance issues to different stages of the House agenda using new issue-level data on all legislation considered by the House Commerce Committee from 1979 to 2002.

Key Actors in House Agenda Setting

The main focus of this chapter is to examine how the president can influence the congressional agenda through the use of State of the Union policy requests and through the use of draft legislation that draws on the expertise of the federal bureaucracy. In order to examine presidential influence, I first assess and control for the other important actors in congressional agenda setting. Thus, I begin by looking at the expected influence of all three of the main actors involved in House agenda setting: (1) the committee leadership, i.e., full committee chair and subcommittee chairs; (2) the Senate; and (3) the president.

It is widely recognized that the committee chair and subcommittee chairs have an extraordinary amount of discretion in making scheduling decisions, which essentially makes them the default committee and subcommittee agenda

Table 6.1 Predicted direct effects of president, committee leaders, and the Senate on stages of the House agenda

---

- **President's State of the Union Issues**

- *Floor Stage:* The president is expected to exercise positive influence over the consideration of issues in later, more public stages of the House agenda, e.g., the floor, with mentions in his State of the Union addresses. This occurs because the president's speeches can influence some conditions in the political environment, such as the public salience of an issue problem, which can in turn affect issue consideration on the floor. But these political environment considerations are somewhat less important at the committee level, where technical expertise plays a significant role.

- *First Congress:* The president is expected to be able to use his State of the Union addresses to exert positive influence over the House agenda only in his first Congress, when he can be held most accountable for the consequences of the issues he raises.*

- **President's Draft Legislative Issues**

- *Hearings and Markup:* The president is expected to exercise positive influence over the issues considered in earlier information-gathering stages of the House agenda, e.g., hearings and markups, by introducing draft legislation, because these early stages make greater use of policy expertise than later stages, e.g., floor consideration, where political environment concerns are more likely to dominate.

- *All Congresses:* The issues the president introduces in draft legislation are expected to exercise positive influence over the agenda in every Congress, because the usefulness of this expertise does not decline in the way the president's potential accountability does throughout his term.

- **Committee Leadership**

- *All Agenda Stages:* Since committees vote by majority rule whether to report legislation to the floor, chairs are expected to have less influence over floor consideration than over whether an issue is scheduled for hearing and markup. Chairs are still expected to have some influence on the floor since they can schedule the vote to report.

- *All Congresses:* Since the committee and subcommittee chairs can unilaterally schedule hearings and markups, they are expected to have a strong and persistent positive influence over the issues considered in committee and subcommittee.

- **Senate**

- *Floor Stage:* Senate issues are more likely to influence later stages of the House legislative process, e.g., the floor, where the concerns for final enactment are more likely to be salient.
- *All Congresses:* The Senate is expected to have a strong and persistent positive influence over the issues considered on the House floor.

In later Congresses, voters will not trust the president to promote a legislative program that is in their best interests, because the president can suffer no direct electoral penalties for ignoring their interests.

setters, respectively (Oleszek 2001; Sinclair 1986; Taylor 1998). Chairs can be overridden by a majority of their committee or subcommittee, but this rarely happens. "Chairs win. . . . The expertise that committee and subcommittee chairs bring to the process, their ability to write the actual language of the bill in the markup process, and their dominant formal and informal participation in White

House negotiations . . . are major and important institutional endowments that validate the many claims made for the power and influence of these chairs" (Weissert and Weissert 2002, 315).

It is less widely recognized that the Senate is an important actor. However, any bill that has already passed in the Senate stands a higher chance of becoming law, since it is has already cleared a difficult hurdle in the legislative process. To the degree that House actors are concerned with the future prospects of their issues and bills in the Senate, the likelihood that the issues covered by Senate-passed bills will advance on the House agenda will increase.

I considered the hypothesized effects of the president in detail in chapters 3 and 4, where I modeled the effects of presidential speeches and draft legislation on the congressional agenda. The expected influence of the president, committee leaders, and the Senate on the House agenda is summarized in table 6.1.

Isolating Presidential Influence on the House Agenda Process

The almost unilateral ability of subcommittee and committee chairs to schedule hearings and markup sessions makes their influence particularly important. Presidents, aware of this power, will often ask committee chairs to sponsor their legislation when it is introduced in Congress. In other words, the president may try to leverage the committee chair's influence in his attempt to get his policy issues on the congressional agenda. Because of this, there is always the danger that any statistical attempt to isolate presidential influence on the congressional agenda that "controls for" or "holds constant" the role of committee chairs is likely to underrepresent the president's influence to the degree that it is exercised through the committee chair. Multivariate regression measures the association between two variables when the effects of other control variables are essentially extracted, but if the president's influence is partly exercised indirectly through his influence on the committee chairs, this indirect influence on the agenda will be extracted by controlling for the committee chair. It may thus be impossible to accurately measure the president's influence while "controlling for the committee chair," exactly because the president may depend on the committee chair's influence to bring more attention for his policy priorities. In this case, simple multiple regression controls for too much. Instead, as shown in figure 6.1, the president may influence any agenda stage either directly or indirectly through his influence on earlier stages. For example, the president can influence markup of an issue directly or through two possible indirect routes: (1) by influencing hearings that subsequently have a direct influence on markup; or (2) by influencing a committee leader who can subsequently have both a direct effect on markup and an indirect effect through hearings.

Figure 6.1 Causal models of House Commerce agenda process

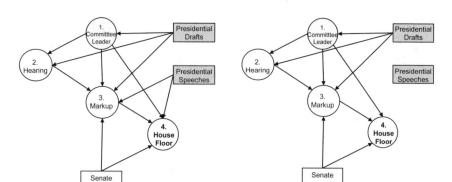

Expected effects in a president's first Congress   Expected effects in a president's later Congresses

To account for the president's indirect effects on the agenda, I perform four distinct regressions in each Congress to determine the president's influence on (1) the committee chair's decision to sponsor a bill concerning a given issue, (2) hearings on the issue, (3) subcommittee markup of the issue, and (4) floor consideration of the issue. The endogenous (explained) variables in each of these regressions are numbered correspondingly in figure 6.1, which summarizes the predicted influences of the theoretical models of presidential influence as well as the expectations about the role of committee leadership and Senate passage from table 6.1.[1]

Each arrow in figure 6.1 represents a predicted positive influence of one variable on an agenda stage. A chain of two or more arrows together represents an indirect influence of the first variable on the last, mediated by those variables between them. The causal diagram on the left represents the expected chain of influences on the agenda in a president's first Congress, and the causal diagram on the right represents a president's subsequent Congresses. The definition and measurement of the complete set of variables used in the four agenda-setting models are given in table 6.2. The results of the four individual regression equations are given in the tables in Appendix F.

An Overview of the President's Influence on the House Agenda

Using the issues covered by all bills referred to the House Commerce Committee from the 96th through the 107th Congresses,[2] table 6.3 summarizes the total agenda-setting effects of the president's State of the Union topics and draft leg-

Table 6.2 Definition and measurement of independent variables for House Commerce models

State of Union—a dichotomous (0, 1) variable indicating whether a given issue was mentioned in the president's State of the Union speeches. Coded by the author.

Draft Legislation—a dichotomous (0, 1) variable indicating whether the president submitted draft legislation covering a given issue. Source: House Commerce Final Calendars and THOMAS legislative database.

Markup—a dichotomous (0, 1) variable indicating whether any bill covering a given issue was subject to subcommittee markup in the House Commerce Committee. Source: House Commerce Final Legislative Calendars, 1979–2002, and THOMAS legislative database.

Hearing—a dichotomous (0, 1) variable indicating whether any bill covering a given issue was subject to subcommittee or full committee hearing in the House Commerce Committee. Source: House Commerce Final Legislative Calendars, 1979–2002, and THOMAS legislative database.

Committee Leader—a dichotomous (0, 1) variable indicating whether any bill covering a given issue had a primary sponsor who was a House Commerce committee or subcommittee chair. Source: House Commerce Final Legislative Calendars, 1979–2002, and THOMAS legislative database.

Senate Bill—a dichotomous (0, 1) variable indicating whether any bill covering a given issue was passed by Senate and referred to House Commerce. Source: House Commerce Final Legislative Calendars, 1979–2002, and THOMAS legislative database.

Request Executive Comment—a dichotomous (0, 1) variable indicating whether an executive comment was requested for any bill covering a given issue. Source: House Commerce Final Legislative Calendars, 1979–2002, and THOMAS legislative database.

Maximum Cosponsors—the maximum number of cosponsors for all bills associated with a given issue and referred to House Commerce. Coded from the final number of cosponsors at the adjournment of a given Congress for each bill, as recorded in the THOMAS legislative database.

Scope (of Issue)—a count of the number of bills referred to House Commerce that cover a given issue. Coded from the CRS-LIV issues assigned to each bill by the Congressional Research Service after compiling this information into a relational database.

Minimum Complexity (of Bills)—the minimum complexity (number of issues) for all bills associated with a given issue and referred to House Commerce. Coded from the CRS-LIV issues assigned to each bill by the Congressional Research Service after compiling this information into a relational database.

Multiply Referred—a dichotomous (0, 1) variable indicating whether any bill covering a given issue was referred to more than one committee. Source: House Commerce Final Legislative Calendars, 1979–2002, and THOMAS legislative database.

Authorization Issue—a dichotomous (0, 1) variable indicating whether an issue concerns authorization or reauthorization of a program. Source: House Commerce Final Legislative Calendars, 1979–2002, and THOMAS legislative database.

(continued)

TABLE 6.2 Definition and measurement of independent variables for House Commerce models *(continued)*

Timing of Introduction—the lowest bill number associated with a given issue divided by the last bill number referred to House Commerce in the same Congress. Source: House Commerce Final Legislative Calendars, 1979–2002, and THOMAS legislative database.

Democrat Sponsor— a dichotomous (0, 1) variable indicating whether the primary sponsor of any bills covering an issue is a Democrat for a given issue. Source: House Commerce Final Legislative Calendars, 1979–2002; THOMAS legislative database; and Swift et al. (2004).

Maximum Sponsor Experience—the highest years of experience in the House of the primary sponsors of all bills associated with a given issue. Source: House Commerce Final Legislative Calendars, 1979–2002; THOMAS legislative database; and Swift et al. (2004).

---

islation as well as the total effects of issues sponsored by committee leaders and issues that are passed by the Senate on House floor consideration. Because the set of Congressional Research Service's Legislative Indexing Vocabulary (CRS-LIV) issues, by which bills are classified into issues, varies from Congress to Congress, the president's effect on the congressional agenda must be analyzed separately for each Congress. The values in table 6.3 are calculated by adding the "statistically significant" direct and indirect effects of each variable on the floor consideration of an issue.[3] Indirect effects are calculated according to the method of path analysis, which is explained in the appendix to this chapter. Technically, the values in table 6.3 are interpreted as indicating the average increase of the probability of floor consideration that is associated with a one-unit increase in the explanatory variable of concern, controlling for all other variables in the model. Since most of the independent variables in the models are dichotomous, the coefficient simply measures the average increase in the probability of an issue reaching a given agenda stage given that a specific condition holds, e.g., the issue covered a bill with a Democratic sponsor, ceteris paribus. More simply, the larger the value in table 6.3, the greater the total expected influence of a given variable on floor consideration in that Congress, controlling for all other factors. Negative values indicate that the probability of floor consideration tends to decrease as the variable is increased, controlling for all other factors.

Table 6.2 reveals some support for the hypothesis that the president only exercises positive total influence over the floor agenda through the legislative programming process (State of the Union addresses) in his first Congress. Nine of the Congresses studied are consistent with this hypothesis, but there are three important exceptions: Reagan fails to exercise significant influence on his first Congress, the 97th, and yet has a small significant effect on his last Congress, the 100th; and Carter experiences significant influence on his second Congress, the 96th. I explore these discrepancies further in individually reported results

TABLE 6.3 Statistically significant (p < .10) total effects from president, committee, and Senate on the House floor agenda for all issues covered by bills referred to House Commerce, 96th–107th

President	Congress	State of Union Address	Draft Legislation	Committee Leader	Senate Bill	Executive Comment Requested	Total Number of Issues
Carter	96	.011	-.012	.035	.342	0.02	1,556
Reagan	97		.085	.438	.144	0.01	1,145
	98	-.008	.057	.508	.135	-0.01	1,362
	99		-.018	.326	.207	-0.05	1,871
	100	.012	.049	.115	.174	-0.04	2,410
Bush I	101	.075	.115	.276	.115	-0.03	2,236
	102		-.074	.427	.067	0.00	2,597
Clinton	103	.041	.243	.247	.069	0.01	2,858
	104		.140	.279	.029	-0.01	3,261
	105		.011	.272	.091	0.00	2,853
	106	-.016	.119	.359	.092	0.03	3,176
Bush II	107	.121	.288	.378	.096	0.01	3,207

for each president. It is important to keep in mind, however, that table 6.3 summarizes *total* effects on the floor agenda, while the predictions listed in table 6.1 and illustrated in figure 6.1 are pitched at the level of *direct* effects on hearings, markup, and floor levels. I will test these more detailed predictions of the president's direct effects on hearings, markup, and the floor in individual sections devoted to each president.

In table 6.1, draft legislation was only hypothesized to have a direct influence on hearings and markup, but it can also be expected to exercise some indirect influence on the floor through these important early stages. Draft legislation does indeed allow the president to exert a positive total influence over the floor agenda in all Congresses, except for a negative total effect on the floor in the 96th, 99th, and 102nd. In each of these Congresses, however, draft legislation exercises a positive influence over early stages of the legislative process. I explore these cases in detail in the individual studies of each president to follow. Overall, the total effects results also support the hypothesis that the president's influence on the congressional agenda is more persistent and at times stronger through the legislative clearance process (draft legislation) than through programming (public speeches).

There is consistent support for the hypothesized influence of the committee leaders and the Senate on the House floor agenda. Both have a persistent, statistically significant, positive influence on the floor agenda in each Congress in the

TABLE 6.4 Expected influence of issue characteristics on the House agenda

1. **Maximum Cosponsors**—The maximum number of cosponsors for bills covering a given issue offers an imperfect measure of the level of support for consideration of an issue in the House, ceteris paribus. The maximum number of cosponsors should therefore have a positive effect on consideration at all stages of the agenda process. Although the number of cosponsors often changes during the life of a bill, the final number of cosponsors as reported in the THOMAS legislative database is used.

2. **Multiply Referred**—Until 1975, the Speaker could refer a bill to only one committee (Oleszek 2001), and the use of multiple referrals grew over the period of our study, reaching a plateau in the late 1980s (Davidson, Oleszek, and Kephart 1988). If any bills on an issue are singly referred, then that issue is more likely to be central to the committee's jurisdiction, and thus more likely to receive consideration in committee.

3. **Authorization Issue**—Most federal programs require reauthorization every two or three years. Reauthorization measures are often considered must-pass legislation, since technically funds cannot be appropriated for programs that have not been authorized (though Congress often finds ways around this (Oleszek 2001)). The CRS-LIV includes separate issue categories for reauthorizations. Thus, there should be a positive relationship between reauthorization issues and consideration at the floor stage.

4. **Timing of Earliest Introduction**—The timing of introduction of an issue in the House is calculated by dividing the number of the earliest bill introduced on that issue by the number of the highest bill introduced in the same Congress. Issues that appear earlier are more likely to see legislative action, all other things being equal, because the legislative calendar gets crowded late in the session. Thus, there should be a negative* relationship between timing of earliest introduction and appearance on the congressional agenda, particularly at earlier stages of the agenda process, such as hearings and markup, since these stages may be circumvented for urgent issues that arise late in the Congress.

5. **Democratic Sponsor**—If the sponsor of any bill covering a given issue is a Democrat, then the issue is more likely to rise on the agenda under Democrat-controlled Houses (96th–103rd) and less likely to appear on the agenda in Republican-controlled Houses (104th–107th).

6. **Maximum Sponsor Experience**—The maximum tenure of primary sponsors in years is an indicator of whether the issue is being advanced by a senior members of the House. Thus, there should be a positive relationship between the maximum sponsor experience of an issue and advancement along each stage of the agenda.

* Here, a negative influence means that on average bills that are introduced later in a given Congress tend to be less likely to reach the floor agenda, controlling for all other factors.

study. The standardized total effect of the committee chair is particularly impressive, usually several times the magnitude of the influence of the president or the Senate. The strength of the committee chairs' influence reaffirms the necessity of using path analysis to calculate the president's indirect influence on each agenda stage that is exercised through the committee chair. I explore this indirect influence in the individual studies of each president to follow.

TABLE 6.5   Statistically significant total effects from selected issue and contextual binary variables on the House floor agenda for all bills referred to House Commerce, 96th–107th

Congress	Maximum Number of Cosponsors*	Multiply Referred	Authorization Issue	Timing of Earliest Introduction*	Sponsored by Democrat	Maximum Main Sponsor Experience*	Total Number of Issues
96	0.0006	0.05	0.00	0.068	0.01	0.001	1,556
97	0.0008	-0.09	0.12	0.304	0.16	0.019	1,145
98	0.0008	-0.31	0.15	-0.103	0.14	0.017	1,362
99	-0.0013	-0.07	0.08	-0.252	0.01	0.044	1,871
100	0.0001	-0.02	0.10	0.109	0.48	0.029	2,410
101	0.0011	-0.18	0.22	0.159	0.11	0.033	2,236
102	0.0010	-0.32	0.08	-0.234	0.22	0.017	2,597
103	0.0008	-0.16	0.02	-0.054	0.35	0.024	2,858
104	0.0015	-0.05	0.04	-0.067	-0.16	0.017	3,261
105	0.0012	-0.15	0.05	-0.065	-0.29	0.017	2,853
106	0.0022	-0.04	0.00	-0.309	-0.13	0.001	3,176
107	0.0013	-0.06	0.14	-0.388	-0.20	0.019	3,207

Not a dichotomous variable.

More ambiguous results arise with respect to the total influence of "requests for executive comment." Requests for executive comment, which are a very preliminary form of legislative action, do not seem to have a predictable total effect on the floor agenda across Congresses. The general role of these requests in policy making is an important question that deserves further attention but is beyond the scope of the present study.

I also expect some issue and primary bill sponsor characteristics to influence whether an issue proceeds through the agenda process. In table 6.4, I summarize the expected total effects of each of these control variables.

Table 6.5 summarizes the total measured effects of key contextual variables on the floor agenda. The direct effects of all variables on each individual stage of the agenda process are available in tables F.1 through F.4 in Appendix F. As in table 6.3, each indirect effect is considered statistically significant only if all links in the causal chain of direct effects are statistically significant. To calculate the total effect, I add up the statistically significant indirect and direct effects that exist between the variable and the floor agenda. Three variables in table 6.5— maximum number of cosponsors, timing of earliest introduction, and maximum main sponsor experience—are not dichotomous (0, 1) variables, but the indirect effects are all calculated by multiplying by intervening variables that are all dichotomous so that they still provide interpretable information. The problems of dichotomous dependent variables and path analysis are discussed in detail in Appendix D, "The Linear Probability Model with Dichotomous Independent Variables," and Appendix E, "Indirect and Total Effects in Path Analysis."

The total measured effects of the maximum number of cosponsors, multiple referral, authorization, Democratic sponsorship, and maximum main sponsor experience are in the predicted direction in all but two cases. The timing of earliest introduction, however, seems to have a less predictable total influence on the House floor agenda. In eight Congresses, the maximum number of cosponsors has the predicted positive effect on the floor agenda, but in the other four Congresses it has a surprising positive total effect on the floor. In tables 6.4 and 6.5, I leave out the total effects for scope and minimum complexity of an issue because these variables are entered mainly as control variables rather than for their isolated effect on the agenda. Their direct effects are available in the tables of regression coefficients in tables F.1 through F.4 in Appendix F.

Having summarized the total effects of each of the control variables on the floor, I now turn in much greater detail to the consideration of main variables of concern: the president, committee leaders, and the Senate. For each Congress I will examine the influence of these variables on the three most important stages of the congressional agenda: hearings, subcommittee markup, and the floor. My main concern, however, is with the influence that the president exercises on the agenda, and I will examine the direct and indirect effects of the president's influence on committee leaders, markups, hearings, and the floor to assess more carefully the hypotheses of presidential agenda setting generated by the formal models of chapters 3 and 4.

Jimmy Carter

Table 6.6 displays the agenda success in the House Commerce Committee of the issues mentioned by Carter in his State of the Union addresses to the 96th Congress. A quick perusal of the table would suggest that Carter did indeed have considerable success with the 96th Congress. Nearly half of the relevant issues mentioned by Carter in his 1979 and 1980 State of the Union addresses reached some stage of the committee agenda process. And many of those issues that were not taken up by the committee, like congressional elections and education, lie outside of the committee's main jurisdiction. This quick perusal, however, can be misleading in at least two ways: (1) The fact that half of Carter's issues were considered by Congress does not reveal whether Carter had influence on the congressional agenda unless it is compared to the fate of issues not mentioned by Carter, while controlling for other factors, like sponsorship by committee chairs

TABLE 6.6   Scope, complexity, and agenda consideration of issues from Carter's State of the Union addresses to the 96th Congress

CRS-LIV Issue	Scope	Average Complexity	Hearing	Markup	Floor
Antitrust law	21	20.2	X	X	X
Atomic weapons	3	7.0			
Capital investments	2	19.0			
Coal	27	13.4			
Competition	14	24.7	X	X	X
Comprehensive health care	13	21.2			
Congressional elections	1	4.0			
Education	3	11.7			
Energy conservation	41	15.0	X	X	X
Energy policy	39	11.7	X	X	X
Executive departments—Management	1	19.0			
Executive reorganization	106	15.3	X	X	X
Exports	15	17.7			
Federal aid to education	5	15.4			
Fossil fuels	8	29.1	X	X	X
Government regulation	23	11.8			
Government regulation—Economic aspects	1	3.0			
Hospital rates	11	18.5	X	X	X
Industrial production	1	6.0			
Intelligence services	1	11.0			
International relations	1	5.0			
Manpower training programs	5	22.4			
Military personnel	2	5.0			
National defense	1	11.0			
National health insurance	10	24.2			
Natural resources	1	7.0			
Nutrition	17	7.6			
Nutrition policy	1	9.0			
Petroleum prices	19	7.9			
Railroads	30	9.7	X	X	
Restrictive trade practices	19	12.6	X	X	X
Rural economic development	7	8.9			X
Savings accounts	1	99.0			
Solar energy	18	27.2	X	X	X
Sunset legislation	8	22.4	X	X	X
Synthetic fuel	15	17.5	X	X	X
Technology	1	40			
Trade agreements	1	59.0			
Trucking	5	3.2			
Urban areas	2	8.5			X
Youth	1	15.0			

and passage by the Senate, which may have also influenced the congressional agenda; and (2) because the set of CRS-LIV issues is hierarchical and overlapping, it is necessary to take into account the scope, or number of associated bills, of each issue. Broad-scope issues are inherently more likely to receive agenda attention regardless of whether the president promotes them because they tend to be more general in coverage. Any attempt to measure the president's influence on the agenda must take into account this inherent advantage of high-scope issues by controlling for the scope of each issue.

A further complication is that some of the issues in table 6.5 do not fit in either the committee's statutory or common law jurisdictions (King 1997). For example, a bill concerning Internet connections in schools, H.R. 4600—"[t]o require schools and libraries to implement filtering or blocking technology for computers with Internet access as a condition of universal service discounts under the Communications Act of 1934"—was referred exclusively to Energy and Commerce in the 106th Congress, even though education is the primary jurisdiction of another committee.[4] This means that part of what is measured here as the president's influence on the committee's agenda includes his influence on issues that are outside of the committee's normal jurisdiction. It is still important, however, to include such issues because, for instance, if the president emphasizes education, this may make committees other than the Education and Labor Committee turn attention to education-oriented legislation.

I am able to control for the fact that an issue is not the committee's primary concern in two ways. First, I control for whether an issue is a component of any bills that get referred solely to House Commerce using the "Multiply Referred" variable from table 6.4. Singly referred issues will generally be more central to the committee's jurisdiction, although the educational dimension of H.R. 4600 shows that even some singly referred issues are outside of House Commerce's traditional jurisdiction. Second, I control for the scope of the issue. Broader issues like education and energy policy that cover more bills will tend to reach across committees. In the analysis that follows, I control for these influences, while at the same time separating the influences of the president, committee leaders, and the Senate on different stages of the agenda.

I begin with a brief summary of significant specific bills and issues promoted by Carter in the 96th Congress and then turn my attention to a more general analysis of the president's influence on the different stages of the agenda process. I begin in Carter's second Congress, the 96th, for a technical reason relating to the way Congress introduces bills, rather than in his first Congress, the 95th[5] Carter conducted steady business with House Commerce because some of his most pressing priorities like energy, transportation regulation, and health care were a part of its jurisdiction. Among issues referred to House Commerce, the 96th Congress passed Carter's request for railroad deregulation and an energy conservation law (S. 1030). Carter did not call for the toxic waste cleanup leg-

FIGURE 6.2 Direct effects on the House agenda for 96th House Commerce issues.

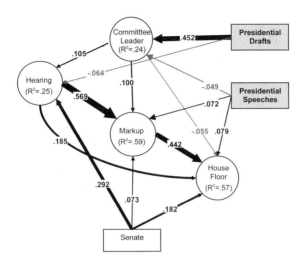

islation now known as "Superfund" in his State of the Union addresses, but he did submit draft legislation that was introduced in the Senate Environment and Public Works Committee. The House and Senate passed an alternate House measure, H.R. 7020, sponsored by Jim Florio of New Jersey instead. Congress failed to pass Carter's requests for national health care, hospital cost control, sunset legislation, and lobbying and campaign reform legislation, but all of these issues reached some stage of the agenda consideration. Congress also passed Carter's requests for a windfall profits tax on oil and a synthetic fuels subsidy through bills that were not referred to the committee.

Ordinary least squares is used for estimation of the direct effects rather than logit or probit, which are more common for dichotomous explained variables, because least squares is less problematic when all or most of the independent variables are also dichotomous and because logit and probit are nonlinear estimators that do not allow the straightforward calculation of the indirect and total effects. The advantages and disadvantages of using ordinary least squares are discussed at length in Appendix D, "The Linear Probability Model with Dichotomous Independent Variables," and Appendix E, "Indirect and Total Effects in Path Analysis." Heteroskedasticity-robust standard errors (White 1980) are used to determine statistical significance because all endogenous variables are dichotomous (0–1) and yield heteroskedastic standard errors under ordinary least squares. The usual t-statistics apply to the robust standard errors. I present the direct effects on the four agenda stages that meet at least the (two-tailed) p $<$ .10 level of statistical significance in the path diagram in figure 6.2, where it is easier to assess the indirect influence of the president, committee leaders, and the Senate, through chains of connected causal arrows. The path diagram also indicates R^2, the amount of variance in each endogenous (explained) variable that is determined by its explanatory variables. An R^2 near 0 indicates that the model has not explained much of the variation in the endogenous variable, and an R^2 near 1 indicates that the model has explained nearly all of the variance in the endogenous variable.

The size of the direct effects on each endogenous variable is also reflected in the thickness of the causal arrows between variables in figure 6.2. In a pattern that will persist, the strongest influences on each agenda stage are the previous agenda stages themselves. The occurrence of hearings on an issue is by far the most important determinant of whether an issue reaches the markup stage. Similarly, the occurrence of a markup session on an issue is the strongest determinant of whether an issue reaches the floor. Hearings have both a direct effect on the floor agenda (.185) and an indirect effect through their influence on markups, which is calculated simply by multiplying the effect of hearings on markup (.569) by the effect of markup on the floor agenda (.442). So the indirect effect of hearings on floor is .251, meaning that if an issue receives hearings this leads to a .251 increase in the probability on floor consideration on average, controlling for all other variables (those listed in the regression table not just those in the path model). The total effect of hearings on the floor agenda is calculated by adding the direct and indirect effects, yielding a .436 value for the total effect. This means that holding a hearing on an issue is associated with a total increase of .436 in the probability of floor consideration, controlling for all other variables. This is a very strong influence indeed.

The path diagram in figure 6.2 for the 96th Congress reveals that Carter's State of the Union addresses had statistically significant direct effects on the appearance of issues in markup and on the floor agenda. This is inconsistent with the theoretical model of chapter 3 that suggested presidents should only be able to exercise such influence in their first Congress. It may be that unified government, where one party controls both the presidency and Congress, plays a role in enhancing the president's influence here. However, there are only two Congresses with completely unified government within the 24 years of the analysis: the 96th and 103rd, and only the 96th offers a look at a president's second Congress. It is therefore difficult to say anything authoritative at this point about the role of unified government in enhancing the president's agenda-setting influence.

Carter was less influential with draft legislation in the 96th House, exercising a negative direct effect on an issue's likelihood of being considered in hearings and a negative total effect on the floor, in spite of having a strong positive influence on committee leader sponsorship. This puzzling result is one of only three cases where the president's draft legislation exercised a negative total effect on the floor. Ironically, Carter's influence on committee chairs is the highest recorded for any Congress in this study. But in this case, this powerful influence does not translate into measurable influence on the floor agenda. In fact, Carter's 96th Congress is one of three cases where the president's draft legislation suffers a negative total influence on the floor agenda. This means that issues in Carter's draft legislation are actually less likely than other issues to be considered on the floor, in spite of the fact that these issues are more likely to be sponsored by committee leaders. The only other Congresses, the 99th and 102nd, where the president's draft legislation suffered a negative total influence on the floor agenda occurred under the much more contentious partisan environment of divided government. However, in neither of these divided government cases did the president's State of the Union addresses exercise a measurable influence on the floor. It may be that focus on the president's more public State of the Union program eclipsed the agenda influence of Carter's draft legislation in the 96th Congress. Facing reelection in troubled times and after only limited policy successes in the 95th Congress, the administration and/or Congress may have decided that success of the president's more public program was more critical than processing the administration's clearance program. To fully resolve the puzzle of the 96th Congress we must look at the policy decisions of the administration and Congress in much more detail. Carter's influence on the 96th Congress shows that it can be misleading to look at either the direct effects alone or at the total effects alone when trying to assess the president's influence on the hearing, markup, and floor stages of the House agenda. I will therefore consider direct, indirect, and total effects in examining each subsequent president's influence on the congressional agenda.

Ronald Reagan

Ronald Reagan's 1980 election victory over incumbent Jimmy Carter brought a Republican majority to the Senate. In this new Congress, Reagan exercised enormous influence in passing both his Economic Recovery Tax Act and dramatic spending reductions that were included in the Omnibus Budget Reconciliation Act of 1981. In addition, the 97th Congress witnessed a significant change in the jurisdiction of the House Commerce Committee, which gained jurisdiction over several new energy policy areas (King 1997). The committee was renamed "Energy and Commerce" to reflect the new jurisdictional focus of the committee, but there is little evidence that Reagan's State of the Union addresses were able to exercise much influence over the agenda of the new House Commerce Committee. This runs counter to the expectation that presidents will be able to use the legislative programming track to influence the floor agenda in their first Congress. The absence of Reagan's influence in the 97th Congress, however, is perhaps easier to explain than Carter's surprising influence in the 96th. Reagan

FIGURE 6.3 Direct effects on the House agenda for 97th House Commerce issues.

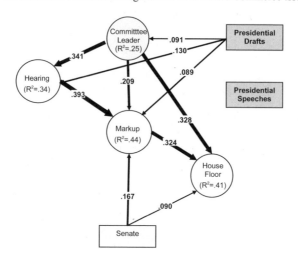

made very few requests in his 1981 economic message that were directly relevant to Energy and Commerce. Only requests to deregulate oil price controls and his call for enactment of Clean Air Act amendments make specific legislative requests of the committee. His 1982 State of the Union also had few policy proposals relevant for House Commerce. Reagan's narrow agenda thus provided little guidance for House Commerce's agenda. Thus, it seems that even the broad jurisdiction of the Energy and Commerce Committee is too limited in this case because Reagan aimed his agenda largely towards other committees. In table C.1 in Appendix C, I compare the bills and issues considered by Energy and Commerce to other committees in the 103rd Congress. While Energy and Commerce is one of the committees that is most representative of the entire chamber, it still has a limited agenda as one of more than 20 standing committees in the House. A study of all issues in the 97th Congress would perhaps demonstrate that the president's speeches did have a positive influence on the floor agenda.

Reagan did, however, exercise the expected influence over the early stages of the House agenda through the legislative clearance process, as shown in figure 6.3. Among prominent issues, the 97th Congress passed the Nuclear Waste Repository Act, for which Reagan submitted draft legislation but which he did not mention in his economic message in 1981 or in his State of the Union address in 1982. But the House failed to consider a Reagan request for revisions to the Clean Air Act and his draft legislation calling for more equitable treatment of health maintenance organizations and other deregulation requests. Reagan's draft legislation exercised the expected positive direct effect on committee leaders, hearings, and markups, and this led to a positive total effect on the House floor.

FIGURE 6.4 Direct effects on the House agenda for 98th House Commerce issues.

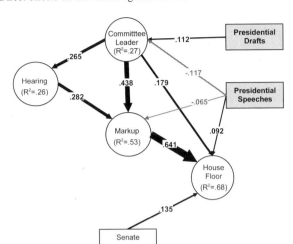

When Reagan delivered a more substantial agenda to Energy and Commerce in the 98th Congress, the issues mentioned in his State of the Union did indeed exercise a direct positive effect on the floor agenda, as shown in figure 6.4. This is remarkable because Reagan lost 26 House seats in the 1982 midterm election between the 97th and 98th Congresses, and yet he wielded a stronger direct influence over the floor agenda in the 98th Congress than in the 97th. But the total effect of Reagan's State of the Union addresses on the floor agenda was negated by their negative influence on the markup of issues and sponsorship by the Democratic committee leaders. Overall, the president's speeches exercised a slight negative total effect on floor consideration. Thus, while the positive direct effect on the floor suggests that Congress's floor decisions were positively influenced by Reagan's State of the Union addresses, the overall floor agenda was dominated by issues arising from committee consideration where the Democratic majority seems to have largely avoided the president's agenda issues. Congress took some form of action on the president's requests for abortion, acid rain, and the Clean Air Act legislation but failed to act on "the skyrocketing cost of health care," or on "catastrophic health insurance for older Americans" (SOTU 1983). Reagan was also able to use his draft legislation to exert the expected positive total influence only on sponsorship by committee leaders, and this was strong enough to yield an indirect positive influence on floor consideration.

In his State of the Union addresses to the 99th Congress, Reagan called for an end to the subsidization of Amtrak, health care vouchers, slowing the growth of Medicare and Medicaid, the expansion of Superfund, the deregulation of natural gas, legislation to restrict abortions, further deregulation of the bus and railroad industries, and announced he was developing his own plan to deal with cata-

FIGURE 6.5 Direct effects on the House agenda for 99th House Commerce issues.

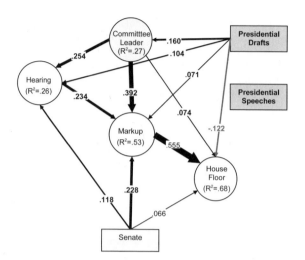

strophic illness. In spite of this ambitious agenda, and his landslide 1984 reelection, he failed to exercise a statistically significant influence over the House Commerce agenda through his State of the Union addresses. This is consistent with the model of legislative programming from chapter 3, which predicted that such influence would only be effective in a president's first Congress.

In the draft legislation he sent to the 99th Congress, Reagan called for revision of the Clean Water Act, provision of voluntary coverage for Medicare beneficiaries, stockpiling of children's vaccines, amendment of health maintenance organization authorities, requiring Medicare providers to accept military and veterans health insurance plans, deregulation of natural gas, and allowing the Environmental Protection Agency and Federal Energy Regulatory Commission to collect user fees. Reagan's influence on the 99th Congress is summarized in figure 6.5. While Reagan was able to use his draft legislative proposals to exercise the predicted positive influence over the committee leader, hearing and markup stages of the House Commerce agenda process, he also experienced a negative direct influence on floor consideration. Thus, these draft proposals actually had a very weak negative total influence on the floor agenda. Only Carter in the 96th and George H. W. Bush in the 102nd also experienced a negative total effect on the floor agenda through his draft legislation. But in each case, the president did exhibit a positive influence on the early agenda stages, where draft legislation is expected to exercise its greatest influence because of the policy expertise it contains. In the 99th and 102nd Congresses, it appears that the expertise provided in draft legislation was useful in committee consideration, but that political con-

FIGURE 6.6 Direct effects on the House agenda for 100th House Commerce issues.

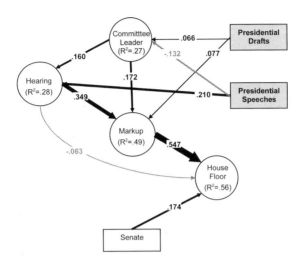

cerns of the Democratic majority became dominant in determining what issues to bring to the floor.

The 100th Congress was in many ways a preview of the revolutionary 104th Congress. In both, the opposing party took over at least one chamber of Congress and an aggressive Speaker of the House forged a bold domestic agenda at odds with the president. In both Congresses, the president also took a decidedly more passive role in congressional agenda setting. Ironically, because they occurred under the most hostile divided government years in my analysis, the 100th and 104th Congresses mark the high water mark for the House Commerce Committee for initiating laws on Mayhew's (1991) index of landmark legislation. James Wright's and Newt Gingrich's Houses provide a counterexample to the conventional wisdom—sometimes originating in Congress itself—that suggests that the Congress is inherently incapable of developing a coherent agenda and seeing it through to passage (e.g., Sundquist 1981). Very few of the items on Mayhew's index that were referred to House Commerce in the 100th and 104th Congresses were passed because of presidential initiative, indicating that Congress was quite capable in these two cases of formulating its own agenda.

In his State of the Union addresses to the 100th Congress, Reagan included calls for catastrophic health insurance for the elderly, "a program of welfare reform through community based demonstration projects" (SOTU 1987), further regulatory reforms, new science and technology centers, a halt in all federal funding for abortion, and a constitutional amendment banning abortion. Reagan was able to use State of the Union messages to exercise a direct positive influence on

105

House Commerce hearings in the 100th, as shown in figure 6.6. Although this direct influence on hearings did give Reagan some indirect influence over sub-committee markups and a very small amount of indirect influence on the floor, this is one of the three cases (96th, 97th, and 100th) that did not fit the predictions of the programming model. Since the 100th was Reagan's fourth Congress, the programming model predicted that he would not have sufficient accountability to use State of the Union speeches to influence the agenda. Reagan's influence, however, was generated indirectly through his influence over hearings rather than directly on the floor, as the programming model would have predicted.

In draft legislation referred to the House Commerce Committee, Reagan included implementation of the U.S.-Canada Free Trade Agreement, establishment of the National Vaccine Injury Compensation Program, the amendment of federal securities laws to facilitate cooperation between the United States and foreign countries in securities law enforcement, and revision of the Clean Air Act "to control hazardous pollutants" (H.R. 5556). Reagan was able to use his draft legislation for direct influence over both committee leader sponsorship and markup, as predicted by the legislative clearance model. He did not experience the predicted direct influence on hearings, but his influence on committee leader sponsorship of an issue led to an indirect positive influence on the floor. One remarkable feature of the 100th Congress is that committee leaders did not experience any measurable direct influence on the floor agenda. Committee chairs with little direct influence over the floor appear again in the highly centralized 104th Congress under Speaker Gingrich. Speaker Wright, like Gingrich later, developed an endogenous House agenda that he tried to guide through the House by using more centralized leadership than his predecessors. As in the divided government of the 104th, to be considered later, it may be that the centralization of agenda setting in the House leadership deprived the floor of some of the valuable expertise provided by committees. In the 104th, the centralization of House agenda setting ironically may have opened the door for the executive expertise in draft legislation to have a direct influence on the floor. I will consider the possibility of this dynamic in the discussion of the Clinton presidency.

George H. W. Bush

In his economic and State of the Union addresses to the 101st Congress, Bush included calls for an increase in funding for the war against drugs, including expanded treatment to the poor and young mothers, funding for AIDS education and research, "legislation for a new, more effective Clean Air Act" (SOTU 1989), funding for clean coal technology, penalties for pollution of the ocean, an increase of funding for Medicaid, mental health facilities, and cleanup of nuclear

FIGURE 6.7 Direct effects on the House agenda for 101st House Commerce issues

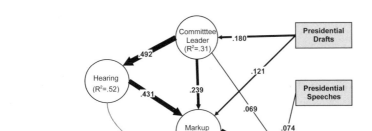

weapons plants. Bush experienced the predicted positive direct effect on the floor agenda through his State of the Union speeches in his first Congress, as shown in figure 6.7.

Bush also experienced the expected positive influence on early stages of the congressional agenda through submission of draft legislative proposals. In draft legislation referred to the 101st House Commerce Committee, Bush included requests for additional enforcement of securities laws, Food and Drug Administration user fees for the review of drugs, deregulation of oil pipelines, a comprehensive drug control plan, and further regulation of the stock market.

In his State of the Union addresses to the 102nd Congress, Bush's requests included drug abuse prevention, elevating the Environmental Protection Agency to a Cabinet position, air pollution control, product liability reform, a review of the nation's health care system, a national energy strategy that included energy conservation and alternative energy, a program of preventative medicine, implementation of the North American Free Trade Agreement (NAFTA), reform of the health insurance market, and welfare reform. Bush experienced the expected pattern of no visible effect on the congressional agenda through these State of the Union issues in his second Congress, as shown in figure 6.8.

Bush also experienced the expected positive influence on early stages of the legislative process through the submission of draft legislation in the 102nd Congress, but this was overridden by a direct negative influence on the floor agenda. In the drafts submitted to the 102nd Congress, Bush included legislation improving procedures for allocating assignment to the electromagnetic spectrum, which

FIGURE 6.8 Direct effects on the House agenda for 102nd House Commerce issues.

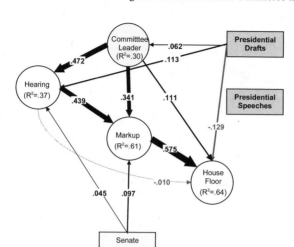

I discussed in chapter one, to expand the nation's drug treatment capacity, to reduce medical liability costs, and a comprehensive health care plan. The spectrum auction issue received consideration at the hearing stage, where presidential expertise is hypothesized to be influential, but did not receive floor consideration in the 102nd.

Bill Clinton

Bill Clinton came to office in the 103rd Congress under the first unified government since Carter's 96th. Clinton's economic and State of the Union addresses to the 103rd Congress included requests for health care reform, increased environmental cleanup, children's vaccinations, welfare reform, an energy conservation program, reform of Superfund, connecting classrooms and libraries to the Internet, a revision of the Safe Drinking Water Act and Clean Water Act, investment in environmental technologies, and campaign finance reform. Like George H. W. Bush in the 101st Congress, Clinton experienced the predicted first-Congress direct influence on the floor agenda through his State of the Union addresses. He also experienced a negative direct effect on hearings, but this did not cancel his total positive effect on the floor agenda.

After the 107th Congress, Clinton's 103rd Congress experienced the second largest total effect on the congressional agenda from his draft legislation of any president in this survey. As indicated in figure 6.9, the direct effect on the floor

FIGURE 6.9 Direct effects on the House agenda for 103rd House Commerce issues

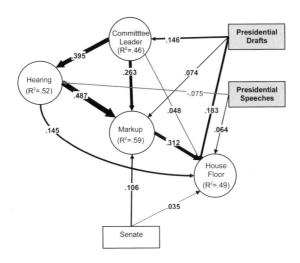

was .183, indicating that submission of draft legislation on an issue was associated with an 18.3 percentage point increase in the chance that the issue would appear on the floor agenda, controlling for other factors. Clinton submitted draft legislation for comprehensive health care reform, the prevention of mineral mining in Antarctica, revision of the Safe Drinking Water Act, enhancement of the safety of nuclear power facilities, development of the Internet, implementation of NAFTA, and regulation of chemical pesticides in food. Like presidential drafts in the 104th and 107th Congresses, these drafts had an unexpected direct positive effect on the floor. The direct influence in the 103rd and 107th Congresses may have occurred because the same party controlled the presidency and the House. In the only other case of a House under the control of the president's party, however, Carter did not experience a direct influence of his draft legislation on the floor in the 96th, his second Congress. Unfortunately, as noted earlier, there is not yet sufficient evidence to say anything authoritative about the influence of unified government on the president's agenda-setting power.

The 104th Congress brought Republican control to the House for the first time in 40 years. The whole legislative process changed under Republican leadership. Committees were eliminated. The House "Energy and Commerce" committee lost jurisdiction over several policy areas and was renamed the "Commerce" Committee (King 1997). Speaker Gingrich employed task forces to expedite consideration of legislation rather than passing it through the traditional legislative channels, because he had pledged the House to pass items on the Contract with America in the first 100 days. The corrections calendar was created to expedite consideration of noncontroversial legislation. The Speaker

FIGURE 6.10 Direct effects on the House agenda for 104th House Commerce issues.

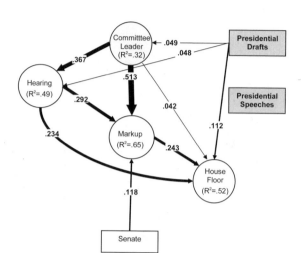

was restricted from making joint referrals unless they were either sequential or split up parts of a bill to go to different committees. And in both types of joint referrals, a primary committee was to be designated. Also, Congress reduced its own ability to generate policy expertise by cutting committee staff by one-third, eliminating funding for the 23 legislative service caucuses, and abolishing the Office of Technology Assessment. In his State of the Union addresses to the 104th Congress, Clinton included requests for lobbying and campaign reform, childhood vaccines, welfare reform, health insurance portability, and the V-Chip for televisions. As shown in figure 6.10, Clinton had the predicted absence of influence on the House agenda through these State of the Union messages.

As in the 103rd Congress, Clinton surprisingly exercised both a positive direct and total influence on the floor agenda from his draft legislation in the 104th. Clinton submitted proposals for nuclear waste disposal, welfare reform, a juvenile crime measure, pipeline safety, increased penalties for environmental crimes, and many others. From the informational perspective of the clearance model of chapter 4, it appears that the way Gingrich opened up the floor, circumvented the committees, and reduced staff and supporting agencies actually weakened Congress with respect to the expertise of the federal bureaucracy wielded in Clinton's draft legislation because it deprived the floor of the valuable expertise traditionally provided by committees. George W. Bush would exercise a similar direct effect on the floor in the 107th Congress, but that case was apparently brought about by the urgent need to bring the president's proposals for responding to the September 11 terrorist attacks to the floor, rather than a weakening of committee expertise.

The change in the majority party also brought in new committee chairs who were less experienced at pushing their policy proposals to the floor and had less policy expertise than their more senior Democratic predecessors. But these new committee chairs were also weakened by the structural changes introduced in the 104th House. With the weakened chairs, hearings played a stronger role in determining what reached the floor and had almost as much direct influence on the floor as committee markups. In this decentralized environment Clinton was able to use draft legislation to exert some influence over the agenda, at the same time ironically that he found himself having to publicly defend the relevancy of the presidency.[6] Clinton exercised this influence mostly in the second session after Gingrich had lost a public relations battle with Clinton over a budget impasse that led to repeated government shutdowns. The Republicans' strategy changed after the government shutdowns, and they started looking for some legislative accomplishments to peddle in their reelection battles. "Some of the 104th's best work came in the session's last months when the committees were more active. For instance, the Commerce Committee pushed through two high-profile environmental bills—a rewrite of the safe water drinking act (PL104–182) and an overhaul of pesticide regulations (PL104–170)" (*CQ Almanac* 1996). While it would be an exaggeration to say that Clinton played a strong agenda-setting role in the 104th, it appears that Gingrich's attempts to make the House legislative process less beholden to committee leaders offered a more open process that Clinton was able to exploit with the expertise in his draft legislation.

By the 105th Congress, committee leaders already began to regain some of their direct influence on the floor agenda and by the 106th the committee leaders would exercise levels of influence comparable to their Democratic predecessors. Part of this regained influence may be due to the experience and expertise the new Republican chairs gradually acquired, but the chairs' influence over the floor continued even in the 107th, when term limits that were initiated in the 104th brought in a new set of committee leaders. More importantly, it seems the party began to return more responsibility to the committee chairs: "After centralizing power in the 104th by writing legislation in task forces instead of committee, by the 105th the GOP was ready to return power to the committee chairs. . . . There was a feeling that the committees had better expertise" (*CQ Almanac* 1998).

Clinton's State of the Union addresses to the Republican Congresses continued to be exercises in futility. In his State of the Union addresses to the 105th Congress that impeached him on two articles, Clinton included requests for AIDS research, health insurance portability, modernization of Medicare, Superfund enhancement, a ban of toxic chemicals, patient's rights, a plan to buy into Medicare before retirement, revision of the Clean Water Act, a ban on cloning of humans, and campaign finance reform. As shown in figure 6.11, these issues did not have a statistically significant effect on any stage of the agenda.

FIGURE 6.11 Direct effects on the House agenda for 105th House Commerce issues.

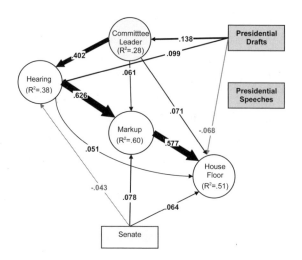

Clinton's draft proposals in the 105th Congress, however, fit the predictions of influence in the early information-gathering stages of the legislative process. Clinton found a significant positive direct influence on both hearings and committee leaders. In draft legislation submitted to the 105th Congress, Clinton included requests for stiffer penalties for environmental crimes, a ban on the cloning of humans, Medicaid and Medicare reform, and the deregulation of the electric power industry. Clinton's drafts experienced a slight negative direct influence on floor consideration, but this was negated by his expected positive influence on earlier stages to yield a net positive influence on the floor.

In his historically lengthy State of the Union addresses to the 106th Congress, Clinton included requests for legislation to save Social Security, reform Medicare, provide a patient's bill of rights, insure privacy of medical records, offer health insurance portability, reform campaign finance, provide health coverage for uninsured children, offer Medicare prescription drug coverage, expand mental health services, develop biomass energy, and much more. As shown in figure 6.12, these appeals had no significant positive impact on the agenda and actually exercised a negative direct influence on hearings.

In draft legislation submitted to the 106th Congress, Clinton included electricity deregulation, pipeline safety, protection of privacy of medical and financial information, health coverage for the uninsured, improvement of nursing home care, and consumer protection in Internet sales of prescription drugs. These draft issues exercised a negative direct influence on the floor but still exhibited a positive total influence on the floor due to their positive impact on earlier stages.

FIGURE 6.12 Direct effects on the House agenda for 106th House Commerce issues.

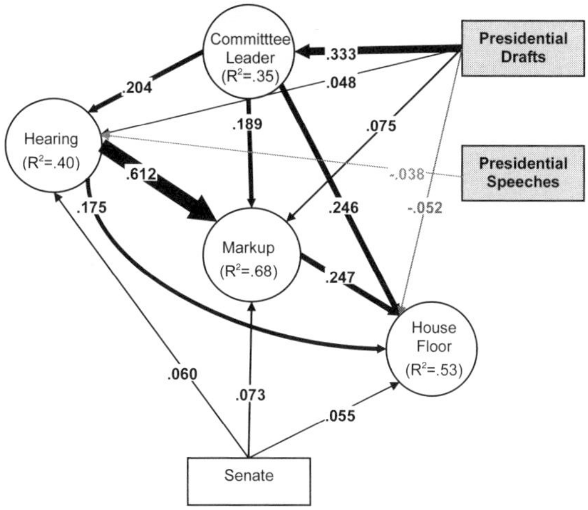

George W. Bush

George W. Bush's 107th Congress was unusual because of the historic mid-session change of leadership in the Senate from the Republicans to the Democrats, after the defection of Senator Jim Jeffords from the Republican Party, but this Congress became extraordinary because of the events of September 11, 2001. Congress responded in urgent fashion to the president's requests to deal with the crisis. For example, the USA PATRIOT Act was enacted even before Bush's second State of the Union. In his State of the Union addresses to the 107th Congress, Bush included legislative requests for Medicare coverage of prescription drugs, a patient's bill of rights, medical malpractice reform, cleanup of toxic brownfields, alternative energy sources, energy conservation, campaign finance reform, vaccines against bioterrorism, welfare reform, and national service. As predicted for his first Congress, Bush was able to exercise a significant direct positive influence on the floor consideration of these issues through his major addresses. Bush's influence on the 107th House agenda is represented in figure 6.13.

Bush's draft proposals exercised an unusual positive direct impact on the floor. In draft legislation referred to the House Commerce Committee, Bush's requests included establishing the Department of Homeland Security, preventing bioterrorism, combating money laundering, and resolving disputes regarding the allocation of the electromagnetic spectrum. But it appears that Bush exercised influence on the floor rather than in the committees for a very different reason

FIGURE 6.13 Direct effects on the House agenda for 107th House Commerce issues.

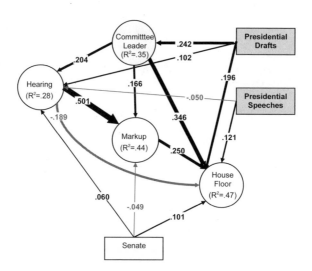

than Clinton. Whereas Clinton was able to play on the vulnerability of a floor operating without the full resources of its committees, several of Bush's proposals were brought to the floor deliberately because of their urgency. In addition, it appears that Congress was not equipped to pull together the kind of comprehensive responses to terrorism that Bush developed through the coordinated efforts of the federal bureaucracy in drafting the USA PATRIOT Act, establishing the Department of Homeland Security, and developing a bioterrorism protection bill. These exceptional measures demonstrate in exaggerated form the kind of expertise that has allowed the president to exercise consistent influence on the congressional agenda through draft legislation.

Conclusion

The results of this chapter generally support the main theoretical predictions of chapters 3 and 4, with some illuminating exceptions. The president is able to use State of the Union speeches and draft legislation to influence the issues on the congressional agenda. State of the Union speeches exert effective agenda-setting influence on later stages of the agenda process, but these speeches are most often effective in a president's first Congress. Although often celebrated as the president's main agenda-setting tool, e.g., Light (1991) and C. Jones (1994), the State of the Union addresses offer the president a very limited means of influencing the congressional agenda. The influence the president exercises through his State of the Union speeches was generally effective only on the floor stage of the legislative process and usually only during a president's first Congress. Surprisingly, Carter was able to use State of the Union speeches to influence the congressional agenda in his second Congress, and Reagan was able to use them in his last Congress after being uninfluential in his first term. Reagan's early ineffectiveness is, at least partly, a function of very small number of his agenda items that were within House Commerce's jurisdiction. Carter's influence in his second Congress hints that unified government may enhance the president's ability to set the congressional agenda through his State of the Union addresses. Presidents are, after all, more likely to share agenda priorities with their fellow partisans in Congress than with the opposite party. However, there are only two Congresses (96th and 103rd) with fully unified government, so there simply are not enough cases here to make a valid inference about the role of unified government without further evidence.

As predicted, the expertise of executive draft legislation from the legislative clearance process provides a more consistent influence on the congressional agenda than the State of the Union addresses, and the influence of drafts tends to act more directly on earlier stages of the legislative process, like committee leader sponsorship, hearings, and markups. In chapter 4, I developed a model that suggested that this influence over the agenda arises from the policy expertise that is embodied in such draft legislation. In all twelve Congresses studied, the president's draft legislation exercised a direct influence over the issues considered in at least one of the three early stages of agenda consideration (committee leader sponsorship, hearings, and markup). Draft legislation also exercised a positive total influence on the floor in nine of the twelve Congresses. In three exceptional cases (103rd, 104th, and 107th Congresses), drafts had a significant direct positive influence on floor consideration. Ironically, it may be because of centralization of the House agenda process in the 104th Congress that committee expertise was used less, thereby providing an opening for the president to exploit with his control of executive expertise. This, however, can only remain a conjecture without further analysis.

The persistent influence of draft legislation and the ephemeral influence of presidential speeches beg the question of whether presidents have a larger overall impact on public policy through the submission of draft legislation than through public speeches. The results of this chapter certainly point in this direction. C. Jones (1994) has pointed out that most of the legislative business of Congress concerns adjustments to already existing legislation, which he calls the "continuing agenda," rather than new policy proposals. It is particularly in determining where to make adjustments to this less prominent continuing agenda that draft legislation may play a more important agenda-setting role than presidential speeches. And the cumulative effect of this agenda control over an entire presidency may leave a more enduring legacy on public policy than the policy agenda the president promotes in his public speeches.

Despite the influence of the president and other actors, by far the most important determinant of each House agenda stage is simply the previous agenda stage, so that the issues that are subject to hearings are the ones most likely to reach markup, and issues that reach markup are the most likely to reach the floor. This has important implications for presidential agenda setting because it means that the president may be able to exercise a larger effect on the floor consideration of an issue by influencing hearings or markup, i.e., indirectly, than he can by directly influencing the floor. For example, the president's draft legislation rarely had a direct positive influence on floor consideration, but it had a positive total effect on the floor agenda in nine of the twelve Congresses because of such indirect effects.

The issue-level data of this chapter have also revealed that committee leaders and the Senate play an important role in determining the House agenda. The committee leaders are the most important agenda actors in the House, often having effects on each of the stages of the congressional agenda that were several times larger than that of other actors like the president and the Senate. This again suggests that the president can wield influence on the floor agenda indirectly, i.e., by influencing which issues are taken up by committee leaders, as he did in all of the Congresses studied.

In addition to revealing the complex nature of the president's influence on the congressional agenda, the issue-level data have reaffirmed the conventional wisdom that committee leaders play by far the most important role in setting the congressional agenda, even in the more open 100th and 104th Congresses, where they still exercised a significant indirect effect on the floor. In each Congress the data have also supported the less widely acknowledged argument that the Senate exercises an important influence on the later stages of the House agenda. In the next chapter I explore this bicameral link further by turning attention to the president's influence on the Senate agenda and the influence of the House on the Senate agenda.

· 7 ·

Presidential Agenda Setting in the Senate

Because the U.S. Constitution requires that bills be passed by the Senate as well as the House before they are presented to the president for signing, analysis of the president's influence on the House agenda alone offers a potentially incomplete picture of his influence on the congressional agenda. The modern Senate provides a challenging test of the president's ability to set the congressional agenda because many politicians enter the Senate in an attempt to wield their own influence on the national agenda (Oleszek 2001; Sinclair 1989). In this chapter I analyze whether the president is nevertheless able to influence the Senate agenda through his public addresses and draft legislation.

Differences in the House and Senate Legislative Processes

In general, bicameralism adds a layer of redundancy to policy making that may reduce the overall efficiency of Congress. Only some special cases of legislation—e.g., treaties, nominations, revenue-raising bills—receive privileged treatment in one of the chambers. In practice, however, the House and Senate operate under an informal division of labor, where issues of high priority to each chamber often receive more serious consideration in that chamber, followed by more perfunctory consideration in the other chamber. This can be seen, for instance, in figures 5.5 and 5.6, by the different route of consideration given in each chamber to bills and issues from the other chamber. Despite this informal division of labor, bills must clear the House in time for Senate consideration before the end

TABLE 7.1 House and Senate committee jurisdictions in 97th Congress

House Energy and Commerce	Senate Commerce, Sci., and Tech.
Foreign commerce	
National energy policy	
Exploration, production, regulation of energy	
Conservation of energy	
Commercial application of energy technology	
Energy information	
Generation and transmission of electrical power	
Interstate energy compacts	
DOE and FERC	
Inland waterways	Inland waterways
Railroads	Railroads
Regulation of interstate and foreign communications	
Securities and exchanges	
Consumer protection	Consumer protection
Travel and tourism	
Public health and quarantine	
Health and health facilities*	
Biomedical research	
	Coast Guard
	Coastal zone management
	Highway safety
	Interstate commerce
	Marine and ocean navigation
	Marine fisheries
	Merchant Marine
	Nonmilitary aeronautical and space sciences
	Ocean, weather, and atmospheric services
	Panama Canal
	Science, technology, research
	Interstate carriers (buses, trucks, pipelines)
	Sports
	Standards and measurements
	Transportation
	Outer Continental Shelf Lands

Except health care supported by payroll deductions

of a Congress and vice versa. This potentially crowds each chamber's agenda with those bills that have already passed in the other chamber. Bicameralism, therefore, although allowing some division of labor in the initiation and serious consideration of issues, also imposes further time and resource constraints on the congressional agenda (Longley and Oleszek 1989).

I analyze the Senate Committee on Commerce, Science, and Transportation (hereafter Senate Commerce Committee). This committee is in one important way the natural Senate counterpart to the House Energy and Commerce Committee. Although Munger and Torrent (1993) show that there really are not powerful committees to the same extent in the Senate, it is the broadest and most active of the Senate policy committees (Evans 1991, 29). The Energy and Commerce Committee developed the same reputation in the House during the period of this analysis (King 1997, 42). Smith and Deering (1990, 82) also report that the House Energy and Commerce and Senate Commerce Committees have more minutes of news coverage than any other policy committees in their respective chambers.[1] And yet the jurisdictional range of Senate Commerce is much smaller than that of House Commerce, because it covers very few of the popular health care, energy, and environmental issues. The jurisdictions of the two committees as they stood in the 97th Congress are compared in table 7.1, which reveals that there is very little overlap in the formal jurisdictions of those committees in spite of their similar names.

Table 7.2 shows, however, that there is somewhat more overlap in the "common law" or informal agendas of House and Senate Commerce because on average 29.5% of the total number of issues considered by either committee are

TABLE 7.2   Overlap in the issues covered by bills referred to House and Senate Commerce Committees, 96th–107th Congresses

Congress	House Commerce Only	Senate Commerce Only	Both House and Senate Commerce	Total Number of Issues
96	64.1%	13.8%	22.0%	1,815
97	61.9%	17.2%	20.9%	1,400
98	64.1%	15.7%	20.2%	1,620
99	67.7%	12.3%	20.0%	2,135
100	67.3%	10.4%	22.3%	2,706
101	55.2%	18.1%	26.7%	2,230
102	51.5%	18.2%	30.3%	2,611
103	43.3%	17.5%	39.2%	2,856
104	50.6%	14.3%	35.1%	3,170
105	49.0%	14.5%	36.5%	2,922
106	53.4%	14.7%	31.9%	3,127
107	50.9%	16.0%	33.0%	3,235
Average	55.3%	15.2%	29.5%	2,485.6

referred to both committees in a given Congress. In fact, the percentage of Senate Commerce issues that are shared with House Commerce is larger than the percentage of Senate Commerce issues that are not shared with House Commerce.

In table C.2 in Appendix C, I also compare characteristics of the bills and issues submitted to Senate Commerce to the characteristics of bills and issues submitted to all other standing committees in the 103rd Senate. As was also true of House Commerce in table C.1, Senate Commerce seems to receive a mix of issues that is representative of the overall set of issues in the chamber.

Since the House and Senate have about the same number of committees, it is not surprising that the House, with more than four times as many representatives introducing legislation, has committees that handle a bigger workload. The House Energy and Commerce Committee contains about twice as many members as its Senate counterpart, and these members have fewer committee assignments than Senators, which aids the House committee in processing its bigger workload.

For a number of reasons, including the smaller size of the Senate, committees and subcommittees do not necessarily have the same importance in the Senate consideration of legislation as they do in the House (Baker 1989, Sinclair 1989; Binder and Smith 1995; Dion 1997). Looser formal rules and the individualistic nature of the Senate also make it much easier for a bill sponsor to circumvent the committees in bringing a measure before the Senate for consideration. A bill, for example, can be offered as a nongermane amendment to another bill under consideration since the Senate has few restrictions on germaneness of amendments and rarely uses restrictive rules in considering legislation. Unlike House members, Senators can also call ad hoc hearings on an issue when a committee refuses to give it consideration, putting public pressure on the committee to act. Most importantly, because Senators can block action on legislation with a filibuster, controversial issues are considered under unanimous consent agreements. Because unanimous consent agreements are often used in the Senate, individual Senators have a greater chance to influence legislation. By contrast, the House considers only noncontroversial legislation under unanimous consent, is more likely to use suspension of the rules that requires only two-thirds approval, and often considers major and controversial legislation under restrictive rules that place limits on debate and amendments.

In the next section I consider recent spatial models of supermajoritarian politics that have been used to capture this unique Senate lawmaking process. I show how these models are better suited for explaining policy outcomes on a single issue than the agenda-setting problem of which issues the Senate considers in committee and on the floor. I then characterize the predictions of the informational models of public addresses and draft legislation for the president's agenda influence in the Senate, in particular noting how it is likely to differ from his influence in the House. Finally, I test the predictions of these models on all legislation referred to the Senate Commerce Committee from 1979 to 2002.

The Filibuster and Supermajoritarian Politics

The explosive growth of the filibuster in the post-reform Congress and the failure of the unified government under Jimmy Carter and Bill Clinton to break the policy gridlock of the divided government that preceded it inspired researchers to extend the basic median voter theorem to take into account the supermajoritarian obstacles to legislative action that arise in the Senate.[2] With the filibuster, a majority's preferred policy can be assured of victory only when there is no group of 41 or more senators who prefer the status quo to the measure being voted on. Any group of 41 or more senators can block cloture votes to end debate, which requires approval of three-fifths of senators, and thus forestall action on legislation they find less appealing than the status quo. Whereas the majority often gets its way in the House, the Senate is essentially a supermajoritarian institution, requiring three-fifths support to overcome the filibuster.

The models of chapters 3 and 4 assumed a median voter in the legislature and thus are not directly designed to model agenda setting in supermajoritarian institutions like the Senate. Here I consider the pivotal model (Krehbiel 1998) of Senate policy making to examine how supermajoritarian procedures affect the president's agenda-setting influence. I show that supermajoritarian procedures have less impact on agenda setting than they have in determining the final bill passed by the Senate.

Consider the general policy issue space represented in figure 7.1, where F_L represents the 41st senator and F_R the 60th senator as they are arranged from left to right by ideal policies along an issue dimension. The determinant of whether gridlock occurs is the location of the status quo relative to these pivotal senators. All of the senators to the left of F_L represent a filibuster group that would be unwilling to let any status quo policy located at or to the right of F_L move further to the right, regardless of the preferences of the other senators. Even if the status quo were located exactly at F_L and all 59 other senators attempted to move it slightly to the right, the filibuster group could block such a move.

Similarly, F_R denotes the location of the ideal policy of the 60th senator (from right to left) and a filibuster group made up of this senator and the 40 senators to the right, who can block any attempt by the Senate to move a status quo located

FIGURE 7.1 The Senate's gridlock region

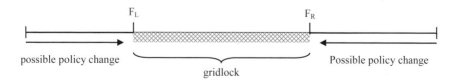

possible policy change   gridlock   Possible policy change

FIGURE 7.2 Range of possible Senate policy outcomes when status quo = 0

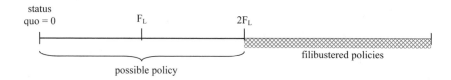

at or to the left of F_R any further to the left. Together these filibuster pivots thus prevent policy from changing at all if the status quo is located between the pivots, F_L and F_R. The region between the pivots is thus called the "gridlock" region by Brady and Volden (1997). The filibuster groups also place restrictions on what happens on issues where the status quo is located outside of the gridlock region; legislation can only move the status quo closer to or into the gridlock region. Once policy is in the gridlock region, of course, it cannot be altered unless this new status quo is subsequently bumped out of the gridlock region through exogenous events or the election of new senators with differing preferences. See Brady and Volden (1997) or Krehbiel (1998) for a fuller explanation of the model.

In agenda-setting models from chapters 3 and 4 with the status quo on each issue located at sq = 0 (see figure 7.2), the right filibuster pivot, F_R, can be ignored because the status quo cannot be moved any further to the left. The left filibuster, F_L, thus plays the key role in determining policy outcomes. This filibuster group, however, can block policy moves only to the right. In particular, the left filibuster group will block any policy that moves the status quo further from the pivot's ideal point, F_L, than the status quo. All possible policies must therefore fall between the status quo and $2F_L$.

The filibuster models are designed to counter the policy predictions of legislative stalemate in divided government that is generated by party-based models of legislative decision making. Sundquist (1988) and Ginsburg and Shefter (1990) found divided government responsible for gridlock because it provides incentives for the president and Congress to undermine each other's initiatives. Mayhew (1991), however, provides a strong case against stalemate in divided government theory by showing there is little change in the amount of major legislation produced by unified vs. divided governments. Conditional party models (Rohde 1991; Aldrich 1995; Aldrich and Rohde 1995) are more subtle models of divided government because they claim that the distribution of the majority party's preferences matters as much as whether the majority party holds the presidency. Fragmented parties, like the Democrats in the House with a host of conservative southerners in the 1980s, thus are unable to form the coalitions necessary to pass their agenda. Dion (1997) finds further that the majority party is actually more cohesive when it is smaller.

FIGURE 7.3 Configuration of ideal points on two issues in bicameral agenda setting

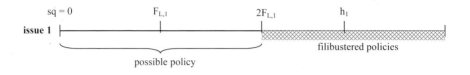

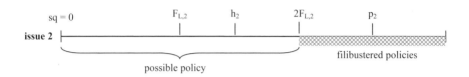

Despite the appeal of the conditional party argument, parties are alarmingly absent in the supermajoritarian models of gridlock I have been considering (Brady and Volden 1997; Krehbiel 1998). But this is by design. The parties holding the presidency and controlling Congress are inconsequential for policy outcomes because gridlock is determined by the preferences of the filibuster pivotal senators on each issue, the president's veto point, and the median voter in the House. All legislative outcomes on a given issue are deducible from this limited amount of information about the issue. Because of its sparseness, however, the gridlock models have more to say about what policies will be blocked than the exact policies that will be passed. For example, if the status quo is located outside the gridlock region, the Senate can pass any policy between the two filibuster pivots.

The Senate filibuster pivots have implications for presidential agenda setting as well as for gridlock. First, notice that in presidential agenda setting the effects of the presidential veto can be ignored in most cases since the president can propose policies where he and both chambers agree about how to move policy with respect to the status quo. Just as the veto was largely inconsequential in the models of chapter 3 and 4, it plays little significant role here.[3]

The supermajoritarian nature of the Senate, however, still places two important restrictions on the issue chosen by the House according to the agenda model considered in chapters 3 and 4. On the issue the president would like Congress to work on, the left Senate filibuster pivot must be to the right of the status quo, $sq = 0 < F_L$, and the final policy enacted must be to the left of the right filibuster pivot, $x < F_R$. If the House chooses action on an issue where the status quo lies in the gridlock region, it is likely to see any policy change blocked in the Senate. Thus, the Senate may have a restrictive effect on the issues that are chosen by the House. For the purposes of the models developed in chapters 3 and 4, however, as long as the left filibuster falls to the right of the status quo, the Senate will not block all possible action. Only policies to the right of $2F_L$ are then likely to be blocked.

Consider the two issues represented in figure 7.3. The Senate will reject any attempt to move policy to the right of $2F_{L,i}$ on either issue i = 1,2. If h_1, the House's median position on issue 1, or p_2, the president's ideal policy on issue 2, are greater than $2F_{L,i}$ on the issue i under consideration, the Senate may thus affect House action on that bill. The House has an interest in finding an agenda issue acceptable to the president where either h_1 is maximized, i.e., the status quo is furthest from its ideal policy, and $h_1 < 2F_{L,1}$ or where $2F_{L,1}$ is maximized when $h_1 > 2F_{L,1}$. Likewise, the president has an interest in choosing an issue acceptable to Congress where p_2 is maximized and $p_2 < 2F_{L,2}$ or where $2F_{L,2}$ is maximized subject to $p_2 > 2F_{L,2}$.

Gridlock theory is agnostic, however, on the question of exactly where policy will be moved when the status quo lies outside the gridlock region. If the gridlock region is relatively large, many possibilities exist, and the gridlock theories relegate such decisions to bargaining and agenda-setting power. In Congress, chamber differences are often resolved with conference committees, which are likely to choose a policy between the House and the Senate medians.[4] While gridlock theory is agnostic on the question of agenda setting, Brady and Volden (1997) suggest that the results of gridlock theory leave agenda setting as the chief role of the president: "The final significant role of the president in the theory of legislative policy making is in bringing the public's attention to an issue. . . . Whereas the revolving gridlock theory argues that legislator preferences and institutions affect *where* policy will end up, the president can help decide *which* issues will be addressed. . . . From this view, the president becomes more an agenda setter than a force influencing policy outcomes" (32).

Brady and Volden, however, fail to explain exactly how the president exercises this influence over the issues addressed. Whenever the status quo on an issue falls between the pivotal members of the Senate on that issue, a filibuster coalition will effectively forestall action on that issue. Thus, only issues where the status quo lies outside of the gridlock region are amenable to the president's agenda-setting power. A similar but less restrictive condition was imposed in chapters 3 and 4, where I modeled Congress by the median voter. In that case, the president's issue had to satisfy the condition that both the president and Congress desired to move policy in the same direction relative to the status quo. The Senate thus adds a possibly more restrictive condition on presidential agenda setting but does not necessarily eliminate it. In fact, when considering the Senate instead of the House, the same results follow from chapters 3 and 4, as long as issues are available to the president that satisfy the gridlock conditions. Still, since the supermajoritarian character of the Senate filibuster may restrict the set of issues available for presidential agenda setting, the gridlock theories lead us to predict that the president may exercise less overall influence over the Senate agenda than over the House agenda. In the next section I join these considerations and other Senate differences with the models of chapters 3 and 4 to generate predictions about the president's likely influence on the Senate agenda that I test in the following section.

Model Predictions

To explore the president's effect on the Senate agenda, all of the issues covered by bills referred to the Senate Commerce Committee in the 96th through 107th Congresses were coded similarly to House bills in the previous chapter. The total of 2,758 bills and 4,229 issues referred to the Senate Commerce Committee, however, represents only a fraction of the 11,379 bills and 7,906 issues that were referred to the House Energy and Commerce Committee during the same Congresses.

In the introduction to this chapter I argued that differences between the visibility of senators and members of Congress made the senators less vulnerable to efforts by the president to set the congressional agenda. The president's public addresses are also less effective in the Senate because only one-third of the Senate is up for reelection in any given election year. The influence of the president's addresses on members in the legislative programming model from chapter 3 occurred because the information provided by the president was used by voters to decide whether to reelect their representative. The dynamics of declining presidential accountability and six-year Senate terms may actually shield a portion the Senate from presidential influence because there is always the possibility that there will be a new president before one-third of the Senate comes up for reelection.

Draft legislation is expected to have a significant impact on the Senate agenda because the executive has an even larger advantage in expertise over the Senate than over the House, which has more manpower and more specialists. I thus expect that the president's draft legislation will have a positive effect on an issue's chance of reaching the floor in the more open floor agenda process of the Senate.

In summary, the two main differences from the expectations in the House in terms of the president's influence are: (1) the president's major addresses are expected to have a less significant impact on all stages of the Senate agenda process; and (2) the president's draft legislation is expected to exercise a stronger direct influence on both the committee and floor agendas in the Senate.

Overall Presidential Influence on the Senate Agenda

In table 7.3, I present the statistically significant total effects on the Senate floor agenda from the president, committee leaders, and the House for all issues covered by bills referred to the Senate Commerce Committee from the 96th to the 107th Congresses. The president's major addresses exercise a positive total influence on the floor agenda in only three Congresses, and they exercise a negative total influence in the same number of Congresses. This influence is weaker and less consistent than in the House. This weaker influence was predicted in part because senators are better equipped to challenge the president's dominance of the agenda through the media as a result of their greater prominence than House members (Sinclair 1989, 214). In the cases where the president exercises a total negative influence on the Senate agenda, issues mentioned by the president are actually less likely to be considered by the Senate, ceteris paribus. Not surprisingly, two of these Congresses, the 100th and 101st, occur in divided government when a Republican controlled the presidency and Democrats controlled the Senate. In the other case, the 98th Congress, Republicans controlled both the presidency and the Senate.

TABLE 7.3 Statistically significant (p <.10) total effects from president, committee, and House on the Senate Commerce floor agenda, 96th–107th

President	Congress	Major Address	Draft Legislation	Committee Leader	House Bill	Request for Executive Comment	Total Number of Issues
Carter	96	.04	.17	.40	.29 + .20t	.03	651
Reagan	97		.06	.32	.21 + .20t	-.03	531
	98	-.15	-.02	.51	.28 + .19t	-.05	580
	99		-.03	.23	.27 - .05t	.15	690
	100	-.07	.00	.03	.19 + .10t	-.08	884
G. W. H. Bush	101	-.03	.13	.05	.25 + .13t	-.05	999
	102		.002	-.04	.09 + .22t	.00	1,264
Clinton	103		.20	.01	.15 + .08t	-.11	1,613
	104		.16	.03	.25 - .02t	-.06	1,552
	105	.05	.12	.15	.10 + .17t	.00	1,377
	106		.06	.33	.22 + .27t	.00	1,353
G. W. Bush	107	.15	N.A.	.24	.27 - .00t	-.17	1,588

Note: Statistically significant total effects are approximately calculated by including only direct or indirect effects that are statistically significant at the $p \leq .10$ level.

TABLE 7.4   Number and origin of Senate issues referred to Senate Commerce, 96th–107th

| Congress | Issues on House bills | | | Total Issues | Percentage of Issues Initiated by House |
	House-Initiated Issues	Senate-Initiated Issues	Total House Issues		
96	8	143	151	656	1.22%
97	17	104	121	542	3.14%
98	16	196	212	590	2.71%
99	27	166	193	689	3.92%
100	23	305	328	903	2.55%
101	60	375	435	999	6.00%
102	45	549	594	1266	3.55%
103	131	889	1020	1629	8.04%
104	136	741	877	1566	8.68%
105	135	367	502	1489	9.07%
106	132	593	725	1456	9.06%
107	135	351	486	1588	8.50%

As predicted, the president is more successful in using draft legislation than public addresses to set the Senate agenda. In the 98th and 99th Congresses, the president's draft legislation had a negative total effect on the floor agenda, but in all other Congresses it was positive and significant. Committee leaders are, on average, also weaker influences on the agenda than their counterparts in the House Commerce Committee. Another significant difference from the House is that the other chamber plays a much stronger agenda-setting role in the Senate, as can be seen in figure 7.16, which presents the average size of the House and Senate agenda influences side-by-side.

The effect of House bills is broken down into two components, e.g., .29 + .20t, where the first term (.29) indicates the influence on the floor agenda of an issue being covered by a House bill that is referred to the Senate only after the issue has already been introduced by a Senate bill. The second term (.20) indicates the additional influence that comes from an issue appearing in the Senate on a House bill before any Senate bills are introduced on the topic. House bills have a positive influence on the Senate agenda in all Congresses, and in 9 of the 12 Congresses House initiation of an issue also exerts an additional positive total effect on floor consideration. Breaking down House issues into those that are introduced before and after the same issue is introduced by Senate bills allows more precise determination of the House's influence on the Senate agenda. Since the House has a larger legislative workload than the Senate, House bills make up a much larger portion of the Senate agenda than is the case for Senate bills on the House agenda. Many of the issues that are introduced in the Senate are introduced through House bills. In table 7.4, I show that anywhere from 1.22% to 9.07% of all of the issues introduced in a given Senate were placed there by a House-passed bill before any Senate bill was even introduced on the topic.[5] By contrast, an insignificant number of issues are introduced into the House for the first time by Senate-passed bills, so it would have been less informative to break down Senate bills in this way when considering the House agenda in chapter 6.

House issues are particularly fascinating because they might serve as a means for the president to exert influence over the Senate agenda in the same way that his influence over House Commerce Committee leaders gives him indirect influence over the House agenda. However, interaction terms multiplying the variable for the president's message or draft legislation by the House bill variables do not indicate any significant total influence on the Senate floor. The House is a major player in Senate agenda setting—perhaps even more important than Senate committee leaders as will be shown in figure 7.16—but given that the president's modest control over even the House Commerce agenda, the detection of such an effect, if it exists, may require a Congress-wide study.

I have largely the same expectations for contextual variables in the Senate as in the House with some notable exceptions. Theoretical explanations for the expectations in the context of the House are presented in table 6.4. In the Senate, (1) the average number of cosponsors should have a positive total effect on the Senate floor agenda; (2) multiply referred issues should have a negative impact on the Senate floor agenda; (3) authorization issues should have a positive effect on the Senate floor agenda; (4) the order of introduction should have a negative effect on the Senate floor agenda; (5) Democratic sponsors should have a positive impact in Democrat-controlled Senates and a negative impact in Republican-controlled Senates; and (6) the average tenure of the main sponsor should have a positive impact on an issue's chance of appearing on the Senate floor agenda. Many of these House expectations are borne out in the Senate data but less consistently than in the House.

I also add a variable in the Senate data that indicates whether the issue is a matter of private rather than public legislation. Much of Congress's legislative production is such private legislation, but in the Senate Commerce Committee almost all of this private legislation concerns documenting merchant ships, such as the following example from the 103rd Congress:

H.R. 2198. A bill to authorize a certificate of documentation for the vessel "Serenity."

Most private legislation is not controversial and passes easily, but I control for it in the analysis to make sure that the agenda effects of public bills are not biased by the inclusion of private bills. Almost no private legislation was referred to the House Commerce Committee, so I ignored this variable in the consideration of

TABLE 7.5   Statistically significant (p < .10) total effects from issue and contextual variables on the Senate Commerce floor agenda, 96th–107th

Congress	Max. Number of Cosponsors	Multiply Referred	Authorization Issue	Private Legislative Issue	Timing of Earliest Introduction	Sponsored by Democrat	Max. Sponsor Experience	Total Number of Issues
96	0.00	-0.24	0.15	0.24	< 0.01	0.17		651
97	< 0.01	-0.37	0.24	-0.08	-0.33	< 0.01	0.03	531
98	0.01	0.23	< 0.01	-0.28	-0.03	< 0.01		580
99	0.01	-0.03	< 0.01	0.08	-0.35	-0.16	0.01	690
100	0.01	-0.003	< 0.01	0.32	< 0.01	0.32	0.03	884
101	0.01	-0.01	-0.06	0.34	0.05	0.14	-0.01	999
102	0.01	-0.06	0.12	0.74	-0.31	0.21	0.01	1,264
103	< 0.01	0.21	-0.04	0.11	-0.17	0.36	0.02	1,613
104	0.01	0.57	< 0.01	-0.31	-0.49	-0.16		1,552
105	0.01	0.31	< 0.01	0.13	-0.20	< 0.01		1,377
106	0.01	0.65	-0.01	-0.16	-0.51	-0.07		1,353
107	0.02	0.58	0.39	0.09	-0.12	0.05		1,588

House agenda setting in chapter 6. I expect a private legislative issue to have a significantly higher probability of reaching the Senate floor agenda but a lower probability of receiving hearings since such matters are noncontroversial and involve particular constituents rather than broad public policy issues, which might elicit public interest. The statistically significant total effect from these control variables are presented in table 7.5.

The maximum number of cosponsors has the expected positive total influence on floor consideration. Multiple referrals have a puzzling positive effect on the Senate floor agenda in the 103rd to 107th Congresses as well as the 98th Congress. Otherwise, they have the expected negative total influence on the floor. Authorization issues have the expected positive total influence on the floor agenda in 9 of the 12 Congresses studied. The timing of earliest introduction has the expected negative association with floor consideration in 9 of the 12 Congresses. But the relation of the proportion of Democratic sponsors to floor consideration does not seem to be driven by the party in control of the Senate in the way that it was in the House. Oleszek (2001, 181) offers a possible explanation for this difference: "Unlike the House, where the majority party led by the Speaker is in charge of scheduling, the majority and minority leaders in the Senate together largely shape the institution's program and agenda." It is not surprising that the Senate thus appears less partisan in its agenda setting, but it is surprising that more evidence of a party bias does not appear. The same inconsistency afflicts the average Senate tenure of bill sponsors for an issue. In the 104th through 107th Congresses, the effect of main-sponsor experience disappears. The results also show that private legislative issues exercise a significant positive influence over the Senate floor agenda in 8 of the Congresses considered but a negative significant influence over the agenda in four Congresses. Next, I examine in detail the influence of the president and the House on the Senate agenda for issues covered by bills referred to Senate Commerce in each Congress from the 96th to the 107th.

Jimmy Carter

Carter's influence over the Senate agenda in his second Congress, the 96th, presents an exception to the two patterns that will characterize the most significant differences between the president's House and Senate influence: (1) the president's speeches rarely have any influence on the Senate agenda; and (2) the president's draft legislation exerts most of its influence on hearings in the Senate rather than on committee leaders.

As shown in figure 7.4, Carter's State of the Union addresses to the 96th Congress exhibit a surprising positive influence on committee markups and yield a positive total influence on the floor agenda. Carter's major addresses also exercised influence in the 96th House, but in that case it was due mainly to direct influence on the floor.

Carter's draft legislation in the 96th Senate exercises a direct positive influence over committee leaders and over markup and a negative direct influence on

FIGURE 7.4 Direct effects on the Senate agenda for 96th Senate Commerce issues

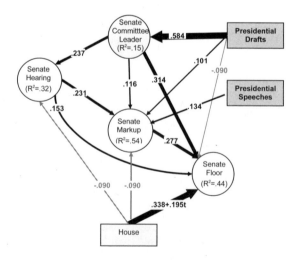

the floor but no direct influence over hearings. In subsequent Congresses, the president will typically experience a more robust direct influence on hearings than on either committee leaders or markup. Carter's draft legislation also exerts a negative direct influence on the floor in the 96th Senate, but this is counterbalanced by the positive indirect effects from committee leaders and markup so that the president has a positive total influence on the Senate floor.

Issues introduced in the Senate on House-passed bills exhibit a slight negative influence on hearings and markup but a powerful positive direct influence on Senate floor consideration. Issues that are first introduced on House-passed bills have a direct positive influence on the Senate floor that is slightly larger than the combined direct influence of Senate committee leaders and markup. This is a strong influence indeed, and the Senate exercised no comparable level of influence over the House floor in the Congresses studied in chapter 6.

Ronald Reagan

Reagan brought with him into office a Republican majority in the Senate. Many of his legislative proposals were introduced first in the Senate in order to gain legislative momentum. As figure 7.5 reveals, Reagan's draft legislation had a direct positive influence on committee leaders and hearings but a negative direct influence on markup. Even in his first Congress, Reagan was not able to positively influence the Senate consideration of issues through his State of the Union addresses, but this may have been partly because he focused on economic issues in his first Congress, as I discussed in the last chapter. Reagan's issues covered

FIGURE 7.5 Direct effects on the Senate agenda for 97th Senate Commerce issues

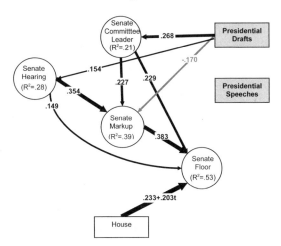

FIGURE 7.6 Direct effects on the Senate agenda for 98th Senate Commerce issues

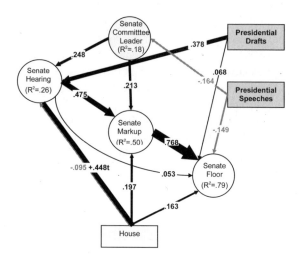

FIGURE 7.7 Direct effects on the Senate agenda for 99th Senate Commerce issues

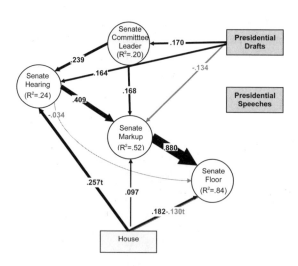

in addresses to the 97th Congress included government regulation, petroleum (with respect to pipelines), and subsidies among issues that fall directly under the committee's official jurisdiction. The Democratic House continued to exercise a very powerful direct positive influence over the Senate floor in the 97th

FIGURE 7.8 Direct effects on the Senate agenda for 100th Senate Commerce issues

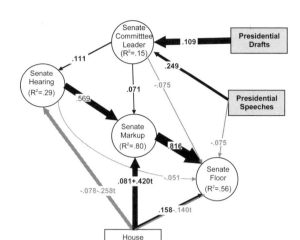

Congress, but the now-Republican Senate's influence over the House weakens, as was shown in figure 6.3.

In the 98th Congress, Reagan surprisingly exercised negative total influence over the Republican Senate Commerce agenda from his State of the Union speeches, as shown in figure 7.6. Reagan's draft legislation, however, exhibited the typical Senate pattern of direct positive influence on hearings. In the 98th Congress, the House exerts a negative direct influence on Senate hearings for issues introduced first on Senate bills but a very powerful positive direct influence for issues first introduced on House-passed bills. The House also exerts a positive direct influence on markup and the floor in the 98th Senate.

As shown in figure 7.7, Reagan's draft legislation in the 99th Congress exhibited the same pattern as in the 97th Senate: a positive direct influence on committee leaders and hearings but a negative direct influence on markup. The House exerts a positive direct influence on hearings in the 99th only for issues that are first introduced by House-passed bills. However, these House-initiated issues exert much less influence on the Senate floor than Senate-initiated issues that are covered by House bills.

As shown in figure 7.8, in the 100th Congress after the Senate was taken back by the Democrats, Reagan again found that his State of the Union addresses exerted a negative direct and total influence on an issue's likelihood of reaching the Senate floor agenda. Reagan's speeches did exercise a direct positive influence on committee leaders, but it was not strong enough to fully counterbalance the negative direct influence his speeches exerted on the Senate floor. Reagan's draft legislation was able to exercise a positive total influence on the floor

133

through its influence on committee leaders. In the unified Democratic 100th Congress, House passage exerts an unusually strong influence on committee markups but mainly for issues first introduced in the Senate by House-passed bills. Other than this, there is little influence that the 100th House and Senate were any more successful in coordinating their agendas than the 3 preceding divided-party Congresses.

George H. W. Bush

Like Reagan in the 98th Congress, Bush experienced a positive direct influence on the Senate floor agenda with his draft legislation in the 101st as shown in figure 7.9. Bush's draft legislation also exercised the predicted positive direct influence on committee leaders and hearings. Bush's speeches, however, exercised only a negative direct influence on the Senate floor agenda, indicating that the Senate and White House were pushing competing agendas. The House exerted a direct positive influence on markup and the floor in the 101st Senate, with an additional positive influence for House-initiated issues on the Senate markup stage.

As shown in figure 7.10, the 102nd Senate stands out as the only case in either chamber where committee leaders did not exercise a direct positive influence on any stage of the agenda-setting process. Bush's draft legislation still exerted the predicted positive direct effect on hearings, but this was nearly nullified by a direct negative influence on the Senate floor agenda and by the indirect negative impact through committee leaders. Bush's speeches exercise no measurable

FIGURE 7.9 Direct effects on the Senate agenda for 101st Senate Commerce issues

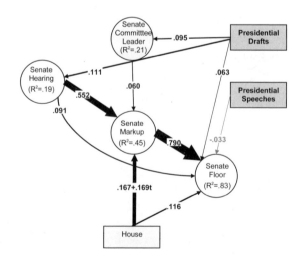

FIGURE 7.10 Direct effects on the Senate agenda for 102nd Senate Commerce issues

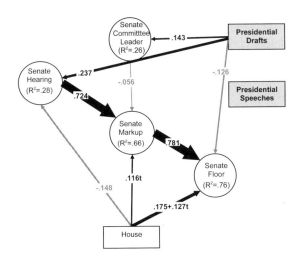

influence on any stage of the 102nd Senate agenda. The influence of the House was negative on Senate hearings in the 102nd Congress but positive on the Senate floor agenda, particularly for House-initiated issues, which also exerted a positive influence on Senate markup.

Bill Clinton

Ironically, the 103rd Congress looks much like the 102nd, even though the Democrats now controlled the presidency. In contrast to the 103rd House, Clinton's speeches evidenced no measurable influence on the 103rd Senate at any stage of the agenda-setting process, as shown in figure 7.11. Furthermore, Clinton's draft legislation experienced a direct negative influence on the Senate floor that somewhat weakened the indirect influence he experienced by way of committee leaders, hearings, and markups. In the 103rd Congress, the House exercised a direct positive influence on markup and the floor in the Senate, and House-initiated issues exercised a direct positive influence on hearings.

The 104th Congress brought Republican leadership to the Senate as well as the House. Clinton's State of the Union addresses to the 104th Congress exercised no measurable influence on the Senate agenda, as shown in figure 7.12. However, Clinton was able to exercise considerable influence over the Senate floor agenda through the submission of draft legislation, particularly at the hearing and markup stages. In the Republican House and Senate of the 104th Congress,

135

FIGURE 7.11 Direct effects on the Senate agenda for 103rd Senate Commerce issues

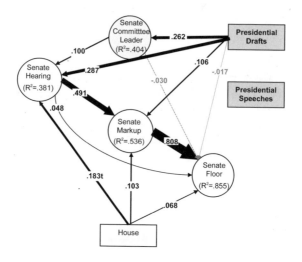

FIGURE 7.12 Direct effects on the Senate agenda for 104th Senate Commerce issues

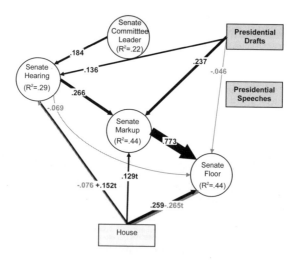

House-initiated issues exerted a surprisingly strong negative additional impact on the Senate floor that negated the positive impact the House exerted on Senate-initiated issues. This suggests that House passage had a direct positive influence on the Senate floor for Senate-initiated issues but a direct positive influence on markup and hearing for House-initiated issues.

It is notable that the House and Senate of the 104th Congress had separate

TABLE 7.6 Republican House and Senate candidate campaign agenda pledges

Contract With America	Seven More in 94
1. Balanced-Budget Amendment and Line-Item Veto	1. Balanced-Budget Amendment
2. Crime Legislation	2. Crime Legislation
3. Welfare reform	3. Welfare Reform
4. Family and Child Legislation	
5. Middle-Class Tax Cuts	5. Middle-Class Tax Cuts
6. Reduce Defense Cuts	6. Reduce Defense Cuts
7. Social Security	7. Social Security
8. Capital Gains Reductions	8. Capital Gains Reductions
9. Product Liability Reform	
10. Term Limits	

uncoordinated agendas, even though the Republicans were in control of the House for the first time in 40 years and in control of the Senate for the first time since 1986. The new Republican control of both chambers might have led one to expect that the House would have played a stronger role in setting the Senate agenda in the 104th Congress, but the House actually had one of its weakest total impacts on the Senate floor agenda in the 104th Congress. Perhaps signals that the House and Senate would not work too closely together were evident in the different 1994 campaign pledges signed by House and Senate Republican candidates; House Republicans had pledged to the 10 elements of the "Contract with America" while the Senators had embraced only the 7 of these elements in their own "Seven More in 94" contract as shown in table 7.6. The disconnect is especially surprising when considering that Gingrich purposefully avoided controversial issues like abortion and school prayer in defining an agenda all Republicans could unite behind. The balanced-budget amendment and the term limit proposal were both defeated in the Senate after passing in the House. Furthermore, the 104th Senate also voted a rule change whereby it would adopt a formal legislative agenda at the beginning of each Congress by a three-fourths vote of all Republican senators in an effort to gain more independent control over its agenda.

Ironically, the measured influence of Clinton's speeches and draft legislation is quite robust in the 105th Congress, in which the House impeached him on two articles. Clinton's drafts and speeches both experienced a direct and total positive influence on the Senate floor agenda, as shown in figure 7.13. This differs markedly from his influence in the House, where his speeches had no measurable impact and his draft legislation exercised a direct negative impact on the floor

FIGURE 7.13 Direct effects on the Senate agenda for 105th Senate Commerce issues

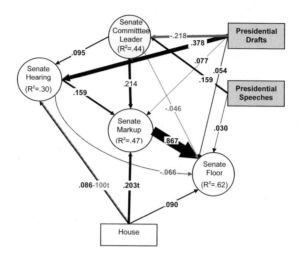

FIGURE 7.14 Direct effects on the Senate agenda for 106th Senate Commerce issues

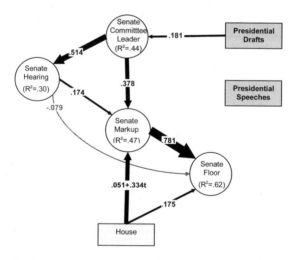

agenda. Clearly, the Senate was not as polarized against Clinton as the House, as became clear in the 106th Congress when the Senate voted to acquit the president on both impeachment articles. In the 105th Congress, the House exercised a positive direct influence on hearings and the floor of the Senate for Senate-initiated issues. The House exercised a positive direct influence on markups and the floor for House-initiated issues.

In the 106th Congress, Clinton's speeches had no direct impact on any stage of the Senate agenda, as shown in figure 7.14. The 106th Senate also experienced one of the lowest levels of influence from draft legislation. Clinton's drafts had a direct positive influence only on the committee-leader stage of the Senate agenda. In terms of House influence on the Senate agenda, the 106th Congress looks similar to the 101st. House-passed issues exert a positive direct influence on markup and the floor in the Senate, and House-initiated issues exert a strong additional influence on Senate markup.

George W. Bush

The 2000 election produced an exact tie in the Senate, which led to a brokered compromise regarding leadership and membership of the Senate committees. Democrats would hold the chairmanships as long as Gore held the decisive tie-breaking vote as vice president, i.e., until the January 20 inauguration of President George W. Bush. Afterwards, the Republicans would chair the committees. But, as mentioned in chapter 6, the 107th Congress was also marked by the historic mid-session change of leadership in the Senate from the Republicans to the Democrats, after the defection of Senator Jim Jeffords from the Republican Party. This sent the leadership of the committees back to the Democrats on June 6, 2001.

As shown in figure 7.15, in the 107th Senate the president's addresses exercise only a positive direct influence over hearings, which leads to a positive total influence on the Senate floor. Unfortunately, the president's draft legislation sub-

FIGURE 7.15 Direct effects on the Senate agenda for 107th Senate Commerce issues

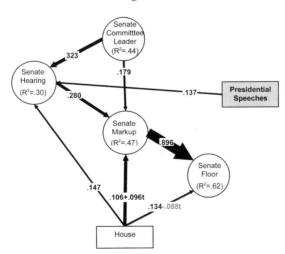

mitted to the Senate Commerce Committee is unavailable, so I am able to measure only the influence of the president's speeches on the agenda. House issues that are initiated by Senate bills in the 107th Congress exert a relatively similar level of direct positive influence on hearings, markup, and the floor in the Senate. House-initiated issues, however, exert a much stronger influence on the markup stage and a much weaker influence on the Senate floor.

Conclusion

Overall, the president exercises little regular influence over the Senate agenda through mentions of an issue in his State of the Union addresses, even in the president's first Congress when he often enjoys such influence in the House. The House, however, does act as a very strong influence on the Senate agenda, so it is possible that the president exerts influence on the Senate indirectly through his influence on the House. The evidence I have collected from a single committee is inadequate, however, for determining whether the president can actually exercise such influence indirectly on the Senate through his influence on the House. Data from multiple committees could offer more insight into this intriguing possibility.

The effects of the president's draft legislation are stronger and look more like the results in the House. In the Senate, draft legislation exercised a significant positive total effect on the floor agenda in 9 of the 11 Congresses where I measure the influence of drafts, compared to 9 of 12 Congresses in the House.

In figure 7.16, I compare the average effects of influences on the House and Senate agendas. The overall internal patterns are similar. In both House and Senate, the strongest influence on the floor agenda comes from markup, and the strongest influence on markup comes from hearings. As would be expected, however, committee leaders exercise more influence in the House than in the Senate. There are also significant differences in the president's overall average influence in the House and Senate. On average the president's speeches have no influence in the Senate, while they have a slight positive overall average influence on the House floor. Draft legislation exercises its strongest average influence on hearings in the Senate, while it has its strongest influence on committee leaders in the House. And in the Senate, the effect of draft legislation on early stages of the agenda tends to be tempered by an occasional negative direct influence on the floor. In both House and Senate, the influence of draft legislation is mostly on earlier stages of the agenda process, i.e., the consideration of issues in committee.

The House also exerts a stronger influence on the Senate agenda than the Senate exerts on the House agenda. For Senate-initiated issues, the Senate looks

FIGURE 7.16 Comparative average influence of president on agenda stages for issues referred to 96th through 107th House and Senate Commerce Committees.

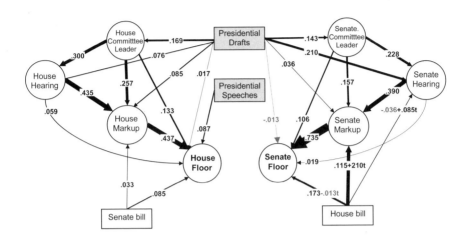

like the House, with House-passed issues having a direct positive influence on markup and the floor. For House-initiated issues, however, there is also evidence of a direct positive influence on Senate hearings and stronger influence on Senate markup.

Overall, the results of this chapter indicate that the president is able to wield significant positive influence over the Senate floor agenda for bills referred to the Senate Commerce Committee but mainly though draft legislation. The model of legislative clearance in chapter 4 suggests that this influence over the agenda arises because of the expertise incorporated into draft legislation. Sinclair's (1989) characterization of the Senate as a body of media entrepreneurs offers an important explanation for the inability of the president to exercise influence over the Senate through public appeals in his State of the Union addresses, but there are other considerations as well, including the small size of the Senate, longer Senate terms of office, and the more open Senate legislative process. A question that remains is whether the president can still exercise such influence indirectly through his influence over the House agenda because House issues make up a large share of the issues in the Senate and because House passage has a strong influence on the Senate agenda. While I have found no evidence that the president exercises an indirect influence on the Senate, the consideration of a single committee in each chamber may be too limited a perspective from which to detect this indirect effect. If it exists, however, the president's overall indirect effect on the Senate agenda through the House is probably very slight since I can detect no evidence of it in any of the Congresses studied here.

·8·

Information and Presidential Agenda Setting

Although the 1787 Constitution enjoined the president annually to recommend to Congress all measures he judges "necessary and expedient," by 1885 Woodrow Wilson had found the presidency so ineffective that he condemned the American system as "Congressional government." However, modern presidents, particularly through the development of the legislative programming and legislative clearance processes detailed in chapters 3 and 4, have recovered much of their constitutionally endowed responsibility. Consequently, today the president is often recognized as the chief agenda setter in Congress (e.g., C. Jones 1994; Light 1991; Peterson 1990). This modern understanding is, however, somewhat misleading. Although the president plays a significant role in setting the congressional agenda, internal congressional forces including committee chairs and the other chamber are more important in determining which issues advance from bill introduction to committee or floor consideration. Much of the president's influence on both the House and the Senate agenda is an indirect result of his influence on committee leaders and committee agendas rather than direct influence on the floor agenda.

Informative Representation

I have developed two informational models that explain how the president has come to exercise agenda-setting influence over Congress, and I have used new multidimensional issue-level data to trace the institutional lineaments of that

142

power. The president is shown to exercise more direct control over the floor agenda through his role in public addresses, yet this influence is short-lived and seems to be effective mainly in the House. The president's control over executive expertise in draft legislation is shown to provide a more consistent influence on the congressional agenda of both chambers, but only for issues which are either relatively noncontroversial or highly technical. The persistent application of this legislative clearance influence throughout the president's term, however, may in the end be more consequential for public policy than the major policy issues the president is able to bring to the congressional agenda through his public addresses.

In both instances the president is able to exercise informal influence through the provision of information. In the case of public addresses the president provides information to voters that may influence the congressional agenda by altering voters' assessment of the most important problems. In the case of draft legislation, the president's control over policy expertise from executive agencies gives him a technical informational advantage over Congress that allows him to influence the issues Congress considers.

I have developed a model of the president's public addresses where the president exercises influence over the congressional agenda and policy outcomes because he provides information to voters about the most important issues facing Congress. Voters may or may not then use the president's policy agenda as a standard for reelecting members of Congress. The president does not directly change the voters' policy preferences in this model but instead uses his policy expertise to provide information about issues on which the voters are not well informed.

This is a much weaker kind of influence than is suggested by arguments that the president can "go public" to force Congress to pass the president's program or arguments that the president possesses a mandate from the electorate because it models voters themselves as strategic agents who are not automatically influenced by the president's message. For example, the president's public addresses are only effective early in his term because voters realize that the president only has a strong incentive to communicate policy information faithfully to them when reelection still looms in the future as a means of holding the president accountable for his leadership.

The result is a sober picture of the president's ability to "go over the heads of Congress" in order to manipulate the congressional agenda via public opinion. Presidents only seem to be able to use public addresses to influence the congressional agenda in their first one or two Congresses in the House and even more infrequently in the Senate. And even in these Congresses, the president is considerably weaker than other actors like committee chairs and the other chamber. Nevertheless, public addresses are the president's chief tool for bringing congressional attention to sweeping and controversial issues like Jimmy Carter's energy plan or Bill Clinton's health care reform. The model bears out the folk wisdom that presidents must introduce any large-scale policy changes at the beginning of their first Congress, though for different reasons than are usually advanced. It is neither a perceived mandate (Conley 2001) nor a honeymoon (Ragsdale 1988), but the president's accountability to the voters that drives his early influence in this model.

Since the development of the legislative clearance process in 1935 (Neustadt 1954), the president has also had the ability to control the policy expertise that flows from the executive agencies to Congress in the form of draft bills. The president is able to influence the agenda through draft legislation because the policy expertise contained in a draft bill makes Congress better informed than it would otherwise be about how to resolve a policy issue. While technical expertise alone is unlikely to sway the congressional agenda towards issues where the president and Congress have fundamental policy disagreements, there are likely to be many issues connected with already-existing government programs like Medicare, the Clean Air Act, and the Public Health Service Act, where their policy preferences are similar. Since this "continuing agenda" accounts for a large portion of the policy bills introduced in Congress, the president's control of executive draft legislation offers a potentially important power to influence the direction of public policy, though in a much more gradual manner than the landmark issues that are more likely to arise in his public addresses.

For example, in each Congress many bills are introduced to extend Medicare coverage to new treatments and diseases. Because of the crowded congressional agenda, very few of these amendments to the Social Security Act receive any attention. However, the president may submit a draft bill of Medicare amendments prepared by the Department of Health and Human Services, which therefore may be more persuasive than any of the bills drawn up by individual members or committees covering other Medicare issues. This kind of alteration in the "continuing agenda" is more likely to be incremental rather than drastic, but because this presidential influence is persistent throughout his term the cumulative effect on public policy may be quite large. A president may, for example, shift the focus of new Medicaid coverage areas to preventive rather than catastrophic care over the course of several Congresses through the submission of a series of draft bills that propose coverage for preventive procedures.

This suggests that it pays for presidents to be mindful of the possible long-term policy change that is possible through the legislative clearance process, as Gilmour noted in the quote opening chapter 4. But it also serves as a caution that a president may be able to use draft legislation to slowly shift national policy agenda in ways that are not highly visible to the public. For example, Ronald Reagan submitted a series of draft bills proposing the deregulation of the financial services industry,[1] which helped precipitate the Savings and Loan crisis that his successor George H. W. Bush inherited. Since the legislative clearance process often involves highly technical issues that are not highly salient, like financial institution regulation, natural gas regulation, and radio spectrum allocations, agenda shifts in these areas are likely to go unnoticed among the general public. The resulting changes in policy are more likely to be unnoticed both because they are gradual rather than dramatic and because they sometimes concern highly technical issues like pollution allowances or spectrum auctions that are not easily understood by the public. This caution, however, is mitigated by the observation that I discussed earlier in this chapter: the president's overall influence on the agenda remains weaker than internal congressional influences like committee chairs and the other chamber. Furthermore, the built-in limitations of this expertise-based agenda setting suggest that the president cannot use draft legislation to redirect the congressional agenda to issues where the president and Congress have fundamental disagreements. Only the president's public addresses can offer dramatic shifts in the policy agenda, and this process necessarily involves voters as well as the president and Congress.

The analysis of the main pathways of bills and issues through the House and Senate in chapter 5 revealed that the agenda-setting process is enormously complex, and that there are many ways that issues can advance on the agenda other than the textbook process, particularly in the House. This complicates the president's job in trying to influence the agenda. The more direct avenues that exist for a bill to go to the floor, the more the president's influence from executive expertise seems to be enhanced because the president's expertise can serve as a substitute for committee expertise for bills that circumvent committee consideration. For example, in the 104th House, where the Republican leadership frequently used ad hoc task forces to prepare bills for the floor instead of standing committees, Clinton's draft legislation had a direct positive influence on the floor consideration of an issue, whereas draft legislation exercised a direct positive influence only on committee consideration in most other Congresses. I argue that Clinton's surprising influence in this case arose because the congressional task forces did not benefit from the same level of technical expertise as the standing committees. Ad hoc task forces thus generally yield bills with more uncertain policy effects than traditional committee bills. In this environment the expertise contained in the president's draft legislation became more valuable at the floor stage of consideration even though the party leadership had centralized policy making.

It is also noteworthy that recent models of supermajoritarian institutions have not yet been generalized to acknowledge this informational advantage at the heart of the legislative clearance process (e.g., Brady and Volden 1997; Krehbiel 1998). Yet, just as legislative committees may use their expertise to secure policies closer to their ideal,[2] the president can use the expertise of the federal bureaucracy to secure policies closer to his own ideal or to place his issue priorities on the congressional agenda.

The Bicameral Hurdle to Presidential Agenda Setting

As a part of the empirical analyses of chapters 6 and 7, I measured the influence of bills passed in one chamber on the issues under consideration in the other chamber. In both the House and the Senate the other chamber proved to be one of the most robust influences on the agenda, particularly for late stages of the agenda like floor consideration. It is still common, however, for models of presidential-congressional interaction to portray the Congress as a single actor or as a unicameral body. The "pivotal" models of Krehbiel (1998) and Brady and Volden (1997) stand out because they model the House and Senate separately, and my analysis suggests further reasons why the unicameral assumption is precarious. The president exercises a different kind of influence in the House than he does in the Senate because of the policymaking differences between the chambers. The picture is also complicated by the fact that each chamber is a very powerful agenda setter in the other chamber, granting the other chamber's bills privileged consideration.

Furthermore, there is little effective formal coordination of the House and Senate agendas. Despite a recent increase in informal meetings between the House and Senate leadership and their staffers to coordinate their policy agendas (Galloway 1994, 288), attempts at such coordination are still rare, even when the same party controls both chambers (Baker 1989; Sinclair 1995). One implication for presidential agenda setting is that the president's influence is weakened because he has to deal with two separate and uncoordinated congressional agendas. However, there are other ways in which the president's influence is actually enhanced by the lack of formal coordination.

The president's influence due to his public addresses stems partly from the advantage the president has over members of Congress in communicating with the public. This advantage might be diminished if the House and Senate work together to promote a common agenda because the Senate already seems to be somewhat immune to this kind of presidential dominance. Since the president's influence due to executive expertise arises from his control of the vast information of the federal bureaucracy, the House and Senate could also diminish the advantage the president holds in policy expertise if they coordinate their hearings and other information gathering actions.[3] In these ways, at least, the inability to coordinate House and Senate agendas actually seems to strengthen the president's ability to influence the agenda in both chambers.

The question remains whether the president can wield influence indirectly in the Senate through his influence over the House agenda or vice versa. House bills, in particular, make up a considerable portion of the legislation and issues introduced in the Senate. While I have found no evidence that the president can influence the one chamber's agenda by setting the agenda in the other chamber, the consideration of a single committee in each chamber may be too limited a perspective from which to detect this indirect effect.

Issues vs. Bills

One of the innovative aspects of this project is the use of issue-level rather than bill-level data for the analysis of the president's influence on the agenda. I analyze issues instead of bills because issues are the fundamental units of agenda setting. Knowing what bills are on the agenda does not necessarily tell us what the agenda is unless we observe the issues covered by those bills as well. This was strikingly evident in the difference between the flow of bills and issues through the legislative process as portrayed in the figures of chapter 5.

The issue-level data were analyzed to explore the influence of the president and other factors on each level of the congressional agenda. The results are largely supportive of the predictions of the agenda-setting models of chapters 3 and 4. The president's public addresses tend to influence the floor stage of the legislative process, and this influence is exercised mainly in the House and in the president's first Congress. The draft bills of the legislative clearance process generally influence earlier stages of the legislative process in both chambers, and they tend to have a more persistent influence throughout the president's term. Yet, it must also be reiterated that other influences on the congressional agenda loom even larger than these presidential mechanisms. For example, committee leaders and the other chamber generally play a more robust role in determining the congressional agenda than the president at most stages.

It is sometimes argued that issues that are not salient go through an incubation period whereby they may become readied for future consideration (Kingdon 1984). It is possible, by this argument, that hearings, markups, and other forms of consideration in one Congress may lead to expedited consideration of an issue in the following Congress. At the bill level, however, it is difficult to identify corresponding bills from Congress to Congress. Here, issue-level data would seem to provide a natural advantage to bill-level analysis because the same issue can easily be identified in each Congress. Unfortunately, however, the Congressional Research Service's Legislative Indexing Vocabulary (CRS-LIV) issues have changed from Congress to Congress, making such cross-Congress analysis difficult. Only 349 (out of 7,906) issues in the CRS-LIV are common across the House Commerce Committee jurisdiction in all twelve Congresses from the 96th through the 107th. Measurement of similar issues across Congresses would also permit easier identification of Jones's "continuing agenda," but such work must await the development of a means of tracking CRS-LIV issues across Congresses.

Agenda Setting and Law Making

Despite the complexity of the legislative process, one can identify a trajectory for the majority of issues that largely reflects the textbook understanding of law making. By dissecting the common pathways of issues, I break the agenda-setting process within either chamber into three main stages: (1) hearings, (2) markup, and (3) floor consideration. I have analyzed the president's influence on committee markups and hearings as well as floor consideration, but I have stopped short of analyzing the president's influence on the passage of bills or issues. Yet, agenda setting is important ultimately because it does in fact have consequences for what is enacted. The president's main influence on policy outcomes may even come from his agenda-setting powers. A long tradition of research explaining the ability of the president to influence the final policy outcome of roll-call votes has yielded mixed results (e.g., Bond and Fleisher 1990; Edwards 1989). Meanwhile, previous empirical studies also have found in different ways that the president is able to influence the congressional agenda (e.g., Edwards and Barrett 2000; C. Jones 1994; Taylor 1998). These results and the models I have presented here suggest that while the president may not always be able to get Congress to vote the way he would like on a particular measure, he has been often able to play a significant hand in determining what kind of measure Congress is considering, which determines in no small degree the final policy outcome.

Because agenda setting can be as important as the president's ability to secure passage of particular measures for public policy outcomes, my findings raise new questions. First, the president's ability to affect the congressional agenda through public addresses is very short-lived, and the admonition by Paul Light and others for the president to "hit the ground running" has all the more urgency. But the findings of the legislative clearance model suggest another path. The president has a more persistent influence on the congressional agenda through the expertise he is able to employ in draft legislation. Although many of these bills involve technical amendments to previously enacted law, the cumulative effect the president can exercise on public policy through the control over this agenda throughout his entire tenure may outpace the effect he is able to wield from his public addresses. It is worth questioning whether presidents interested in having a policy impact should direct more of their attention to the potential influence of the vast expertise of the federal bureaucracy, channeled through the legislative clearance process, particularly in later years of their presidency when their public address agenda-setting influence seems to falter.

Appendix A

Proof of Legislative Programming Equilibrium

Definition of Equilibrium Solution Concept

I simplify the analysis of the infinitely repeated legislative programming game by restricting attention to stationary strategies, i.e., strategies that require each actor to choose the same action when he faces structurally identical conditions. Since I assume that presidents can serve only two terms, the first Congress of a presidential administration presents the president, Congress, and voter with choices that are structurally identical to the choices they face in the first Congress of other presidential administrations. I restrict attention to equilibria in which the president, Congress, and voter will make identical decisions in each of these structurally identical conditions. In a similar way, the conditions in the second, third, and fourth Congresses of a president's tenure yield structurally identical choices in Congresses of other presidents. I restrict attention to equilibria in which actors in the second, third, and fourth Congresses of a president's tenure are also restricted to stationary strategies. Without this restriction, strategies can become enormously complicated and perhaps less realistic because they can depend on all previous actions in the game. One way of thinking about stationarity in this game is that Congress and the voter forget everything that happened before the current presidential administration began.

I find a Perfect Bayesian equilibrium in stationary strategies, which requires that the stationary strategies are "sequentially rational" given the voter's beliefs and given that the voter's beliefs that are updated rationally (by Bayes's rule). A **Perfect Bayesian equilibrium** in the legislative programming game satisfies the following conditions for some specified common discount factor $0 < \delta < 1$ and wage $k \geq 0$:

1. The president chooses a strategy, specifying a sequence of signals $\{m_t\}_{t=1,\ldots,4}$ that maximizes the president's utility Eu_p given the equilibrium strategies of Congress and the voter and the voter's equilibrium beliefs.

2. Congress chooses a strategy, specifying a sequence of pairs of legislative policies $\{b_{1,t}, b_{2,t}\}_{t=1,\ldots}$ that maximizes Congress's utility Eu_c given the equilibrium strategies of the president and the voter and the voter's equilibrium beliefs.

3. The voter chooses a strategy, specifying a sequence of pairs of reelection decisions $\{r_{m,t}, r_{p,t}\}_{t=1,\ldots}$ that maximizes the voter's utility Eu_v given the equilibrium strategies of the president and Congress and the voter's equilibrium beliefs.

4. The voter's prior beliefs about the value of $v_{2,t}$ in each period t are rational and updated using Bayes's rule whenever possible, i.e.,

$$\text{Prob}(v_{2,t} = \bar{v}_2 \mid m_t) = [\text{Prob}(v_{2,t} = \bar{v}_2)\text{Prob}(m_t \mid v_{2,t} = \bar{v}_2)]/[\text{Prob}(v_{2,t} = \bar{v}_2)\text{Prob}(m_t \mid v_{2,t} = \bar{v}_2) + \text{Prob}(v_{2,t} = 0)\text{Prob}(m_t \mid v_{2,t} = 0)]$$

The voter observes neither the value of her ideal point, $v_{2,t}$, chosen by nature in each period t nor the exact policies $b_t = \{b_{1,t}, b_{2,t}\}$ chosen by Congress in each period. The voter does observe the policy issue signaled by the president and the policy issue chosen by Congress. The voter also directly observes the utility accruing from the policy enacted by Congress, but she observes this information one period after the policy is enacted. The voter can use information about the utility observed from a policy to partially determine whether Congress has chosen policies that benefit the voter, but only with hindsight. Messages from the president, however, may help the voter determine whether Congress has pursued the voter's policy interests before she decides whether to reelect Congress.

Perfect Bayesian Equilibrium of Legislative Programming Game

The following strategies and beliefs constitute a Perfect Bayesian equilibrium in stationary strategies of the legislative programming game:

- **President:**
  First Congress: $m_t = v_{2,t}$
  Later Congresses: $m_t = p_2$

- **Congress:**
  First Congress of a president:
  $b_t = \{v_1, 0\}$ for $m_t = 0$; and $v_{2,t} = 0$;
  $b_t = \{v_1, 0\}$ for $m_t = 0$; and $v_{2,t} = \overline{v}_2$;
  $b_t = \{0, \overline{v}_2\}$ for $m_t = \overline{v}_2$ and $v_{2,t} = \overline{v}_2$;
  $b_t = \{0, c_2\}$ for $m_t = \overline{v}_2$ and $v_{2,t} = 0$;
  $b_t = \{c_1, 0\}$ otherwise

  Later Congresses:
  $b_t = \{v_1, 0\}$

- **Voter Reelection of Congress:**
  First Congress:
  $r_{m,t} = 1$ for $b_{1,t} \neq 0$ if $m_t = 0$ or $b_{2,t} \neq 0$ if $m_t = \overline{v}_2$;
  $r_{m,t} = 0$ otherwise

  Later Congresses:
  $r_{m,t} = 1$ for $u_{v,t-1}$ in $\{0, -v_1^2\}$;
  $r_{m,t} = 0$ otherwise

- **Voter Reelection of President:**
  $r_{p,t} = 1$ for $u_{v,t-1}$ in $\{0, -v_1^2\}$;
  $r_{p,t} = 0$ otherwise

- **Voter's Prior Beliefs:**
  $\text{Prob}(v_{2,t} = \overline{v}_2) = \frac{1}{2}$
  $\text{Prob}(v_{2,t} = 0) = \frac{1}{2}$

- **Voter's Posterior Beliefs:**

$\text{Prob}(v_{2,t} = \bar{v}_2 \mid m_t = \bar{v}_2) = 1$

$\text{Prob}(v_{2,t} = 0 \mid m_t = \bar{v}_2) = 0$

$\text{Prob}(v_{2,t} = \bar{v}_2 \mid m_t = 0) = 0$

$\text{Prob}(v_{2,t} = 0 \mid m_t = 0) = 1$

under the following conditions:

IC_p: $p_2 > (1/\delta^3)(\bar{v}_2(\delta^3 + \delta^2 + \delta + 1) - (-p_1^2\delta^6 + \bar{v}_2^2 + 2\bar{v}_2^2\delta + 3\bar{v}_2^2$
$\delta^2 + \delta^5(\bar{v}_2^2 + v_1^2 - 2p^1v^1) + (2\bar{v}_2^2 + v_1^2 - 2p_1v_1)\delta^4 + (3\bar{v}_2^2 + v_1^2 - 2p_1v_1)\delta^3)^{1/2})$.

When IC_p fails, the president prefers to send message $m_t = 0$ when $v_{2,t} = \bar{v}_2$.

IC_{p2}: $p_2 > 1/(2(1 + \delta + 3\delta^2 + \delta^3))(2c_2 + 2c_2\delta^2 + \bar{v}_2\delta^2 + \frac{1}{2}(4(2c_2(1 + \delta^2) + \bar{v}_2\delta^2)^2 - 8(1 + \delta + 3\delta^2 + \delta^3)(2c_1^2(1 + \delta^2) + 2c_2^2(1 + \delta^2) + 2k\delta^2 + 2k\delta^3 + 2k\delta^4 + 2k\delta^5 - 4c_1(1 + \delta^2)p_1 + 2p_1^2 - 2p_1^2\delta + 2p_1^2\delta^2 - 2p_1^2\delta^3 + 4p_1v_1 + 4p_1v_1\delta + 6p_1v_1\delta^2 + 4p_1v_1\delta^3 - 2v_1^2 - 2v_1^2\delta - 3v_1^2\delta^2 - 2v_1^2\delta^3 + \bar{v}_2^2\delta^2))^{1/2}))$.

When IC_{p2} fails, the president prefers to send message $m_t = \bar{v}_2$ when $v_{2,t} = 0$.

IC_1: $c_1 < (1/(2\delta^4 - 2))(-2v_1 - \delta^2v_1 + \delta^3v_1 + 2\delta^4v_1 (-(\delta - 1)\delta^2(4(1 + d)(1 + \delta^2)^2k + (2 + \delta^2 - \delta^3 - 2\delta^4)v_1^2 + 2(\delta^4 - 1)(2c_2 - \bar{v}_2)\bar{v}_2)))^{1/2})$.

When IC_1 fails, Congress prefers to pass policy $b_t = \{c_1, 0\}$ when $v_{2,t} = 0$ and $m_t = 0$.

IC_2:* $c_1 < (\delta v_1 + (c_2^2 - c_2^2\delta + k\delta - k\delta^2 + v_1^2\delta)^{1/2})/(\delta - 1)$.

When IC_2 fails, Congress prefers to pass policy $b_t = \{c_1, 0\}$ when $v_{2,t} = 0$ and $m_t = \bar{v}_2$.

IC_3:* $c_1 < (1/(2\delta^4 - 2))(-2v_1 - \delta^2v_1 + \delta^3v_1 + 2\delta^4v_1 (-(\delta - 1)\delta^2(4(1 + d)(1 + \delta^2)^2k + (2 + \delta^2 - \delta^3 - 2\delta^4)v_1^2 + 2(\delta^4 - 1)(2c_2 - \bar{v}_2)\bar{v}_2)))^{1/2})$.

When IC_3 fails, Congress prefers to pass policy $b_t = \{c_1, 0\}$ when $v_{2,t} = \bar{v}_2$ and $m_t = 0$.

IC_4: $c_1 < (1/(2(\delta - \delta^2 + \delta^3 - 1)))(v_1\delta^3 - v_1\delta^2 + (\frac{1}{2})(4 v_1^2 (\delta - 1)^2\delta^4 - 8(2(c_2 - \bar{v}_2)\bar{v}_2 + (2k + v_1^2 - 2c_2\bar{v}_2 + \bar{v}_2^2)\delta^3 + 2(k + \bar{v}_2(\bar{v}_2 - 2c_2))\delta - (v_1^2 + \bar{v}_2^2(\bar{v}_2 - 2c_2))\delta^2)(-1 + \delta - \delta^2 + \delta^3))^{(\frac{1}{2})})$.

When IC_4 fails, Congress prefers to pass policy $b_t = \{c_1, 0\}$ when $v_{2,t} = \bar{v}_2$ and $m_t = \bar{v}_2$.

IC_5: $c_1 < ((2)^{\frac{1}{2}}(-\delta^2(1 + \delta)^2(-2 - \delta - \delta^2 - \delta^3 + 3\delta^4 + 2\delta^6)k)^{\frac{1}{2}} + 2(-1 - \delta + \delta^4 + \delta^5)v_1)/(2(\delta^4 + \delta^5 - 1 - \delta))$.

When IC_5 fails, Congress prefers to pass policy $b_t = \{c_1, 0\}$ in later periods when $v_{2,t} = 0$.

Denotes a constraint on an off-the-equilibrium-path strategy.

Proof of Legislative Programming Equilibrium

1. President maximizes his utility:

President's message in his first Congress: $m_1^* = v_2$.

Case 1: $v_{2,1} = \bar{v}_2$. In response to the president's equilibrium message $m_1^* = \bar{v}_2$, Congress chooses equilibrium policy $b_t^* = \{0, \bar{v}_2\}$, and the voter's equilibrium strategy reelects the president, which yields the president expected utility[1] $Eu_p = -p_1^2 - (p_2 - \bar{v}_2)^2 + [\frac{1}{2}(-(p_1 - v_1)^2 - p_2^2) + \frac{1}{2}(-p_1^2 - (p_2 - \bar{v}_2)^2)](\delta^4/(1 - \delta^4)) + [-(p_1 - v_1)^2 - p_2^2]((\delta + \delta^2 + \delta^3)/(1 - \delta^4)) + k(1 + \delta + \delta^2 + \delta^3)$.

Suppose instead the president sends message $m_1 = 0$. According to its equilibrium strategy, Congress will pass $b_t^* = \{v_1, 0\}$. In this case, according to the voter's equilibrium strategy, Congress will be reelected in the midterm because it follows the president's agenda, and the voter will reelect the president and Congress in the next presidential election because the utility she observes from this policy meets her expectation, i.e., $u_{v,t-1}$ in $\{0, -v_1^2\}$. In this case, the president and Congress essentially collude in order to avoid working on issue 2, the voter's preferred issue. This yields the president expected utility $Eu_p = -(p_1 - v_1)^2 - p_2^2 - [(p_1 - c_1)^2 - p_2^2]\delta + [\frac{1}{2}(-(p_1 - v_1)^2 - p_2^2) + \frac{1}{2}(-p_1^2 - (p_2 - \bar{v}_2)^2)](\delta^4/(1 - \delta^4)) + [-(p_1 - v_1)^2 - p_2^2]((\delta + \delta^2 + \delta^3)/(1 - \delta^4)) + k(1 + \delta + \delta^2 + \delta^3)$, which offers the president strictly greater utility whenever the president's participation constraint IC_p fails: $p_2 > (1/\delta^3)(\bar{v}_2(\delta^3 + \delta^2 + \delta + 1) - (-p_1^2\delta^6 + \bar{v}_2^2 + 2\bar{v}_2^2\delta + 3\bar{v}_2^2\delta^2 + \delta^5(\bar{v}_2^2 + v_1^2 - 2p_1v_1) + (2\bar{v}_2^2 + v_1^2 - 2p_1v_1)\delta^4 + (3\bar{v}_2^2 + v_1^2 - 2p_1v_1)\delta^3)^{\frac{1}{2}})$. When this constraint is satisfied, Congress and the president have sufficiently *different* interests that they do not have an interest in colluding to hide information from the voter. By contrast, in the next chapter, the presidential agenda influence arising from legislative clearance will be shown to depend on the president and Congress having *similar* preferences.

Case 2: $v_{2,1} = 0$. In response to the president's equilibrium message $m_1^* = 0$, Congress chooses equilibrium policy $b_t^* = \{v_1, 0\}$, and the voter's equilibrium strategy reelects the president, which yields the president expected utility $Eu_p = -(p_1 - v_1)^2 - p_2^2 + [\frac{1}{2}(-(p_1 - v_1)^2 - p_2^2) + \frac{1}{2}(-p_1^2 - (p_2 - \bar{v}_2)^2)](\delta^4/(1 - \delta^4)) + [-(p_1 - v_1)^2 - p_2^2]((\delta + \delta^2 + \delta^3)/(1 - \delta^4)) + k(1 + \delta + \delta^2 + \delta^3)$.

Suppose instead that the president sends message $m_1 = \bar{v}_2$. According to its equilibrium strategy, Congress would then deliver policy $b_t^* = \{0, c_2\}$. In this case, according to the voter's equilibrium strategy, Congress would be reelected in the midterm, but Congress and the president would be thrown out in the following election for failing to meet the voter's utility expectations. This yields the president expected utility $Eu_p = -p_1^2 - (p_2 - c_2)^2 - [(p_1 - c_1)^2 - p_2^2]\delta + [\frac{1}{2}(-(p_1 - v_1)^2 - p_2^2) + \frac{1}{2}(-p_1^2 - (p_2 - \bar{v}_2)^2)](\delta^2/(1 - \delta^4)) + [-(p_1 - v_1)^2 - p_2^2]((\delta^3 + \delta^4 + \delta^5)/(1 - \delta^4)) + k(1 + \delta)$. The president will prefer his equilibrium strategy whenever IC_{p2} fails, i.e., $p_2 > 1/(2(1 + \delta + 3\delta^2 + \delta^3))(2c_2 + 2c_2\delta^2 + \bar{v}_2\delta^2 + \frac{1}{2}(4(2c_2(1 + \delta^2) + \bar{v}_2\delta^2)^2 - 8(1 + \delta + 3\delta^2 + \delta^3)(2c_1^2(1 + \delta^2) + 2c_2^2(1 + \delta^2) + 2k\delta^2 + 2k\delta^3 + 2k\delta^4 + 2k\delta^5 - 4c_1(1 + \delta^2)p_1 + 2p_1^2 - 2p_1^2\delta + 2p_1^2\delta^2 - 2p_1^2\delta^3 + 4p_1v_1 + 4p_1v_1\delta + 6p_1v_1\delta^2 + 4p_1v_1\delta^3 - 2v_1^2 - 2v_1^2\delta - 3v_1^2\delta^2 - 2v_1^2\delta^3 + \bar{v}_2^2\delta^2))^{\frac{1}{2}}))$.

President's message in his later Congresses: $m_1 = p_2$. In equilibrium, Congress and the voter ignore the president's message to later Congresses, so his message can have no impact on his utility.

2. Congress maximizes its utility:

Congress's strategy in a president's first Congress:

Case 1: $v_{2,1} = 0$; $m_1 = 0$. Congress's equilibrium strategy is $b_1{}^* = \{v_I, 0\}$, which leads to reelection by the voter. This yields Congress expected utility $Eu_C = -(c_I - v_I)^2 - c_2^2 + k + [\frac{1}{2}(-(c_I - v_I)^2 - c_2^2 + k) + \frac{1}{2}(-c_1^2 - (c_2 - \bar{v}_2)^2 + k)](\delta^4/(1 - \delta^4)) + [-(c_I - v_I)^2 - c_2^2 + k]((\delta + \delta^2 + \delta^3)/(1 - \delta^4))$.

Suppose Congress chooses policy $b_1 = \{c_I, 0\}$. The voter's equilibrium strategy does not throw Congress out in the midterm election because it works on issues indicated by president, but Congress is thrown out in the following election for failing to deliver the voter's expected utility. If Congress also passes its optimal policy $b_2 = \{c_I, 0\}$ after the midterm, this yields expected utility $Eu_C = (-c_2^2 + k)(1 + \delta) + [\frac{1}{2}(-(c_I - v_I)^2 - c_2^2) + \frac{1}{2}(-c_1^2 - (c_2 - \bar{v}_2)^2)](\delta^2/(1 - \delta^4)) + [-(c_I - v_I)^2 - c_2^2]((\delta^3 + \delta^4 + \delta^5)/(1 - \delta^4))$. This is strictly less than its equilibrium utility, $Eu_C(b^*)$, whenever the incentive constraint IC_1 is satisfied: $c_I < (1/(2\delta^4 - 2))(-2v_I - \delta^2 v_I + \delta^3 v_I + 2\delta^4 v_I (-(\delta - 1)\delta^2(4(1 + d)(1 + \delta^2)^2 k + (2 + \delta^2 - \delta^3 - 2\delta^4)v_1^2 + 2(\delta^4 - 1)(2c_2 - \bar{v}_2)\bar{v}_2)))^{1/2})$.

Suppose Congress chooses $b_1 = \{0, c_2\}$. Since the voter's equilibrium strategy throws Congress out at the midterm for not following the president's agenda, this yields expected utility $Eu_C = -c_1^2 + k + [\frac{1}{2}(-(c_I - v_I)^2 - c_2^2) + \frac{1}{2}(-c_1^2 - (c_2 - \bar{v}_2)^2)](\delta^2/(1 - \delta^4)) + [-(c_I - v_I)^2 - c_2^2]((\delta^3 + \delta^4 + \delta^5)/(1 - \delta^4))$, which is strictly less than its expected utility for $b_1 = \{c_I, 0\}$ by definition of the agenda setting problem.

Suppose Congress chooses $b_t = \{0, \bar{v}_2\}$. Since the voter's equilibrium strategy throws Congress out at the midterm for not following the president's agenda, this yields Congress strictly less expected utility than $b_1 = \{0, c_2\}$.

Case 2: $v_{2,1} = 0$; $m_1 = \bar{v}_2$. Congress's equilibrium strategy in this case is $b_1{}^* = \{0, c_2\}$. The voter's equilibrium strategy then dictates that Congress be reelected in the midterm election for following the president's agenda, but thrown out of office in the following election for not achieving the voter's utility expectation. This yields Congress $Eu_C = -c_1^2 + k + (-c_2^2 + k)\delta + [\frac{1}{2}(-(c_I - v_I)^2 - c_2^2) + \frac{1}{2}(-c_1^2 - (c_2 - \bar{v}_2)^2)](\delta^2/(1 - \delta^4)) + [-(c_I - v_I)^2 - c_2^2]((\delta^3 + \delta^4 + \delta^5)/(1 - \delta^4))$.

If Congress instead delivers $b_1 = \{c_1, 0\}$, it gets thrown out at the midterm election for ignoring the president's agenda. This yields Congress expected utility $Eu_C = -c_2^2 + k + [\frac{1}{2}(-(c_1 - v_1)^2 - c_2^2) + \frac{1}{2}(-c_1^2 - (c_2 - \bar{v}_2)^2)](\delta^2/(1 - \delta^4))$ $+ [-(c_1 - v_1)^2 - c_2^2]((\delta + \delta^3 + \delta^4)/(1 - \delta^4))$, which is strictly less than the equilibrium policy whenever incentive constraint IC_2 is satisfied: $c_1 < (\delta v_1 + (c_2^2 - c_2^2)$ $\delta + k\delta - k\delta^2 + v_1^2 \delta)^{\frac{1}{2}})/(\delta - 1)$.

If Congress instead delivers the policy $b_1 = \{v_1, 0\}$, the voter's equilibrium strategy throws it out in the midterm because the policy does not match the president's message. Thus this policy offers Congress strictly less utility than $b_1 = \{c_1, 0\}$.

If Congress instead delivers $b_1 = \{0, \bar{v}_2\}$, the voter's equilibrium strategy reelects in the midterm and throws it out in the second election for not meeting the voter's utility expectations. This is the same electoral result as the equilibrium policy $b_1 = \{0, c_1\}$, but it yields strictly less utility to Congress.

Case 3: $v_{2,1} = \bar{v}_2$; $m_1 = 0$. Congress's equilibrium strategy in this case is $b_1^* = \{v_1, 0\}$, which allows Congress to be reelected in both the midterm and following elections by following the president's agenda and satisfying the voter's expected utility. This yields Congress expected utility $Eu_C = (-(c_1 - v_1)^2 - c_2^2 + k) + [\frac{1}{2}(-(c_1 - v_1)^2 - c_2^2 + k) + \frac{1}{2}(-c_1^2 - (c_2 - \bar{v}_2)^2 + k)](\delta^4/(1 - \delta^4)) + [-(c_1 - v_1)^2 - c_2^2 + k]((\delta + \delta^2 + \delta^3)/(1 - \delta^4))$.

If Congress instead delivers policy $b_1 = \{c_1, 0\}$, its optimum single-period policy, it is reelected in the midterm but not in the second election. Suppose that Congress chooses policy $b_2 = \{c_1, 0\}$ in the second period as well. This yields expected utility $Eu_C = (-c_2^2 + k)(1 + \delta) + [\frac{1}{2}(-(c_1 - v_1)^2 - c_2^2) + \frac{1}{2}(-c_1^2 - (c_2 - \bar{v}_2)^2)](\delta^2/(1 - \delta^4)) + [- (c_1 - v_1)^2 - c_2^2]((\delta^3 + \delta^4 + \delta^5)/(1 - \delta^4))$, which is strictly less than the equilibrium policy whenever constraint IC_3 holds: $c_1 < (1/(2\delta^4 - 2))(-2v_1 - \delta^2 v_1 + \delta^3 v_1 + 2\delta^4 v_1 (-(\delta - 1)\delta^2(4(1 + d)(1 + \delta^2)^2 k + (2 + \delta^2 - \delta^3 - 2\delta^4) v_1^2 + 2(\delta^4 - 1)(2c_2 - \bar{v}_2)\bar{v}_2)))^{1/2})$, which is the same as constraint IC_1.

If Congress delivers policy $b_1 = \{0, c_2\}$ or $b_1 = \{0, \bar{v}_2\}$, it will be thrown out of office in the midterm election according to the voter's equilibrium strategy. These policies yield strictly less utility than the policy $b_1 = \{c_1, 0\}$.

Case 4: $v_{2,1} = \bar{v}_2$; $m_1 = \bar{v}_2$. Congress's equilibrium strategy is $b_1^* = \{0, \bar{v}_2\}$, which yields expected utility $Eu_C = -c_1^2 - (c_2 - \bar{v}_2)^2 + k + [\frac{1}{2}(-(c_1 - v_1)^2 - c_2^2 + k) + \frac{1}{2}(-c_1^2 - (c_2 - \bar{v}_2)^2 + k)](\delta^4/(1 - \delta^4)) + [-(c_1 - v_1)^2 - c_2^2 + k]((\delta + \delta^2 + \delta^3)/(1 - \delta^4))$.

Suppose Congress chooses $b_1 = \{c_l, 0\}$. Since the voter's equilibrium strategy throws out Congress at the midterm for not following the president's agenda, this yields expected utility $Eu_C = -c_2^2 + k + [\frac{1}{2}(-(c_l - v_l)^2 - c_2^2) + \frac{1}{2}(-c_1^2 - (c_2 - \overline{v}_2)^2)](\delta^2/(1 - \delta^4)) + [-(c_l - v_l)^2 - c_2^2]((\delta + \delta^3 + \delta^4)/(1 - \delta^4))$. This is strictly less than her equilibrium utility, $b_1^* = \{0, \overline{v}_2\}$, whenever incentive constraint IC_4 is satisfied: $c_l < (1/(2(\delta - \delta^2 + \delta^3 - 1)))(v_l\delta^3 - v_l\delta^2 + (\frac{1}{2})(4v_1^2 (\delta - 1)^2\delta^4 - 8(2(c_2 - \overline{v}_2)\overline{v}_2 + (2k + v_1^2 - 2c_2\overline{v}_2 + \overline{v}_2^2)\delta^3 + 2(k + \overline{v}_2(\overline{v}_2 - 2c_2))\delta - (v_1^2 + \overline{v}_2^2(\overline{v}_2 - 2c_2))\delta^2)(-1 + \delta - \delta^2 + \delta^3))^{(1/2)})$.

Suppose Congress chooses $b_1 = \{0, c_2\}$. This yields expected utility $Eu_C = (-c_1^2 + k)(1 + \delta) + [\frac{1}{2}(-(c_l - v_l)^2 - c_2^2) + \frac{1}{2}(-c_1^2 - c_2 - \overline{v}_2)^2)](\delta^2/(1 - \delta^4)) + [-(c_l - v_l)^2 - c_2^2]((\delta + \delta^3 + \delta^4)/(1 - \delta^4))$, which is strictly less that its expected utility for $b_1 = \{c_l, 0\}$ under the agenda-setting assumption $c_l > c_2$.

Suppose Congress chooses $b_t = \{v_l, 0\}$. Since this does not match the president's message, the voter will throw out Congress at the midterm election. This yields Congress expected utility $Eu_C = -(c_l - v_l)^2 - c_2^2 + k + [\frac{1}{2}(-(c_l - v_l)^2 - c_2^2) + \frac{1}{2}(-c_1^2 - (c_2 - \overline{v}_2)^2)](\delta^2/(1 - \delta^4)) + [-(c_l - v_l)^2 - c_2^2]((\delta + \delta^3 + \delta^4)/(1 - \delta^4))$, which is strictly less that its expected utility from the policy $b_t = \{c_l, 0\}$.

Congress's strategy in a president's second Congress: $b_t^* = \{v_l, 0\}$:
Since the president's message is ignored by the voter's equilibrium strategy in a president's second Congress, we need only consider two cases: $v_{2,t} = 0$ and $v_{2,t} = \overline{v}_2$.

Case 1: $v_{2,t} = 0$. Congress's equilibrium strategy is $b_t^* = \{v_l, 0\}$. This yields Congress expected utility $Eu_C = [\frac{1}{2}(-(c_l - v_l)^2 - c_2^2 + k) + \frac{1}{2}(-c_1^2 - (c_2 - \overline{v}_2)^2 + k)](\delta^3/(1 - \delta^4)) + [-(c_l - v_l)^2 - c_2^2 + k]((1 + \delta + \delta^2)/(1 - \delta^4))$.

Suppose Congress chooses $b_t = \{c_l, 0\}$. According to the voter's equilibrium strategy, Congress will be thrown out of office after another period for failing to satisfy the voter's utility expectation for the second Congress. If Congress chooses its optimal policy $b_t = \{c_l, 0\}$ in both periods it holds office, this yields expected utility $Eu_C = (-c_2^2 + k)(1 + \delta) + [\frac{1}{2}(-(c_l - v_l)^2 - c_2^2) + \frac{1}{2}(-c_1^2 - (c_2 - \overline{v}_2)^2)](\delta^3/(1 - \delta^4)) + [-(c_l - v_l)^2 - c_2^2]((\delta^2 + \delta^4 + \delta^5)/(1 - \delta^4))$. This is strictly less than her equilibrium utility, $Eu_C(b^*)$, in the second Congress whenever incentive constraint IC_5 is satisfied: $c_l < ((2)^{\frac{1}{2}}(-\delta^2(1 + \delta)^2(-2 - \delta - \delta^2 - \delta^3 + 3\delta^4 + 2\delta^6)k)^{\frac{1}{2}} + 2(-1 - \delta + \delta^4 + \delta^5)v_l)/(2(\delta^4 + \delta^5 - 1 - \delta))$.

Suppose Congress chooses $b_t = \{0, c_2\}$ in the second period. Congress is thrown out after the second period by the voter's equilibrium strategy, and this policy yields utility that is strictly less than that expected from Congress's equilibrium policy $b_t{}^* = \{c_1, 0\}$.

Suppose Congress chooses $b_t{}^* = \{0, \bar{v}_2\}$ in the second Congress. Congress is thrown out after the next period by the voter's equilibrium strategy, and this also yields strictly less utility than its expected utility for $b_t{}^* = \{c_1, 0\}$.

Case 2: $v_{2,t} = \bar{v}_2$. Congress's equilibrium strategy is $b_t{}^* = \{v_1, 0\}$. Since the value of $v_{2,t}$ does not directly affect Congress's utility function and Congress's equilibrium policy remains the same as in Case 1, most of the arguments from Case 1 apply in this case as well. There is one exception. Congress will be reelected in this case if it chooses policy $b_t = \{0, \bar{v}_2\}$ instead of the equilibrium policy $b_t{}^* = \{v_1, 0\}$, but this always offers Congress less utility under the agenda-setting preference structure I assume.

Congress's strategy in a president's third and fourth Congresses: $b_t{}^* = \{v_1, 0\}$: Similar arguments hold in the third and fourth Congresses of a presidency. In general, if there is an incentive for Congress to defect from the equilibrium policy in a late round, there will be an even stronger incentive to defect in the first or second Congress.

3. Voter maximizes her utility:

As long as the president and Congress always deliver their equilibrium policies, the voter is indifferent between reelecting them and replacing them with a new president and Congress who also follow the equilibrium strategies. Since she is indifferent, we can assume that she picks a reelection strategy that offers the president and Congress the proper incentives to provide informative representation. That is, she can condition the president's reelection on his sending correct policy information in the first Congress and condition Congress's reelection on its following the president's cue in the first Congress and fulfilling her expected utility in all Congresses. Since the voter will be indifferent between this strategy and any other reelection strategy, we can assume that this strategy maximizes her utility given the equilibrium strategies of the president and Congress.

4. Voter updates her beliefs using Bayes's rule:

The voter updates her initial beliefs that v_2 is uniformly distributed in $\{0, \overline{v}_2\}$ according to Bayes's Rule, whenever possible.

Case 1: m = 0. Bayes's rule dictates that the voter's belief about the value of v_2 after observing the message m = 0 is given by Prob($v_2 = \overline{v}_2$ | m = 0) = Prob($v_2 = \overline{v}_2$)Prob(m = 0 | $v_2 = \overline{v}_2$)/[Prob($v_2 = \overline{v}_2$)Prob(m = 0 | $v_2 = \overline{v}_2$) + Prob($v_2 = 0$)Prob(m = 0 | $v_2 = 0$)] = 0/1 = 0. Thus, after receiving message m = 0, the voter believes that $v_2 = 0$.

Case 2: m = $\overline{v}_2$. Bayes's rule dictates that the voter's belief about the value of v_2 after observing the message m = $\overline{v}_2$ is given by Prob($v_2 = \overline{v}_2$ | m = $\overline{v}_2$) = Prob($v_2 = \overline{v}_2$)Prob(m = $\overline{v}_2$ | $v_2 = \overline{v}_2$)/[Prob($v_2 = \overline{v}_2$)Prob(m = $\overline{v}_2$ | $v_2 = \overline{v}_2$) + Prob($v_2 = 0$)Prob(m = $\overline{v}_2$ | $v_2 = 0$)] = 1/1 = 0. Thus, after receiving message m = $\overline{v}_2$, the voter believes that $v_2 = \overline{v}_2$.

Appendix B

Proof of Legislative Clearance Equilibrium

Congress's utility u_c and the president's utility u_p are calculated as the sum of the negative quadratic distances between their ideal points and the policy outcomes on each issue, where $x_{-i} = sq = 0$ if i is the issue chosen by Congress and $-i$ represents all other issues:

$$u_c = -\Sigma_i(c_i - x_i)^2$$
$$u_p = -\Sigma_i(p_i - x_i)^2$$

Structure of the Game

1. Nature chooses and reveals the value of the exogenous random variable ω_2 from $\{0, 1\}$ to the president.
2. For each possible value of ω_2, the president sends a message $m(\omega_2)$ from $\{0, 1\}$ to Congress. This message may or may not reveal some of his private information about ω_2 to Congress. The most informative strategy the president can choose would reveal the exact value of the exogenous random variable ω_2 to Congress in each state of the world, but nothing about ω_1. The president's message can use a mixed strategy.
3. Congress observes the president's message, $m(\omega_2)$, but not the underlying state of the world, ω_2, and updates its initial belief that ω_2 is uniformly

distributed in {0, 1} according to Bayes's rule whenever possible. Congress then chooses the optimal location of a bill b_i on each issue i subject to the time and resource constraint that at most one bill can be nonzero. On all other issues, the status quo prevails. Congress is restricted to choosing bills and issues in pure strategies.

Strategies and Equilibrium

A strategy for the president specifies a message m for each possible state of the world ω_2. A strategy for Congress specifies a bill b_i on each issue for each possible presidential message m. No more than one of Congress's bills can be nonzero. The number of contingencies specified by a congressional strategy will vary depending on the number of partitions in the president's signaling strategy. That is, the number of policy decisions Congress has to make will depend on the number of different signals the president sends in equilibrium. A strategy must specify a pair of bills for each different signal.

The solution concept used is Perfect Bayesian Equilibrium, which requires that the players always choose optimal strategies and that Congress's beliefs be consistent and rational.

An equilibrium solution of the legislative clearance game consists of (1) a messaging strategy for the president, m*; (2) a policy strategy for Congress, b*; and (3) Congress's beliefs μ^* about the value of ω_2, given the president's message. A Perfect Bayesian Equilibrium is a set of strategies that are "sequentially rational" given the beliefs and a set of beliefs that are updated rationally (by Bayes's rule) given the strategies. Such a set of strategies and beliefs satisfies the following conditions.

1. The president's equilibrium message m* offers him more expected utility than any other possible message m, given Congress's equilibrium strategy b*( ), i.e., $Eu_p(m^*(\omega_2) \mid b^*) \geq Eu_p(m(\omega_2) \mid b^*)$ for all messages m ≠ m* and all possible ω_2.
2. Congress's equilibrium policy b* offers it more expected utility than any other possible policy b, given the president's equilibrium strategy m*( ) and Congress's equilibrium beliefs μ^*, i.e., $Eu_c(b^*(m^*) \mid \mu^*(m)) \geq$ $(b(m^*) \mid \mu^*(m))$ for all policies b ≠ b* and all possible messages m.
3. Congress updates its initial beliefs that ω_2 is uniformly distributed in {0, 1} according to Bayes's Rule, whenever possible, e.g. $\text{Prob}(\omega_2 = \varpi_2 \mid m)$ $= \text{Prob}(\omega_2 = \varpi_2)\text{Prob}(m \mid \omega_2 = \varpi_2)/[\text{Prob}(\omega_2 = \varpi_2)\text{Prob}(m \mid \omega_2 = \varpi_2) +$ $\text{Prob}(\omega_2 = 0)\text{Prob}(m \mid \omega_2 = 0)]$

Proof of Perfect Bayesian Equilibrium in Table 4.1

I prove that each of the three conditions of a Perfect Bayesian Equilibrium holds whenever ICL, ICH, and PC are satisfied.

1. The president's optimal strategy:

CASE 1: $\omega_2 = 0$. The president sends message m* = 0 in equilibrium. Congress's equilibrium policy given that m = 0 is b* = $\{c_1 + \varpi_1/2, 0\}$. This yields the president expected disutility $Eu_p(m^*) = (\frac{1}{2})[-(c_1 + \varpi_1/2)^2 - (p_2)^2] + (\frac{1}{2})[-(c_1 - \varpi_1/2)^2 - (p_2)^2]$. Suppose instead, the president sends message m = ϖ_2. Congress's equilibrium policy given that m = ϖ_2 is b* = $\{c_1 + 0, \varpi_2\}$. Under $\omega_2 = 0$, this yields the president expected disutility $Eu_p = -(p_2 - \varpi_2)^2$. The president will weakly prefer the equilibrium message whenever $Eu_p(m^*) \geq Eu_p(m = \varpi_2)$, or when $-(c_1 + \varpi_1/2)^2 - (p_2)^2 \geq -(p_2 - \varpi_2)^2$. Solving for ϖ_2 yields the constraint $\varpi_2 \leq p_2 + (\frac{1}{2})[4(p_2)^2 + 4(c_1)^2 - \varpi_1^2]^{\frac{1}{2}}$, which is always satisfied when constraint ICL is satisfied.

CASE 2: $\omega_2 = \varpi_2$. The president sends message m = ϖ_2 in equilibrium. Congress's equilibrium policy given that m = ϖ_2 is b* = $\{0, \varpi_2\}$. This yields the president expected disutility $Eu_p(m^*) = (\frac{1}{2})[-(p_2)^2] + (\frac{1}{2})[-(\varpi_1)^2 - (p_2)^2]$. Suppose instead, the president sends message m = 0. Congress's equilibrium policy given that m = 0 is b* = $\{c_1 + \varpi_1/2, 0\}$. Under $\omega_2 = \varpi_2$, this yields the president expected disutility $(\frac{1}{2})[-(c_1 + \varpi_1/2)^2 - (p_2 + \varpi_2)^2] + (\frac{1}{2})[-(c_1 - \varpi_1/2)^2 - (p_2 + \varpi_2)^2]$. The president will weakly prefer the equilibrium message whenever $Eu_p(m^*) \geq Eu_p(m = 0)$, or when $(\frac{1}{2})[-(p_2)^2] + (\frac{1}{2})[-(\varpi_1)^2 - (p_2)^2] \geq (\frac{1}{2})[-(c_1 + \varpi_1/2)^2 - (p_2 + \varpi_2)^2] + (\frac{1}{2})[-(c_1 - \varpi_1/2)^2 - (p_2 + \varpi_2)^2]$. Solving for ϖ_2 yields the constraint $\varpi_2 \leq -p_2 + (\frac{1}{2})[4(p_2)^2 - 4(c_1)^2 - \varpi_1^2]^{\frac{1}{2}}$, which is always satisfied when constraint ICH is satisfied.

2. Congress's optimal strategy:

CASE 1: m = 0. Since the president sends message m = 0 according to its equilibrium strategy when the state of the world is either $\{0, 0\}$ or

$\{\varpi_1, 0\}$, Congress must choose a policy on either issue 1 or issue 2 that maximizes its utility given an equal likelihood that either of the values of ω_2 occurs. I consider the optimal policy for Congress on each issue and then determine which issue offers Congress the greatest expected utility.

Policy change on issue 1: Given that Congress believes that $\omega_1 = 0$ or $\omega_1 = \varpi_1$ with equal probability, and that Congress is risk averse (utility is measured in squared distance from ideal policy), its ideal policy on issue 1 is $c_1 + \varpi_1/2$, which yields it expected disutility $-(\varpi_1/2)^2$.

Policy change on issue 2: Given that Congress believes that $\omega_2 = 0$, its ideal policy on issue 2 is 0, which yields it expected disutility $(\frac{1}{2})[-(c_1)^2] + (\frac{1}{2})[-(c_1 + \varpi_1)^2]$.

Congress will thus weakly prefer its equilibrium policy, $b^*(m = 0) = \{c_1 + \varpi_1/2, 0\}$ whenever $-(\varpi_1/2)^2 \geq (\frac{1}{2})[-(c_1)^2] + (\frac{1}{2})[-(c_1 + \varpi_1)^2]$. This holds for all positive values of c_1 and ϖ_1, so this case does not constrain the conditions under which the equilibrium exists.

CASE 2: $m = \varpi_2$. Since the president sends message $m = \varpi_2$ according to its equilibrium strategy when the state of the world is either $\{0, \varpi_2\}$ or $\{\varpi_1, \varpi_2\}$, Congress must choose a policy on either issue 1 or issue 2 that maximizes its utility given an equal likelihood that either of the states of the world obtains. I consider the optimal policy for Congress on each issue and then determine which issue offers Congress the greatest expected utility.

Policy change on issue 1: Given that Congress believes that $\omega_1 = 0$ or $\omega_1 = \varpi_1$ with equal probability, and that Congress is risk averse (utility is measured in squared distance from ideal policy), its ideal policy on issue 1 is $c_1 + \varpi_1/2$, which yields it expected disutility $-(\varpi_1/2)^2 - \omega_2^2$.

Policy change on issue 2: Given that Congress believes that $\omega_2 = \varpi_2$, its ideal policy on issue 2 is ϖ_2, which yields it expected disutility $(\frac{1}{2})[-(c_1)^2] + (\frac{1}{2})[-(c_1 + \varpi_1)^2]$.

Congress will thus weakly prefer its equilibrium policy, $b^*(m = \varpi_2) = \{0, \varpi_2\}$ whenever $(\frac{1}{2})[-(c_1)^2] + (\frac{1}{2})[-(c_1 + \varpi_1)^2] \geq -(\varpi_1/2)^2 - \varpi_2^2$. Solving for ϖ_2, this holds when $\varpi_2 \geq (\frac{1}{2})(2c_1 + \varpi_1)$, which is always satisfied when the Congress's participation constraint (PC) is satisfied.

3. Congress's beliefs updated using Bayes's Rule when possible: Congress updates its initial beliefs that ω_2 is uniformly distributed in $\{0, 1\}$ according to Bayes's Rule, whenever possible.

CASE 1: m = 0. Prob($\omega_2 = \varpi_2$ | m = 0) = Prob($\omega_2 = \varpi_2$) Prob(m | $\omega_2 = \varpi_2$) / [Prob($\omega_2 = \varpi_2$)Prob(m | $\omega_2 = \varpi_2$) + Prob($\omega_2 = 0$) Prob(m | $\omega_2 = 0$)] = 0/1 = 0. Thus, after receiving message m = 0, Congress believes that $\omega_2 = \varpi_2$.

CASE 2: m = ϖ_2. Prob($\omega_2 = \varpi_2$ | m) = Prob($\omega_2 = \varpi_2$)Prob(m | $\omega_2 = \varpi_2$)/[Prob($\omega_2 = \varpi_2$)Prob(m | $\omega_2 = \varpi_2$) + Prob($\omega_2 = 0$)Prob(m | $\omega_2 = 0$)] = 1/1 = 1. Thus, after receiving message m = ϖ_2, Congress believes with certainty that $\omega_2 = \varpi_2$.

Appendix C

Tables of Comparative Characteristics of House and Senate Committees

TABLE C.1 Comparative characteristics of House committees in the 103rd Congress

Committee	MCs	Chair's Ideology (DW Nominate)	Public Bills (H.R. and S.)	Average Bill Complexity	Issues	Average Issue Scope	Percent of Bills Multiply Referred	Percent of Bills Sponsored by Democrat
Agriculture	37	−0.26	249	28.6	1744	69.9	46.6	67.9
Appropriations	60	−0.36	67	121.4	2572	48.2	16.4	74.6
Armed Services	55	−0.68	263	34.5	2322	56.9	46.8	63.5
Banking, Finance, and Urban Affairs	51	−0.51	348	33.3	2224	59.3	36.8	65.5
Budget	43	−0.59	2	331.5	630	121.6	100.0	50.0
District of Columbia	10	−0.70	37	14.5	317	146.7	40.5	32.4
Education and Labor	42	−0.54	496	37.6	2431	55.1	44.2	71.6
Energy and Commerce	44	−0.44	835	28.3	2827	49.3	50.9	69.5
Foreign Affairs	43	−0.16	229	36.0	2314	55.1	50.2	69.0

continued next page

TABLE C.1 *(cont'd.)* Comparative characteristics of House committees in the 103rd Congress

Committee	MCs	Chair's Ideology (DW Nomi-nate)	Public Bills (H.R. and S.)	Average Bill Complexity	Issues	Average Issue Scope	Percent of Bills Multiply Referred	Percent of Bills Sponsored by Democrat
Government Operations	42	−0.76	250	32.3	1858	68.5	66.0	45.6
Administration	18	−0.32	197	22.3	1142	89.1	54.8	43.1
Intelligence (Permanent Select)	19	−0.20	16	87.1	864	98.9	68.8	68.8
Judiciary	32	−0.42	820	29.0	3265	44.0	30.7	60.4
Merchant Marine and Fisheries	37	−0.52	339	17.6	1513	71.2	31.3	65.2
Natural Resources	42	−0.64	429	20.9	2056	60.7	30.3	63.9
Post Office and Civil Service	24	−0.67	265	22.1	1609	73.2	47.9	59.2
Public Works and Transportation	63	−0.52	369	22.7	2126	58.1	42.0	67.2
Rules	13	−0.43	153	34.7	1347	85.0	90.8	37.3
Science, Space, and Technology	55	−0.51	133	40.7	1587	72.9	63.2	72.9
Small Business	44	−0.39	53	28.4	690	122.2	32.1	71.7
Standards of Official Conduct	14	−0.66	2	20.5	28	265.6	100.0	100.0
Veterans' Affairs	35	−0.03	152	26.8	1273	84.3	19.7	75.7
Ways and Means	38	−0.37	1424	18.8	2875	48.8	30.4	57.7
House committee average	37.4	−0.46	310	28.6	1722	82.8	46.6	65.5
House overall average (H.R. bills only)	NA	−0.15*	5310	18.9	6875	22.7	20.6	64.3

* *indicates House median rather than average.*

TABLE C.2 Comparative characteristics of Senate committees in the 103rd Congress

Committee	MCs	Chair's Ideology (DW Nominate)	Public Bills (H.R. and S.)	Average Bill Complexity	Issues	Average Issue Scope	Percent of Bills Multiply Referred	Percent of Bills Sponsored by Democrat
Agriculture, Nutrition, and Forestry	18	−0.46	99	22.4	1276	109.4	3.0	74.7
Appropriations	29	−0.26	14	37.1	304	136.7	14.3	78.6
Armed Services	20	−0.12	78	63.3	1228	78.9	3.8	80.8
Banking, Housing, and Urban Affairs	19	−0.44	129	25.4	873	99.9	1.6	68.2
Budget	21	−0.36	31	31.3	553	132.9	96.8	38.7
Commerce, Science, and Transportation	19	−0.21	190	23.8	1441	72.6	3.2	66.3
Energy and Natural Resources	19	−0.17	224	15.8	1093	83.6	2.2	62.9
Environment and Public Works	17	−0.24	184	23.3	1165	83.5	2.7	76.1
Finance	20	−0.42	610	16.7	1751	70.1	0.7	56.2
Foreign Relations	19	−0.48	77	33.9	1132	78.8	2.6	71.4
Governmental Affairs	13	−0.36	199	22.2	1413	79.3	18.1	61.3
Indian Affairs	19	−0.37	50	18.6	399	154.7	10.0	56.0
Intelligence (Select)		−0.22	14	39.5	203	193.3	14.3	64.3
Judiciary	18	−0.36	266	20.0	1178	86.6	1.9	58.3
Labor and Human Resources	17	−0.58	251	22.9	1448	75.3	2.0	70.9
Rules and Administration	16	−0.22	37	18.8	293	147.7	0.0	70.3
Small Business	21	−0.38	17	34.1	392	157.9	11.8	70.6
Veterans' Affairs	12	−0.37	72	15.7	353	154.5	1.4	88.9
Senate committee average	18.7	−0.33	141	26.9	916	110.9	10.6	67.5
Senate overall average (S. bills only)	NA	−0.19*	2569	21.9	5011	30.5	2.1	64.6

indicates Senate median rather than average.

Appendix D

The Linear Probability Model with Dichotomous Independent Variables

The application of ordinary least squares to models with dichotmous dependent variables has been termed the linear probability model (LPM) because the regression coefficients for such models can be interpreted as indicating the increase in the probability of occurrence of the dependent variable that is associated with a one-unit increase in the corresponding independent variable, ceteris paribus. It is well known, however, that the LPM fails to meet the Gauss-Markov assumption of homoskedasticity and the further assumption of normally distributed errors required for statistical inference. When regression is performed on a dichotomous dependent variable, it has become standard practice in the social sciences to fit such regression models using nonlinear logit or probit models. Although ordinary least squares estimators are still unbiased with dichotomous dependent variables, the standard errors used in significance testing are biased because of nonconstant error variance. This makes standard statistical tests invalid. Furthermore, OLS sometimes will produce predictions for the probability of occurrence of the dependent variable that are less than 0 or greater than 1. And since the errors of the LPM are nonnormal, the standard errors of the regression slopes will not generally follow the students-t distribution unless the sample size is large, in which case the central limit theorem can be invoked again. The most serious problems with the LPM are heteroskedasticity, the possibility of predicted probabilities less than 0 or greater than 1, and the assumption that the independent variable has a constant effect on the occurrence of the dependent variable. For instance, if an

FIGURE D.1. LPM and logit regression slopes for dummy independent variables.

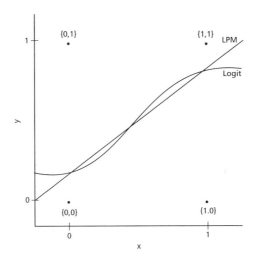

increase of one unit in a dependent variable is associated with a .1 increase in the probability of the dependent variable occurring, this holds at both $y = .5$ and $y = .95$, where it is nonsensical, because it would lead to a probability of 1.05. Logit and probit resolve the problems of predicted probabilities outside of the {0, 1} interval and the problem of constant effects across this interval by positing a non-linear relationship between x and y as shown in figure D.1.

The advantages of logit and probit come at a price. Anderson (1987) has shown that observation-specific dummy variables cannot be estimated by either logit or probit. For example, private bills play a large role in the Senate data that I consider in Appendix E. If I control for these private bills by introducing a dummy variable for the single CRS-LIV topic "private legislation," then the model will either fail or drop this variable under logit or probit. Thus, there is no direct way to measure the effect of private legislation on the agenda using logit or probit. Observation-specific dummy variables, however, pose no problems for the LPM, and I calculate the influence of private legislation on the agenda in this way in Appendix E. Caudill (1988) extended Anderson's result to show that group variables will also drop out of logit and probit if all members of the group have the same value of the dependent variable. For instance, if all issues that receive markup reach the floor, then the influence of markup on the floor cannot be gauged. This is also a condition that occurs occasionally in the Senate data of chapter 7. The LPM can still provide estimates in this case.

The greatest disadvantage of logit and probit models, however, is that the estimated coefficients have no useful interpretation on their own. The logit model comes closest, offering the increase in the log-odds ratio associated with a one-unit increase in a given independent variable. Researchers sometimes just discuss the sign and statistical significance of these estimates because there is not a standard way to interpret the meaning of the coefficients. Not only is it not possible to estimate a single constant slope for each independent variable, but it is not even possible to "hold other variables constant" in determining the effect of a single variable. For example, the president's effect on the agenda will not be constant across levels of the other variables I include in the model. It necessarily changes depending on the levels of all other variables, in this case not because of some specified interaction term between these variables, but because of the curvilinear relationship imposed by logit and probit models. If the values of these other variables are such that they lead to a very high probability of agenda consideration, then the president's influence will necessarily be diminished because the logit and probit curves flatten as y approaches 1.

As shown in firgure D.1, when an LPM model has only a single dichotomous independent variable, we do not need to be concerned with whether the relationship between x and y changes as y approaches 1 because there are only two possible values for x. Thus, the only predictions of importance are the predicted y when x = 0 and when x = 1, and the only change of relevance is the change from x = 0 to x = 1, which is taken in one step. This means that there can be one constant slope for the dichotomous independent variable. Recall that the logit and probit curves flatten as y → 1, because otherwise a constant slope would sometimes yield predicted probabilities to be greater than 1 as the values of the other variables pushed the probability close to 1. When additional dichotomous independent variables are added, logit and probit will guard against predicted values outside of the unit internal, but the curvilinear slope will add little to the interpretation of the influence of each individual variable.

The greatest advantages of the LPM over logit and probit are the easily interpreted slope coefficients and the ceteris paribus nature of these slopes. If all independent variables are dichotomous, then the main disadvantages of using the LPM are that the errors do not have constant variance and they are not normally distributed. This means that the Gauss-Markov theorem does not apply and statistical inference is invalid.[1] Nonconstant error variance can be remedied by using a weighted-least squares approach introduced by Goldberger (1964) or by using heteroskedasticity-robust standard errors introduced by Huber and White (1984). Neither of these techniques recovers the Gauss-Markov conditions, but asymptotic inference (for very large samples) does become valid. Logit and probit are also only valid asymptotically, and so they offer few advantages when all independent variables are dichotomous. When most, but not all, independent variables are dichomtous, the LPM's advantages in interpretation can still overshadow the problems of invalid predicted y values (Woodridge 2003, 456). When most of the variables are continuous, then the advantages of the logit and probit models become more persuasive. In my models of the House and Senate agendas, all of the main independent variables are dichotomous (presidential speech, presidential draft, markup, hearing, committee chair, and Senate/House), and most of the control independent variables are dichotomous. In these models, the advantages of the LPM outweigh those of logit and probit. Furthermore, an additional penalty of losing the ceteris paribus interpretation of slopes in the logit and probit models is that it is no longer possible to calculate indirect and total effects in path models, which play a crucial role in my attempt to untangle to exact mechanisms by which the president influences that agenda. I discuss the importance of measuring these direct and indirect effects in Appendix E on path analysis.

Appendix E

Indirect and Total Effects in Path Analysis

The multiple-equation technique of path analysis presents an elegant solution to the countervailing problems of "controlling for too much" and "omitted variable bias." The more general technique of structural-equation modeling allows for nonrecursive causal conditions as well, but it presents other technical complications. In path analysis, first the president's influence on the committee chair, α_1, is estimated using ordinary multiple regression. Then the direct influences of both the president, β_1, and the committee chair, β_2, on the agenda are assessed by ordinary multiple regression, holding the influences of each other constant. The president's total effect on the agenda is then a simple sum, $\beta_1 + \alpha_1\beta_2$, of his direct effect, β_1, and his indirect effect, $\alpha_1\beta_2$, which is calculated as the product of his influence on the committee chair multiplied by the chair's effect on the agenda. Furthermore, the president's direct and indirect effects on each subsequent stage of the legislative process can be considered in the same way. For instance, to measure the president's influence on the floor agenda, while controlling for whether issues reach markup, may underestimate the president's total influence on the floor because he may exercise influence on the floor indirectly by influencing the prior markup stage. Again using path analysis, separate regressions can sort out the president's direct and indirect effects on the markup and floor stages and can thereby be used to calculate his total effect on the floor.[1]

There is some debate about how the statistical significance should be determined for indirect and total effects in path models (e.g., Kline 1998, 150). Here, I use the simple technique of identifying only those indirect effects as statistically significant where all of the links in the path are statistically significant. By this standard, the president's speeches exercise a statistically significant indirect influence over markup through the committee leader if and only if the president's speeches have a statistically significant influence on the committee leaders and the committee leaders have a statistically significant influence on markups. To calculate the total effect of a variable on the floor agenda, I add up the statistically significant, indirect and direct effects that exist between the variable and the floor agenda.

The role of Senate-initiated legislation in the House (and likewise House-initiated legislation in the Senate) presents a potential endogeneity problem for the attempt to create a causal model of the House agenda process. Most of the explanatory or exogenous variables I consider are determined prior to the agenda process. For instance, each bill has a primary sponsor who introduced the measure in the House. The main characteristics of a bill's primary sponsor—such as the sponsor's party, ideology, and years of experience—do not change much in a given Congress. But the answer to the question of whether the Senate has passed a bill covering an issue is subject to change throughout the course of a given Congress. For some issues that are introduced in the House via Senate-passed bills, Senate passage may occur before any House action takes place—and that is the presumption of the model in this appendix—but for other issues a Senate-passed bill may not arrive in the House until after the House has already begun active consideration of it. In the latter case, it is not easy to assess whether Senate passage had an effect on House stages that have already taken place. The problem of the mutual influence of the House and Senate on each other's agenda would seem to call for nonrecursive simultaneous-equation modeling; but since evidence of House-Senate coordination is almost nonexistent (Joint Committee 1993), the Senate is unlikely to be significantly influenced by prefloor actions in the House. In other words, there does not seem to be a problem of circularity where House hearings or markup influence Senate passage, which then further influences House hearings, markup, and floor consideration, because the only House action that seems to have measurable influence on Senate consideration is House passage, at which point consideration of resulting Senate influence on earlier stages for the same issue is usually moot. Only a small percentage of House-passed bills will be resubmitted in the House in the form of Senate-passed substitutes. Here, I assume that the influence of the House hearings and markup on Senate passage is negligible because House issues seem to make an impact only after they are passed and then introduced in the Senate. I take up the question of House influence on the Senate in more detail in chapter 7.

Appendix F

Tables of Regression Coefficients for Direct Effects on House Agenda

TABLE F.1. LPM Regression slopes (and t-statistics for White-Huber robust standard errors) for determinants of floor consideration of House Commerce Committee issues in the House

	CONGRESS											
VARIABLE	96th	97th	98th	99th	100th	101st	102nd	103rd	104th	105th	106th	107th
Markup	.44 (10.0)	.32 (7.9)	.64 (21.0)	.56 (22.6)	.55 (27.2)	.54 (19.9)	.58 (24.6)	.31 (13.2)	.24 (9.6)	.58 (23.6)	.25 (9.3)	.25 (12.9)
Hearing	.19 (5.9)	−.02 (−0.5)	−.03 (−1.4)	.03 (1.5)	−.06 (−3.1)	−.07 (−2.7)	> −.01 (−.04)	.15 (5.8)	.23 (10.4)	.05 (1.9)	.18 (6.4)	−.19 (−7.0)
Committee leader	−.06 (−5.1)	.33 (9.5)	.18 (6.2)	.08 (3.3)	.02 (1.1)	.07 (2.6)	.11 (4.9)	.05 (2.0)	.04 (1.7)	.07 (3.4)	.25 (12.4)	.35 (16.9)
Senate bill	.18 (6.7)	.09 (2.1)	.14 (4.3)	.07 (2.4)	.17 (7.7)	.12 (5.2)	−.01 (−0.7)	.04 (1.8)	.03 (1.6)	.06 (2.7)	.06 (2.7)	.10 (4.4)
President's speech	.08 (2.2)	.05 (0.6)	.09 (2.4)	> −.01 (−0.1)	.03 (0.6)	.08 (1.9)	< .01 (< .01)	.06 (1.9)	−.02 (−0.6)	.02 (0.6)	−.01 (−0.8)	.12 (2.3)
President's draft	.02 (0.7)	.03 (0.6)	−.03 (−0.7)	−.12 (−4.1)	.02 (0.8)	.02 (0.6)	−.13 (−6.9)	.18 (12.2)	.11 (6.9)	−.07 (−2.9)	−.05 (−2.0)	.20 (10.0)
Maximum cosponsors	< .01 (−0.8)	< .01 (1.7)	> −.01 (−4.8)	> −.01 (−9.9)	< .01 (−1.2)	> −.01 (−1.3)	< .01 (2.6)	< .01 (1.7)	< .01 (4.9)	< .01 (3.5)	< .01 (10.7)	< .01 (6.3)
Scope of issue	< .01 (0.8)	< .01 (2.4)	< .01 (2.2)	< .01 (0.7)	> −.01 (−3.0)	> −.01 (−2.4)	< .01 (−2.1)	> −.01 (−4.8)	> −.01 (−6.9)	> −.01 (−4.4)	> −.01 (−6.3)	> −.01 (−6.6)
Minimum complexity	< .01 (0.4)	< .01 (1.3)	< .01 (4.0)	< .01 (15.2)	< .01 (14.2)	< .01 (0.3)	< .01 (10.3)	< .01 (8.2)	< .01 (−13.4)	< .01 (−1.0)	< .01 (−3.9)	< .01 (7.0)
Multiply referred	.02 (1.1)	.08 (3.4)	−.07 (−3.3)	−.01 (−0.3)	.04 (2.5)	−.05 (−2.5)	−.18 (−12.7)	< .01 (.03)	.04 (2.3)	.01 (0.8)	.06 (3.4)	.03 (1.9)
Authorization issue	−.07 (−1.6)	.04 (0.4)	.01 (0.2)	−.01 (−0.3)	−.03 (−0.5)	.14 (2.1)	.01 (0.1)	< .01 (.07)	.09 (1.2)	−.08 (−1.3)	−.09 (−1.2)	.15 (1.5)
Timing of introduction	.08 (4.6)	.29 (6.4)	−.02 (−0.6)	−.11 (−3.0)	.11 (3.6)	.19 (6.0)	.06 (1.9)	.13 (4.3)	−.38 (−12.8)	−.13 (−4.6)	−.23 (−8.8)	−.12 (−4.1)
Democratic sponsor	.01 (1.4)	.13 (6.4)	.09 (4.6)	.04 (1.5)	.33 (17.2)	.10 (4.4)	.18 (11.4)	.32 (18.3)	−.14 (−8.6)	−.18 (−10.8)	−.10 (−6.0)	−.20 (−10.6)
Max. sponsor experience	< .01 (2.3)	.02 (5.51)	.01 (2.9)	.04 (19.7)	.03 (14.1)	.03 (19.0)	.02 (11.0)	.02 (17.5)	.01 (6.7)	.02 (9.7)	< .01 (2.3)	−.20 (12.6)
Constant	−.06 (−4.4)	−.30 (−7.9)	−.02 (−0.5)	−.09 (−2.6)	−.29 (−10.1)	−.24 (−8.7)	−.09 (−3.7)	−.30 (−12.3)	.34 (11.6)	.25 (10.1)	.30 (12.5)	.19 (6.9)
N	1556	1145	1362	1871	2410	2236	2597	2858	3261	2853	3176	3207
R^2	.572	.363	.286	.574	.558	.529	.637	.490	.520	.349	.343	.364

TABLE F.2. LPM Regression slopes (and t-statistics for White-Huber robust standard errors) for determinants of subcommittee markup of House Commerce Committee issues in the House

VARIABLE	CONGRESS											
	96th	97th	98th	99th	100th	101st	102nd	103rd	104th	105th	106th	107th
Hearing	.57 (18.9)	.39 (12.3)	.28 (10.5)	.23 (8.9)	.35 (14.5)	.43 (16.0)	.44 (19.0)	.49 (20.8)	.29 (15.5)	.63 (31.1)	.61 (31.0)	.50 (17.8)
Committee leader	.10 (6.9)	.21 (6.9)	.44 (15.1)	.39 (14.9)	.17 (7.4)	.24 (9.3)	.34 (15.4)	.26 (11.5)	.51 (24.5)	.06 (2.6)	.19 (10.2)	.17 (10.3)
Senate bill	.07 (3.1)	.17 (4.8)	.04 (1.1)	.23 (6.2)	−.01 (−.05)	.04 (1.6)	.10 (4.7)	.11 (4.5)	.12 (6.3)	.08 (4.0)	.07 (4.2)	−.01 (−0.5)
President's speech	.07 (2.7)	−.08 (−1.5)	−.07 (−1.8)	−.04 (−1.0)	.02 (0.4)	−.01 (−.4)	.02 (0.4)	.01 (0.2)	−.05 (−1.5)	−.02 (−0.6)	−.01 (−0.7)	−.04 (−1.0)
President's draft	−.04 (−1.5)	.09 (1.8)	−.05 (−1.0)	.07 (2.0)	.08 (2.8)	.12 (3.7)	<.01 (0.2)	.07 (4.8)	−.02 (−1.5)	.04 (1.5)	.08 (3.1)	.02 (1.2)
Request executive comment	<.01 (0.1)	.07 (3.0)	.02 (1.0)	−.05 (−2.2)	−.07 (−4.2)	−.06 (−4.2)	−.02 (−1.1)	−.06 (−5.0)	−.06 (−5.6)	−.01 (−0.4)	.04 (2.7)	.06 (4.8)
Maximum cosponsors	>−.01 (−1.4)	>−.01 (−3.2)	<.01 (2.2)	<.01 (1.4)	<.01 (2.7)	<.01 (7.6)	<.01 (2.2)	<.01 (0.2)	<.01 (1.5)	<.01 (.01)	<.01 (3.0)	>−.01 (−3.4)
Scope of issue	<.01 (4.3)	.01 (4.3)	<.01 (1.8)	>−.01 (−0.8)	<.01 (2.1)	<.01 (1.6)	<.01 (0.6)	<.01 (2.1)	<.01 (1.5)	<.01 (.41)	>−.01 (−0.6)	<.01 (4.6)
Minimum complexity	.001 (2.9)	<.01 (1.5)	<.01 (11.6)	>−.01 (−0.2)	<.01 (8.0)	<.01 (0.3)	<.01 (5.7)	>−.01 (−0.3)	>−.01 (−0.3)	<.01 (0.3)	<.01 (0.5)	>−.01 (−2.3)
Multiply referred	−.03 (−1.2)	<.01 (0.2)	−.07 (−2.1)	−.02 (−1.3)	−.01 (−0.6)	−.01 (−1.1)	−.02 (−1.3)	−.03 (−2.0)	−.03 (−2.1)	−.02 (−1.7)	.02 (2.0)	−.06 (−5.1)
Authorization	.02 (0.5)	.07 (1.0)	.15 (2.1)	.14 (2.0)	.12 (1.7)	.15 (2.1)	.13 (1.8)	.04 (1.1)	.02 (0.6)	.01 (0.2)	−.01 (−0.2)	.23 (2.3)
Timing of introduction	−.01 (−0.7)	.06 (1.7)	−.08 (−2.1)	−.26 (−7.8)	−.42 (−13)	>−.01 (−0.1)	−.17 (−6.1)	.02 (1.0)	−.15 (−6.9)	−.11 (−6.3)	−.08 (−4.3)	−.06 (−3.7)
Democratic sponsor	−.03 (−2.8)	.06 (4.2)	.05 (2.0)	−.02 (−0.9)	.26 (11.4)	−.01 (−0.6)	.03 (1.8)	.04 (3.8)	−.04 (−3.0)	−.10 (−7.3)	−.01 (−1.1)	−.02 (−1.2)
Avg. sponsor experience	>−.01 (−2.1)	<.01 (0.7)	.01 (3.6)	.01 (2.6)	>−.01 (−0.4)	<.01 (0.2)	>−.01 (−1.1)	−.01 (−4.8)	>−.01 (−2.0)	<.01 (1.7)	>−.01 (−3.1)	<.01 (4.8)
Constant	.01 (0.6)	−.12 (.03)	−.08 (−2.0)	.20 (5.5)	.18 (5.4)	>−.01 (−0.5)	.09 (3.8)	.06 (3.4)	.14 (6.2)	.12 (6.5)	.04 (2.7)	.06 (3.1)
N	1556	1145	1362	1871	2410	2236	2597	2858	3261	2853	3176	3207
R^2	.59	.44	.53	.49	.49	.58	.61	.59	.65	.60	.68	.44

TABLE F.3. LPM Regression slopes (and t-statistics for White-Huber robust standard errors) for determinants of hearings of House Commerce Committee issues in the House

	CONGRESS											
VARIABLE	96th	97th	98th	99th	100th	101st	102nd	103rd	104th	105th	106th	107th
Committee leader	.11 (4.7)	.34 (10.4)	.26 (8.8)	.25 (9.4)	.16 (6.6)	.49 (21.5)	.47 (23.2)	.40 (17.5)	.37 (17.7)	.40 (17.5)	.20 (9.5)	.142 (11.5)
Senate bill	.29 (8.5)	.03 (0.7)	−.01 (−0.3)	.12 (3.0)	−.03 (−1.3)	−.01 (−0.4)	.04 (1.7)	.03 (1.2)	.01 (0.5)	−.04 (−1.8)	.06 (2.6)	.08 (3.5)
President's speech	.02 (0.4)	−.01 (−0.2)	−.01 (−0.3)	−.02 (−0.3)	.21 (3.4)	.06 (1.5)	< .01 (0.1)	−.07 (−2.1)	−.04 (−0.8)	.01 (0.3)	−.05 (−1.8)	−.04 (1.0)
President's draft	−.06 (−1.7)	.13 (2.2)	.05 (1.0)	.10 (2.4)	.04 (1.2)	.01 (0.4)	.11 (4.2)	> −.01 (−0.1)	.05 (2.7)	.10 (4.1)	.10 (3.4)	−.02 (−1.3)
Request executive comment	.04 (1.8)	−1.0 (−3.7)	−.07 (−2.4)	−.04 (−1.8)	> −.01 (> −0.1)	.02 (1.3)	.02 (1.0)	.10 (7.4)	.03 (2.1)	−.02 (−1.4)	.06 (3.2)	.08 (6.1)
Maximum cosponsors	< .01 (4.4)	< .01 (8.8)	< .01 (8.6)	< .01 (1.9)	< .01 (3.1)	< .01 (11.5)	< .01 (5.8)	< .01 (10.8)	< .01 (18.6)	< .01 (12.9)	< .01 (21.5)	< .01 (1.62)
Scope of issue	.01 (3.9)	< .01 (1.9)	< .01 (3.2)	.01 (4.5)	< .01 (2.6)	< .01 (1.1)	< .01 (1.9)	> −.01 (−1.3)	> −.01 (−7.7)	> −.01 (−0.3)	> −.01 (−1.7)	< .01 (7.3)
Minimum complexity	> −.01 (−2.6)	> −.01 (−3.7)	> −.01 (−6.0)	> −.01 (−10.3)	< .01 (5.0)	> −.01 (−4.1)	> −.01 (−2.2)	> −.01 (−3.1)	> −.01 (−8.3)	> −.01 (−1.2)	> −.01 (−3.6)	> −.01 (−8.4)
Multiply referred	.15 (3.4)	−.06 (−2.3)	.03 (0.9)	.02 (1.1)	−.25 (−11)	−.14 (7.9)	.05 (2.9)	−.11 (−5.2)	< .01 (0.1)	−.16 (−8.6)	−.05 (−3.1)	.01 (1.0)
Authorization	.07 (1.1)	−.001 (−0.1)	−.22 (−3.1)	−.10 (−1.4)	−.10 (−1.1)	−.08 (−1.3)	−.12 (−1.4)	−.03 (−1.1)	−.05 (−0.8)	.11 (1.5)	.07 (0.9)	.02 (0.3)
Democratic sponsor	.05 (2.5)	.11 (4.4)	.10 (2.9)	.09 (3.3)	.08 (2.8)	.09 (7.0)	.11 (6.8)	.04 (2.6)	−.04 (−2.7)	−.14 (−7.8)	−.09 (−5.4)	−.03 (−2.8)
Avg. sponsor experience	< .01 (1.0)	.01 (3.5)	.01 (2.5)	.01 (2.1)	.03 (11.6)	> −.01 (−1.7)	< .01 (0.7)	.01 (6.6)	.02 (11.31)	< .01 (2.4)	> −.01 (−2.0)	< .01 (2.3)
Constant	−.03 (−1.7)	.03 (1.0)	.09 (2.5)	.05 (1.8)	.10 (3.3)	.06 (4.0)	−.03 (−1.8)	< .01 (0.1)	−.02 (−0.8)	.28 (12.6)	.18 (9.3)	−.01 (−.06)
N	1556	1145	1362	1871	2410	2236	2597	2858	3261	2853	3176	3207
R^2	.25	.34	.26	.26	.29	.52	.37	.52	.49	.38	.40	.28

TABLE F.4. LPM Regression slopes (and t-statistics for White-Huber robust standard errors) for determinants of committee leader sponsorship of House Commerce Committee issues in the House

	CONGRESS											
VARIABLE	96th	97th	98th	99th	100th	101st	102nd	103rd	104th	105th	106th	107th
President's speech	−.09 (−1.5)	−.08 (−1.2)	−.12 (−2.4)	−.05 (−1.0)	−.13 (−2.1)	−.04 (−0.9)	> −.01 (−0.1)	.01 (0.4)	> −.01 (−.01)	.05 (1.2)	> −.01 (−0.1)	.02 (0.4)
President's draft	.45 (16.0)	.09 (1.8)	.11 (2.3)	.16 (3.7)	.07 (1.8)	.18 (5.3)	.06 (2.6)	.15 (8.4)	.05 (2.8)	.14 (5.1)	.33 (13.3)	.24 (12.1)
Maximum cosponsors	< .01 (0.1)	< .01 (3.4)	< .01 (6.1)	> −.01 (−4.2)	< .01 (1.0)	< .01 (6.4)	< .01 (2.7)	< .001 (2.0)	< .01 (8.8)	< .01 (7.3)	< .01 (10.0)	< .01 (5.2)
Scope of issue	.01 (2.8)	.01 (4.2)	.01 (3.7)	.01 (5.6)	.01 (4.0)	< .01 (2.7)	< .01 (3.3)	< .001 (4.1)	< .01 (6.6)	< .01 (5.7)	< .01 (3.8)	< .01 (3.5)
Minimum complexity	< .01 (0.6)	> −.01 (−0.1)	< .01 (7.3)	> −.01 (−9.6)	> −.01 (−13)	> −.01 (−4.3)	< .01 (1.5)	< .01 (1.4)	> −.01 (−2.9)	> −.01 (−4.0)	> −.01 (−2.0)	< .01 (4.2)
Multiply referred	−.42 (−17)	−.36 (−14)	−.39 (−14)	−.23 (−10)	−.28 (−16)	−.39 (−22)	−.35 (−19)	−.50 (−27)	−28 (−17)	−.26 (−16)	−.25 (−15)	−.20 (−11)
Authorization	.14 (2.1)	.27 (4.1)	.19 (2.3)	.07 (0.9)	.32 (4.2)	−.02 (−0.2)	.11 (1.1)	.07 (2.7)	.13 (2.1)	.20 (2.0)	.10 (1.5)	.22 (2.3)
Timing of introduction	−.27 (−5.4)	.02 (0.4)	−.10 (−2.3)	−.33 (−8.5)	−.03 (−1.4)	−.11 (−3.2)	−.45 (−12)	−.22 (−7.7)	−.11 (−4.2)	−.04 (−1.5)	−.17 (−6.5)	−.66 (−24)
Constant	.45 (14.0)	.39 (11.5)	.50 (16.9)	.56 (19.9)	.39 (18.0)	.49 (20.9)	.67 (30.4)	.62 (33.9)	.35 (17.3)	.30 (16.8)	.35 (20.0)	.53 (30.1)
N	1556	1145	1362	1871	2410	2236	2597	2858	3261	2853	3176	3207
R^2	.24	.25	.27	.27	.27	.31	.30	.46	.32	.28	.35	.35

Appendix G

Tables of Regression Coefficients for Direct Effects on Senate Agenda

TABLE G.1. LPM Regression slopes (and t-statistics for White-Huber robust standard errors) for determinants of floor consideration of Senate Commerce Committee issues in the Senate

VARIABLE	CONGRESS											
	96th	97th	98th	99th	100th	101st	102nd	103rd	104th	105th	106th	107th
Markup	.28 (7.1)	.38 (10.5)	.77 (20.2)	.88 (44.4)	.82 (35.0)	.79 (29.9)	.78 (32.6)	.81 (35.0)	.77 (41.1)	.87 (45.1)	.78 (41.3)	.90 (59.3)
Hearing	.15 (4.0)	.15 (3.7)	.05 (2.3)	−.03 (−3.0)	−.05 (−2.9)	.09 (3.7)	−.02 (−0.8)	.05 (2.2)	−.07 (−3.7)	−.07 (−3.9)	−.08 (−5.0)	−.01 (−0.5)
Committee chair	.31 (7.2)	.23 (6.3)	.02 (1.5)	−.01 (−0.5)	−.07 (−5.3)	−.03 (−1.5)	.02 (0.9)	−.03 (−3.8)	−.01 (−0.5)	−.05 (−3.4)	> −.01 (−0.1)	> −.01 (−0.2)
House bill	.34 (8.8)	.23 (4.3)	.16 (5.2)	.18 (5.8)	.16 (7.6)	.12 (5.3)	.18 (9.7)	.07 (6.8)	.26 (16.3)	.09 (5.0)	.18 (9.6)	.13 (6.3)
President's speech	.03 (0.4)	−.08 (−0.8)	−.15 (−2.0)	−.07 (−1.2)	−.08 (−3.0)	−.03 (−2.8)	−.01 (−0.5)	−.01 (−0.9)	.05 (1.0)	.03 (2.3)	.01 (0.5)	.02 (0.8)
President's draft	−.09 (−2.6)	< .01 (0.1)	.07 (2.2)	−.02 (−1.0)	−.01 (−0.8)	.06 (3.4)	−.01 (−6.4)	−.01 (−2.2)	.05 (−2.4)	.05 (3.5)	−.01 (−0.3)	N.A.
Maximum cosponsors	−.01 (−3.4)	< .01 (0.9)	< .01 (2.5)	< .01 (2.4)	< .01 (0.9)	< .01 (2.2)	< .01 (1.4)	> −.01 (−5.2)	> −.01 (−0.5)	< .01 (3.8)	> −.01 (−5.2)	< .01 (3.3)
Scope of issue	< .01 (1.0)	−.01 (−1.8)	> −.01 (−0.9)	> −.01 (−0.3)	> −.01 (−2.5)	> −.01 (−3.4)	< .01 (1.1)	< .01 (1.3)	< .02 (3.4)	> −.01 (−1.2)	< .01 (2.6)	> −.01 (−5.4)
Minimum complexity	.01 (3.8)	.02 (11.4)	< .01 (5.2)	< .01 (2.5)	< .01 (4.2)	< .01 (1.6	< .01 (8.9)	< .01 (4.1)	> −.01 (−13.9)	< .01 (4.5)	< .01 (5.3)	< .01 (2.6)
Joint referral	−.13 (−2.7)	−.44 (−10.8)	.08 (3.8)	.10 (2.2)	< .01 (.04)	.05 (1.3)	−.06 (−3.2)	.05 (2.6)	.27 (11.0)	−.01 (−0.4)	.16 (6.6)	.02 (0.8)
Authorization issue	.15 (2.1)	.24 (2.6)	−.02 (−0.9)	−.02 (−0.6)	.06 (1.3)	−.06 (−2.3)	.03 (0.3)	−.04 (−2.4)	.13 (1.5)	.05 (1.6)	> −.01 (−.01)	.01 (0.3)
Timing of introduction	.11 (1.9)	−.24 (−3.6)	.07 (2.2)	.02 (0.7)	.04 (1.4)	.06 (2.3)	−.22 (−6.0)	−.17 (−7.1)	−.18 (−5.2)	−.18 (−4.0)	−.22 (−6.1)	.05 (2.4)
Democratic sponsor	.14 (2.4)	−.06 (−1.5)	−.01 (−0.5)	−.04 (−2.0)	.15 (5.6)	.01 (0.6)	.07 (5.9)	.08 (4.6)	−.16 (−9.7)	< .01 (0.3)	−.07 (−3.8)	−.04 (−2.3)
Avg. sponsor experience	−.01 (−1.2)	> −.01 (−0.3)	> −.01 (−1.6)	.01 (2.9)	.01 (5.9)	< .01 (1.1)	> −.01 (−2.0)	> −.01 (−0.6)	−.02 (−8.7)	> −.01 (−0.5)	.01 (3.1)	< .01 (1.7)
Private legislation	.08 (1.4)	.43 (6.6)	.02 (1.0)	−.09 (−3.7)	−.07 (−4.0)	.30 (5.6)	.13 (3.7)	−.05 (−5.0)	.04 (1.1)	.07 (3.3)	−.10 (−4.5)	−.07 (−3.8)
House X Earlier introduction	.20 (2.2)	.20 (2.8)	.06 (0.8)	−.13 (−5.4)	−.14 (−5.9)	.02 (0.5)	.13 (2.5)	−.01 (−0.8)	−.27 (−6.9)	−.04 (−1.5)	−.03 (−1.0)	−.09 (−5.1)
Constant	.14 (2.2)	.31 (5.5)	.04 (1.5)	.01 (0.2)	−.12 (−4.2)	−.03 (−1.1)	.09 (3.3)	.10 (4.8)	.58 (13.2)	.12 (4.2)	.16 (5.3)	> −.01 (−.01)
N	651	531	580	690	884	999	1264	1613	1552	1377	1353	1588
R^2	.44	.53	.79	.83	.80	.83	.76	.85	.68	.74	.77	.90

TABLE G.2. LPM Regression slopes (and t-statistics for White-Huber robust standard errors) for determinants of committee markup of Senate Commerce Committee issues in the Senate

	CONGRESS											
VARIABLE	96th	97th	98th	99th	100th	101st	102nd	103rd	104th	105th	106th	107th
Hearing	.23 (6.6)	.35 (7.71)	.48 (11.8)	.41 (12.3)	.57 (17.4)	.55 (17.6)	.72 (30.9)	.49 (15.6)	.27 (9.4)	.16 (6.5)	.17 (5.2)	.28 (8.1)
Committee chair	.12 (2.6)	.23 (4.7)	.21 (6.4)	.17 (5.4)	.07 (2.7)	.06 (1.8)	−.06 (−1.7)	.04 (1.5)	.05 (1.5)	.21 (9.7)	.38 (11.9)	.18 (5.4)
House bill	−.09 (−2.3)	−.06 (−1.0)	.20 (4.3)	.10 (2.6)	.08 (2.6)	.17 (5.3)	.03 (1.5)	.10 (4.3)	−.04 (−1.4)	.03 (1.1)	.05 (1.8)	.11 (3.6)
Executive comment requested	−.03 (−0.5)	−.03 (−0.5)	−.01 (−0.2)	.17 (5.3)	−.04 (−1.1)	−.11 (−3.8)	.01 (0.3)	−.06 (−2.5)	−.10 (−4.3)	.05 (1.4)	.04 (1.1)	−.19 (−4.9)
President's speech	.13 (1.7)	−.08 (−0.9)	−.03 (−0.5)	.02 (0.4)	−.07 (−1.2)	−.04 (−0.8)	.03 (0.7)	−.01 (−0.5)	−.09 (−1.5)	.04 (0.8)	.01 (0.1)	.14 (2.0)
President's draft	.10 (2.3)	−.17 (−3.4)	.08 (1.2)	−.13 (−2.9)	>−.01 (−0.1)	.03 (1.0)	.02 (0.7)	.11 (5.9)	.24 (8.7)	.08 (2.9)	.04 (1.2)	N.A.
Maximum cosponsors	.03 (9.3)	.01 (4.1)	<.01 (4.0)	.01 (5.7)	<.01 (7.5)	.01 (7.8)	<.01 (4.0)	<.01 (2.1)	.01 (3.0)	.01 (11.1)	.01 (10.7)	.01 (6.6)
Scope of issue	.02 (3.1)	.02 (2.0)	>−.01 (−0.9)	>−.01 (−0.4)	<.01 (0.5)	<.01 (1.8)	<.01 (2.0)	<.01 (0.2)	>−.01 (−1.2)	>−.01 (−4.8)	>−.01 (−4.5)	<.01 (0.2)
Minimum complexity	.02 (15.0)	.01 (3.5)	.01 (8.0)	.01 (8.0)	.01 (7.9)	<.01 (1.6)	<.01 (4.1)	<.01 (4.1)	>−.01 (−5.4)	>−.01 (−0.4)	<.01 (1.2)	<.01 (1.7)
Joint referral	−.14 (−4.1)	.05 (0.6)	.19 (5.0)	.06 (0.9)	.04 (0.8)	.07 (1.6)	.14 (4.0)	.16 (5.8)	.36 (10.0)	.36 (10.6)	.65 (16.2)	.76 (18.3)
Authorization issue	−.11 (−1.5)	−.04 (−0.5)	−.01 (−0.2)	.03 (0.3)	.12 (1.3)	.11 (1.3)	.06 (1.0)	−.01 (−0.1)	.02 (0.3)	.01 (0.11)	.10 (0.8)	.43 (3.8)
Timing of introduction	−.22 (−4.1)	.01 (0.2)	−.04 (−0.6)	−.33 (−6.1)	−.04 (−0.8)	−.05 (−0.8)	−.12 (−2.8)	.03 (0.8)	−.40 (−8.1)	−.04 (−0.5)	−.19 (−3.4)	−.08 (−1.9)
Democratic sponsor	.11 (2.3)	.02 (0.3)	−.06 (−1.5)	−.09 (−2.6)	.14 (3.3)	.02 (0.6)	.08 (2.8)	.14 (3.4)	−.03 (−1.3)	−.03 (−1.1)	−.01 (−.03)	.08 (2.7)
Avg. sponsor experience	<.01 (0.2)	.02 (4.3)	>−.01 (−0.1)	.01 (1.4)	.01 (2.1)	−.01 (−1.9)	.01 (3.8)	.02 (6.2)	.01 (3.5)	>−.01 (−0.5)	−.01 (−3.4)	<.01 (1.0)
Private legislation	.93 (18.3)	−.46 (−5.1)	.22 (4.7)	.55 (11.9)	.72 (21.2)	.79 (8.6)	.93 (26.8)	.07 (2.5)	−.11 (−1.9)	.61 (15.0)	.80 (24.0)	.11 (3.6)
House X Earlier introduction	.07 (0.7)	.20 (1.5)	−.07 (−.06)	.08 (1.2)	.42 (5.8)	.17 (3.0)	.12 (3.1)	−.01 (−0.2)	.13 (4.6)	.20 (6.0)	.34 (9.2)	.10 (2.8)
Constant	−.07 (−1.3)	−.18 (−2.8)	.20 (3.1)	.26 (4.6)	−.06 (1.3)	.13 (2.2)	−.11 (−2.5)	−.20 (−3.8)	.46 (8.7)	.49 (10.2)	.34 (7.0)	.08 (1.9)
N	651	531	580	690	884	999	1264	1613	1552	1377	1353	1588
R^2	.54	.39	.50	.52	.56	.45	.66	.54	.44	.30	.47	.44

180

TABLE G.3. LPM Regression slopes (and t-statistics for White-Huber robust standard errors) for determinants of committee hearings of Senate Commerce Committee issues in the Senate

	CONGRESS											
VARIABLE	96th	97th	98th	99th	100th	101st	102nd	103rd	104th	105th	106th	107th
Committee chair	.24 (5.0)	.06 (1.24)	.25 (5.87)	.24 (6.71)	.11 (3.1)	−.05 (−1.3)	.03 (1.0)	.10 (4.6)	.18 (6.2)	.10 (3.9)	.51 (19.0)	.32 (11.0)
House bill	−.09 (−2.2)	−.09 (−1.4)	−.09 (−1.7)	.01 (0.3)	−.08 (−2.1)	.05 (1.4)	−.15 (−4.8)	−.04 (−1.6)	−.08 (−2.4)	.09 (2.7)	.04 (1.4)	.15 (5.5)
Executive comment requested	.12 (3.3)	−.10 (−1.8)	−.11 (−2.2)	−.02 (−0.4)	−.19 (−4.1)	.08 (2.3)	−.03 (−0.8)	−.12 (−4.9)	.15 (5.0)	.06 (1.1)	−.01 (−0.4)	−.05 (−1.0)
President's speech	.04 (0.5)	−.08 (−.70)	−.10 (−1.1)	.04 (0.4)	.07 (.08)	−.06 (−1.0)	.08 (1.3)	.02 (0.6)	.02 (0.3)	−.03 (−0.6)	.04 (0.9)	.12 (1.8)
President's draft	.02 (.05)	.15 (3.2)	−.05 (−0.6)	.16 (3.5)	.05 (1.5)	.11 (3.6)	.24 (7.6)	.29 (17.5)	.14 (4.3)	.38 (10.33)	−.05 (−1.3)	N.A.
Maximum cosponsors	.04 (15.5)	.02 (6.4)	.01 (7.4)	<.01 (0.5)	.01 (10.76)	.01 (11.2)	.01 (10.4)	.01 (11.1)	.01 (7.3)	.01 (14.1)	.01 (7.0)	.01 (14.2)
Scope of issue	>−.01 (−0.5)	.03 (2.4)	.03 (3.0)	.04 (5.3)	.02 (3.3)	<.01 (1.5)	.01 (1.8)	>−.01 (−0.6)	>−.01 (−1.3)	>−.01 (−3.8)	<.01 (0.2)	>−.01 (−0.4)
Minimum complexity	>−.01 (−1.2)	.01 (3.7)	<.01 (2.1)	.01 (3.6)	.01 (9.1)	>−.01 (−0.2)	<.01 (0.7)	<.01 (4.7)	<.01 (6.2)	>−.01 (−14.2)	>−.01 (−1.9)	<.01 (8.2)
Joint referral	−.01 (−.03)	.25 (3.3)	.39 (7.2)	−.30 (−4.6)	−.09 (−1.5)	.10 (1.4)	−.20 (−3.6)	.07 (2.4)	.22 (5.5)	.33 (7.8)	.93 (37.2)	−.17 (−4.7)
Authorization issue	.12 (1.6)	−.14 (−1.6)	.14 (1.5)	.14 (1.4)	.05 (0.4)	−.11 (−0.8)	.22 (2.1)	.05 (0.6)	−.02 (−0.1)	.01 (0.1)	−.26 (−3.4)	.11 (0.8)
Democratic sponsor	−.07 (−1.2)	−.08 (−1.4)	.02 (0.5)	−.14 (−3.3)	.14 (2.6)	.27 (5.7)	.12 (3.2)	.37 (6.9)	−.05 (−1.6)	.04 (1.2)	−.04 (−1.7)	.05 (2.0)
Avg. sponsor experience	.01 (1.1)	.02 (3.0)	.01 (1.9)	−.01 (−1.4)	.02 (4.8)	>−.01 (−0.2)	.01 (3.7)	.01 (2.0)	.04 (10.2)	.01 (1.9)	.01 (5.8)	<.01 (1.0)
Private legislation	−.36 (−6.7)	.34 (4.27)	.32 (3.1)	−40 (−7.6)	−.56 (−12.4)	−.72 (−6.0)	−.66 (−13)	.21 (8.5)	.20 (2.3)	−.33 (−8.2)	−.18 (−5.8)	.35 (11.9)
House X Earlier introduction	.17 (1.4)	.17 (1.5)	.45 (5.6)	.26 (3.0)	−.26 (−2.6)	.04 (0.7)	.08 (1.2)	.18 (6.2)	.15 (4.7)	−.10 (−2.0)	−.04 (−0.9)	.06 (1.5)
Constant	.37 (5.8)	.21 (4.0)	.30 (5.2)	.48 (9.6)	.17 (3.1)	.28 (5.5)	.22 (4.7)	.10 (6.2)	.02 (0.4)	.24 (7.9)	−.03 (−0.9)	−.14 (−5.2)
N	651	531	580	690	884	999	1264	1613	1552	1377	1353	1588
R^2	.32	.28	.26	.24	.29	.19	.28	.38	.29	.34	.47	.51

TABLE G.4. LPM Regression slopes (and t-statistics for White-Huber robust standard errors) for determinants of committee leader sponsorship of Senate Commerce Committee issues in the Senate

	CONGRESS											
VARIABLE	96th	97th	98th	99th	100th	101st	102nd	103rd	104th	105th	106th	107th
President's speech	.04 (0.5)	−.11 (−1.6)	−.07 (−0.7)	−.10 (−1.04)	.25 (2.3)	.12 (1.6)	.03 (0.4)	.08 (1.5)	.05 (0.7)	.16 (2.3)	.03 (0.6)	−.02 (−0.2)
President's draft	.58 (16.5)	.27 (4.7)	−.16 (−2.0)	.17 (2.7)	.11 (2.4)	.10 (2.6)	.14 (4.4)	.26 (10.8)	<.01 (0.2)	−.22 (−4.3)	.18 (4.8)	N.A
Maximum cosponsors	−.01 (−1.7)	−.01 (5.0)	>−.01 (−1.1)	>−.01 (−1.2)	<.01 (0.5)	<.01 (4.0)	<.01 (1.3)	.01 (8.1)	>−.001 (−1.4)	<.01 (2.3)	<.01 (2.7)	.01 (17.3)
Scope of issue	.02 (3.6)	.04 (6.3)	.06 (5.6)	.04 (5.7)	.03 (5.6)	.02 (6.6)	.02 (9.2)	<.01 (3.0)	.02 (7.4)	.01 (5.9)	<.01 (4.0)	<.01 (1.1)
Minimum complexity	.01 (4.1)	<.01 (0.5)	.01 (3.6)	.01 (6.8)	<.01 (2.2)	<.01 (3.2)	>−.01 (−3.8)	<.01 (4.8)	>−.01 (−8.5)	<.01 (8.2)	>−.01 (−3.4)	<.01 (6.0)
Joint referral	−.17 (−4.8)	−.04 (−0.6)	−.33 (−10.4)	−.14 (−3.1)	−.11 (−3.0)	−.24 (−8.5)	−.06 (−3.4)	−.27 (−6.3)	.04 (2.1)	−.17 (−3.5)	−.22 (−11.6)	−.27 (−9.9)
Authorization issue	.07 (0.9)	.05 (0.5)	.05 (0.5)	.01 (0.1)	.04 (0.4)	−.04 (−0.3)	−.04 (−0.7)	.12 (1.7)	.01 (.01)	.08 (0.5)	−.02 (−0.1)	.04 (0.3)
Timing of introduction	−.15 (−2.4)	−.29 (−4.1)	−.19 (−2.9)	−.24 (−4.3)	−.10 (−2.3)	−.27 (−6.2)	−.10 (−2.6)	−.36 (−8.3)	−.07 (−2.2)	−.10 (−1.6)	−.46 (−8.1)	−.40 (−9.2)
Constant	.25 (5.9)	.35 (7.6)	.27 (4.9)	.15 (3.2)	.14 (4.5)	.15 (5.1)	.12 (4.2)	.23 (7.1)	.14 (5.8)	.35 (10.1)	.50 (15.9)	.44 (16.2)
N	651	531	580	690	884	999	1264	1613	1552	1377	1353	1588
R^2	.43	.21	.17	.20	.15	.21	.26	.40	.22	.47	.43	.42

Notes

Notes to Chapter 1

1. Since 1981, the use of radio frequencies had been offered for a nominal license fee and allocated through a lottery. In return for nearly free use of the spectrum, broadcasters were expected to provide emergency broadcasting and other public services.

2. Although Bush's spectrum auctions did not pass in the 102nd Congress, they were enacted in the 103rd Congress under Clinton.

3. Spectrum auctions were first proposed by economists Herzel (1951) and Coase (1959).

4. Reagan's 1988–90 budget proposals included revenue from spectrum auctions, although Reagan did not submit separate draft legislation on the issue (Hazlett 1998). In the last months of Reagan's last Congress (100th), Phil Gramm had introduced S. 2807 in the Senate and Don Ritter introduced H.R. 5166 in the House to implement spectrum auctions. Gramm reintroduced his Senate bill at the beginning of the 101st Congress as S. 170, but not in the 102nd.

5. See Canes-Wrone (2001a); Edwards and Barrett (2000); Edwards, Barrett, and Peake (1997); C. Jones (1994); Light (1991); Peterson (1990); Taylor (1998); and Theriault (2002).

6. For example, Fishel (1985); Huntington (1973); B. Jones (1994); Light (1991); Rohde (1991); Sinclair (1995); Sundquist (1981); Wayne (1978).

7. In his critique of Kingdon's model, Gary Mucciaroni (1992) provides further evidence in the case of the 1986 tax reform that solutions can be linked more closely to problems than Kingdon suggests.

8. Sniderman, Brody, and Tetlock (1991), Popkin (1994), and Lupia and McCubbins (1998), among others, argue that poorly informed voters may still be able to make reasonable vote choices through the use of heuristics, and I argue that the president may provide one of the most powerful heuristics in their voting calculus, since he is the most visible actor in national politics.

Notes to Chapter 2

1. If there is a monopoly agenda setter, it will be able to achieve policies other than the median legislator's by making take-it-or-leave-it policy choices to the floor that do not include the median's position. In such cases, it is inappropriate to use the median voter theorem. In the House, although the Rules Committee can report closed rules prohibiting amendments, these rules must be adopted by majority vote, so it is still appropriate to use the median voter theorem to model the House.

2. Lacy (2001) considers nonseparable preferences in the context of survey analysis.

3. In repeated interaction, however, it may be rational for the president to veto bills in order to build a reputation or in order to force Congress to rewrite a bill in a way that is more favorable to the president (Cameron 2000). Unfortunately, I must ignore such repeated-game concerns in the simple model I construct in this chapter. Nevertheless, veto threats offer very little agenda influence even in the repeated-game models of chapter 3.

Notes to Chapter 3

1. Technically, the ability of House committee and subcommittee chairs to schedule hearings and markups is subject to being overruled by a majority of the panel, but this rarely occurs.

2. Riker (1993) goes one step further and claims that an issue is salient if the voter uses it in her decision making. This suggests that another precondition of salience is that it orders preferences. An issue cannot be salient if the voter is indifferent between all outcomes. But by claiming that salient issues are those that voters use in their decision calculus, Riker assumes away the problem I would like to ask: how does salience affect vote choice?

3. Coherent preferences are defined to be both complete and transitive, as explained in chapter 2.

4. A discount factor less than 1 also helps represent the fact that the voter and her representatives do not expect to live forever in the infinitely repeated game.

Notes to Chapter 4

1. Further deregulation of natural gas was later enacted under President George H. W. Bush in the Natural Gas Wellhead Decontrol Act of 1989 (Public Law No: 101–60).

2. Congress's ability to invite or subpoena experts from the federal bureaucracy to its hearings and to require special reports are less direct mechanisms for such access than the president's control over all draft legislation written by the federal agencies, and modern presidents have maintained some control over these mechanisms, as I discuss in the next section.

3. Requests for executive comment are formal congressional requests for executive agency expertise and recommendations on a pending legislative bill.

4. Congress does have its own institutional sources of expertise, such as the Congres-

sional Budget Office and the General Accounting Office as well as lobbyists and interest groups, but with more than one million civilian employees in the federal bureaucracy (Light 1999) the executive generally holds an informational advantage.

5. "Cheap-talk" models involve signals that impose no direct cost or benefit to the sender or receiver of such signals. The only way such signals can affect the welfare of the agents who send and receive them is if the information conveyed in them leads to a change in behavior that influences their welfare.

6. Another way to characterize agenda setting is as an ordering problem where Congress may take more than one action, i.e., send more than one bill to the president for approval, but it may not take all possible actions at once (Cox and McCubbins 1993). This ordering decision becomes an agenda problem with the introduction of time discounting in repeated play so that actions chosen later will result in lower payoffs than they would if chosen in the present period, thus forcing the scheduler to prioritize actions.

7. Another way for the president to affect the outcome is through the use of the veto or the threat of the veto. The president would only veto Congress's ideal policy if it were further from the president's ideal policy than the status quo is. The veto plays a very limited role in restricting the conditions under which legislative clearance can influence the congressional agenda, as shown in the proof of the legislative clearance equilibrium in Appendix B.

Notes to Chapter 5

1. The other key House committee, Energy and Commerce, however, failed to even bring a bill to markup, because chair John Dingell could not get enough supporters to agree to report a bill from committee that would be acceptable to the president (*CQ Almanac* 1995, 335–36).

2. However, the size of the discretionary budget, which is the subject of Canes-Wrone's studies, is a small fraction of the total federal budget, which is dominated by non-discretionary items like entitlements and interest on the national debt (Schick 1995).

3. I can then also measure to some degree whether the scope exercises a moderating influence on the president's agenda power by introducing an interaction effect (Jaccard and Turrisi 2003). Such tests show that there is no support for the idea that the president's effect on the agenda differs by the level of scope, once scope is controlled for.

4. The following analysis is of the House; I briefly look at the House and Senate together at the end of this chapter. Unlike the House, the Senate has almost no restrictions on nongermane amendments.

5. If committee markup adds nongermane amendments to a bill, these nongermane amendments can be incorporated into a new "clean bill" in order to take advantage of the fact that the original provisions of a bill are immune to the germaneness rule. But such a clean bill must then be introduced in the House and referred back to the committee (Oleszek 2001). This is not so in the more informal environment of the Senate, as I will discuss in the chapter 7.

6. In figures 5.3 and 5.4, I exclude bills already passed in the Senate, which elicit a different pattern to be shown in figures 5.5 and 5.6.

7. I consider committee and subcommittee actions that occur exclusively in House

Commerce. If a jointly referred bill reaches the floor after being reported from another committee, it is not available for floor consideration unless House Commerce also reports or discharges the bill.

8. What I call the textbook legislative process is that usually portrayed in introductory American politics textbooks and includes bill introduction, hearing, markup, floor consideration under a special rule, floor vote, consideration by the other chamber, and signing or vetoing by the president.

9. Oleszek does, however, consider requests for executive comment in his co-authored study of joint referrals (Davidson, Oleszek, and Kephart 1988).

10. I argue that the preferences of the administration rather than the agency matter here, since the administration controls to some degree the information provided by the agency in its comment, even if only indirectly as described by Neustadt (1954).

11. In investigative hearings, the committee may have to rely on executive officials as the only source of information, but it may request testimony under sworn oath, so that it can use sanctions to elicit more truthful testimony.

12. The Corrections Calendar was added in the 104th Congress, when an earlier calendar was eliminated. Neither of these calendars has played an important role in the congressional agenda.

Notes to Chapter 6

1. Exogenous or explanatory variables in figure 6.1 are those that have no causal arrows pointing to them. The levels of these variables are assumed to be set by forces other than those represented in the model. Variables that have causal arrows pointing to them are called endogenous because they are influenced by variables within the model.

2. The committee was called "Interstate and Foreign Commerce" in the 96th, "Energy and Commerce" from the 97th through the 103rd and from the 107th on, and "Commerce" from the 104th through the 106th, but I shall almost always refer to it as just the "House Commerce" Committee in order to avoid confusion.

3. In this case, statistical significance means that if we were able to take repeated independent and identically distributed samples of the same size in the hypothetical case where there is no associaton between the variables, then we would expect less than 10% of these samples to have effects (association) as large as they are in our actual sample.

4. Many of the Public Health Service bills that the House Commerce Committee deals with also have an educational dimension.

5. Before the 96th Congress, no bill could have more than 25 sponsors, so additional sponsors were added by introducing duplicate bills. This makes analysis of the agenda at the bill level misleading, but it also complicates analysis at the issue level because it changes the way that important control variables, like the party of the chief sponsor or the maximum number of sponsors, are measured.

6. "The Constitution gives me relevance. The power of our ideas gives me relevance. The record we have built up over the last two years and the things we're trying to do to implement it, give it relevance. The President is relevant here, especially an activist President. And the fact that I am willing to work with the Republicans. The question is, are they willing to work with me?" (William J. Clinton, Presidential Press Conference, April 18, 1995).

Notes to Chapter 7

1. Only each chamber's Foreign Affairs and Judiciary Committees received more television coverage.

2. Most notably, Brady and Volden (1997) and Krehbiel (1998).

3. The danger still exists that Congress could act on the issue the president indicates but offer legislation that is unacceptable to the president compared to the status quo. It is undeniable that sometimes Congress presents legislation to the president that it is confident he will veto. This was a conscious strategy of the Democratic leadership under Speaker James Wright in the 100th Congress. Similarly, the president also often requests action on policy issues, such as the line-item veto under Reagan and Bush, which he is confident that the Congress will not deliver. Such position taking can serve strategic purposes for both the president and Congress. The role of such "blame-game" legislation is ignored here for the purpose of analyzing the president's influence on the congressional agenda. See Groseclose and McCarty (2001).

4. The role of conference committees in policy making is considered at length in Longley and Oleszek (1989) and treated formally in Tsebelis and Money (1997).

5. In figure 5.6, I plot all issues that were covered by all House bills referred to Senate Commerce rather than just those issues initiated by House bills.

Notes to Chapter 8

1. In particular, Reagan submitted H.R. 6720, "[a] bill to authorize the formation of a bank securities affiliate to deal in, underwrite and purchase government and municipal securities, to sponsor and manage investment companies and underwrite the securities thereof" in the 97th Congress; H.R. 3537, "[a] bill to authorize depository institution holding companies to engage in activities of a financial nature, insurance underwriting and brokerage, real estate development and brokerage, and certain securities activities," in the 98th Congress; and H.R. 1603, "[a] bill to amend the Securities Exchange Act of 1934 to authorize the Securities and Exchange Commission to subject banks, associations, and other entities that exercise fiduciary powers, to the same regulations as broker-dealers" in the 99th Congress.

2. The model of draft legislation in chapter 4 also suggests that the informational advantage of the executive branch offers the president a more permanent influence over the congressional agenda than public addresses. While public addresses are only effective in a president's early Congresses, the influence he exercises through draft legislation can persist through his last Congress.

3. Legislative organizations, such as the General Accounting Office and the Congressional Research Service, are essentially bicameral organizations that provide common resources to the House and Senate, offering some counterpoint to executive policy expertise.

Note to Appendix A

1. The payoff for each action is calculated to include all of the actions in the remaining periods of the infinite game, assuming the other actors play their equilibrium strate-

gies. I take advantage of a property of infinite sequences to simplify these infinite-period payoffs. The sum of an infinite sequence of terms like the discount factor δ^k, where $0 < \delta < 1$ and $k = 0, 1, 2, \ldots \infty$, is simply $1/(1 - \delta)$ and the sum from $k = 1, 2, \ldots \infty$ is $\delta/(1 - \delta)$. For sequences of numbers that occur only periodically, like presidents' first Congresses, we can summarize for $k = 0, 4, \ldots \infty$ in the case where all presidents serve two terms, yielding $1/(1 - \delta^4)$, or for $k = 4, \ldots \infty$ the sum is $\delta^4/(1 - \delta^4)$. Non-presidential election years can be summarized simply by subtracting the sum for presidential election years from the sum for all years, e.g., $[\delta/(1 - \delta)] - [\delta^4/(1 - \delta^4)] = (\delta + \delta^2\delta^3)/(1 - \delta^4)$. There will be variations on these sums depending on whether the president is reelected after two Congresses.

Note to Appendix D

1. Amundsen (1973) and Amemiya (1977) have also shown that if the LPM includes only dichotomous variables and all possible interactions among the independent variables, then it is the same as the maximum likelihood estimator, which means that it is guaranteed to be an ideal estimator for large samples.

Note to Appendix E

1. One may also calculate the direct effect of the president on the agenda in the previous example simply by omitting the committee leader control variable. The president's total effect , $\beta_1 + \alpha_1\beta_2$ is equal to the slope of a bivariate regression that does not "hold constant" the committee chair's influence. This does indeed produce an unbiased estimate of the president's total (direct + indirect) effect, but because the committee leader's influence is absorbed in the error term (unexplained causes), this model has errors that are correlated with presidential agenda independent variables, a condition called "endogeneity," which leads to invalid standard errors and statistical tests.

Bibliography

Achen, Christopher H., and W. Philips Shively. 1995. *Cross-Level Inference.* Chicago: University of Chicago Press.

Aldrich, John H. 1995. *Why Parties? The Origin and Transformation of Party Politics in America.* Chicago: University of Chicago Press.

Aldrich, John H., and David Rohde. 1995. "Theories of Party in the Legislature and the Transition to Republican Rule in the House." Paper presented at the Annual Meeting of the American Political Science Association, Chicago, IL.

Allard, Nicholas W. 1993. "The New Spectrum Auction Law." *Seton Hall Legislative Journal* 18:13.

Amemiya, Takeshi. 1977. "Some Theorems in the Linear Probability Model." *International Economic Review* 18(3):645–650.

Amundsen, H. T. 1974. "Binary Variable Multiple Regression." *Scandinavian Journal of Statistics* 1:59–70.

Anderson, Donald K. 1991. *Rules of the House of Representatives.* Washington, DC: U.S. Government Printing Office.

Atkeson, Lonna Rae, and Randall W. Partin. 1995. "Economic and Referendum Voting: A Comparison of Gubernatorial and Senatorial Elections." *American Political Science Review* 89:99–107.

Austen-Smith, David. 1990. "Information Transmission in Debate." *American Journal of Political Science* 34:124–52.

Austen-Smith, David. 1992. "Explaining the Vote: Constituency Constraints on Sophisticated Voting." *American Journal of Political Science* 36:68–95.

Baker, Ross K. 1989. *House and Senate.* New York: W. W. Norton.

Banks, Jeffrey S. 1990. "Monopoly Agenda Control and Asymmetric Information." *Quarterly Journal of Economics* 105:445–64.

Banks, J., Mark Olsen, David Porter, Stephen Rassenti, and Vernon Smith. 2003. "Theory, Experiment, and the Federal Communications Commission Spectrum Auctions." *Journal of Economic Behavior and Organization* 51:303–50.

Barone, Michael, Grant Ujifusa, and Richard E. Cohen. 1997. *The Almanac of American Politics, 1998.* Washington, DC: National Journal.

Baumgartner, Frank R., and Bryan D. Jones. 1993. *Agendas and Instability in American Politics.* Chicago: University of Chicago Press.

Baumgartner, Frank R., Bryan D. Jones, and Michael MacLeod. 1998. "Lessons from the Trenches: Ensuring Quality, Reliability, and Usability in the Creation of a New Data Source." *The Political Methodologist* 8:1–10.

Binder, Sarah A., and Steven S. Smith. 1995. *Politics or Principle: Filibustering in the United States Senate.* Washington, DC: Brookings Institution Press.

Bond, Jon R., and Richard Fleisher. 1990. *The President in the Legislative Arena.* Chicago: University of Chicago Press.

Bowles, Nigel. 1987. *The White House and Capitol Hill: The Politics of Presidential Persuasion.* Oxford: Oxford University Press.

Brady, David W., and Craig Volden. 1997. *Revolving Gridlock: Politics and Policy from Carter to Clinton.* Boulder, CO: Westview Press.

Brandt, Patrick T. 2001. "Lawmaking and Separated Powers: Agenda Setting in Executive-Congressional Relations and Budgeting." Ph.D. diss., Indiana University.

Brown, William, and Charles Johnson, III. 1996. *House Practice: A Guide to the Rules, Precedents, and Procedures of the House.* Washington, DC: U.S. Government Printing Office.

Cameron, Charles M. 2000. *Veto Bargaining: Presidents and the Politics of Negative Power.* Cambridge: Cambridge University Press.

Canes-Wrone, Brandice. 2001. "A Theory of Presidents' Public Agenda Setting." *Journal of Theoretical Politics* 13(2):183–208.

Canes-Wrone, Brandice, M. C. Herron, and K. W. Shotts. 2001. "Leadership and Pandering: A Theory of Executive Policymaking." *American Journal of Political Science* 45(3):532–50.

Carmines, Edward G., and James H. Kuklinski. 1990. "Incentives, Opportunities, and the Logic of Public Opinion in American Political Representation." In *Information and Democratic Processes,* ed. John A. Ferejohn. Urbana: University of Illinois Press.

Caudill, Steven B. 1988. "An Advantage of the Linear Probability Model over Probit or Logit." *Oxford Bulletin of Economics and Statistics* 50(4):425–27.

Chamberlain, Lawrence. 1946. *The President, Congress, and Legislation.* New York: AMS Press.

Clarke, Harold D., and Marianne C. Stewart. 1994. "Prospections, Retrospections, and Rationality: The 'Bankers' Model of Presidential Approval Reconsidered." *American Journal of Political Science* 38:1104–23.

Coase, R. H. 1959. "The Federal Communications Commission." *Journal of Law and Economics* 2:1–40.

Cohen, Jeffrey E. 1997. *Presidential Responsiveness and Public Policy-Making.* Ann Arbor: University of Michigan Press.

Cohen, Jeffrey , J. R. Bond, R. Fleisher, and J. A. Hamman. 2000. "State-Level Presidential Approval and Senatorial Support." *Legislative Science Quarterly* 25:577–90.

Cohen, M. D. , J. G. March, and J. P. Olsen. 1972. "A Garbage Can Model of Organizational Choice." *Administrative Science Quarterly* 17:1–25.

Collier, Kenneth, and Terry Sullivan. 1995. "New Evidence Undercutting the Linkage of Approval with Presidential Support and Influence." *Journal of Politics* 57:197–209.

Collier, Kenneth E. 1997. *Between the Branches: The White House Office of Legislative Affairs.* Pittsburgh: University of Pittsburgh Press.

Committee on Commerce, House. 1995–2000. *Final Legislative Calendar.* Washington, DC: U.S. Government Printing Office.

Committee on Commerce, Science, and Transportation, Senate. 1979–1996. *Final Legislative Calendar.* Washington, DC: U.S. Government Printing Office.

Committee on Energy and Commerce, House. 1981–1994, 2001–2002. *Final Legislative Calendar.* Washington, DC: U.S. Government Printing Office.

Committee on Interstate and Foreign Commerce, House. 1979–1980. *Final Legislative Calendar.* Washington, DC: U.S. Government Printing Office.

Congressional Quarterly. 1977–2002. *CQ Almanac.* Washington, DC: Brookings Institution Press.

Conley, Patricia. 2001. *Presidential Mandates: How Elections Shape the National Agenda.* Chicago: University of Chicago Press.

Cooper, Joseph. 1970. *The Origins of the Standing Committees and the Development of the Modern House.* Houston, TX: Rice University Studies.

Cover, Albert D. 1985. "Presidential Evaluations and Voting for Congress." *American Journal of Political Science* 30:786–801.

Covington, Cary, J. Mark Wrighton, and Rhonda Kinney. 1995. "A Presidency-Augmented Model of Presidential Success on House Roll Call Votes." *American Journal of Political Science* 39:1001–24.

Cox, Gary W., and Matthew D. McCubbins. 1993. *Legislative Leviathan.* Berkeley: University of California Press.

Crawford, Vincent P., and Joel Sobel. 1982. "Strategic Information Transmission." *Econometrica* 50:1431–51.

Dahl, Robert. 1990. "The Myth of the Presidential Mandate." *Political Science Quarterly* 105:355–72.

Davidson Roger H., Walter J. Oleszek, and Thomas Kephart. 1988. "One Bill, Many Committees: Multiple Referrals in the U.S. House of Representatives." *Legislative Studies Quarterly* 13:3–28.

Deschler, Lewis. 1977. *Precedents of the United States House of Representatives.* Washington, DC: U.S. Government Printing Office.

Deschler, Lewis, and William Holmes Brown. 1984. *Procedures in the U.S. House of Representatives: A Summary of the Modern Precedents and Practices of the House.* Washington, DC: U.S. Government Printing Office.

Dion, Douglas. 1997. *Turning the Legislative Thumbscrew: Minority Rights and Procedural Change in Legislative Politics.* Ann Arbor: University of Michigan Press.

Downs, Anthony. 1957. *An Economic Theory of Democracy.* New York: Harper and Row.

Edwards, George C., and Andrew Barrett. 2000. "Presidential Agenda Setting in Congress." In *Polarized Politics: Congress and the President in a Partisan Era,* ed. Jon R. Bond and Richard Fleisher, 109–33. Washington, DC: CQ Press.

Edwards, George C., Andrew Barrett, and Jeffrey Peake. 1997. "The Legislative Impact of Divided Government." *American Journal of Political Science* 41:545–63.

Edwards, George C., William Mitchell, and Reed Welch. 1995. "Explaining Presidential Approval: The Significance of Issue Salience." *American Journal of Political Science* 39:108–34.

Edwards, George C., and B. Dan Wood. 1999. "Who Influences Whom? The President, Congress, and the Media." *American Political Science Review* 93:327–44.

Edwards, George C. 1980. *Presidential Influence in Congress.* San Francisco, CA: W. H. Freeman and Co.

Edwards, George C. 1989. *At The Margins: Presidential Leadership of Congress.* New Haven, CT: Yale University Press.

Eisinger, Robert M. 2003. *The Evolution of Presidential Polling.* Cambridge: Cambridge University Press.

Epstein, David, and Sharyn O'Halloran. 1999. *Delegating Powers: A Transaction Cost Politics Approach to Policy Making Under Separate Powers.* Cambridge: Cambridge University Press.

Evans, C. Lawrence. 1991. *Leadership in Committee: A Comparative Analysis of Leadership Behavior in the U.S. Senate.* Ann Arbor: University of Michigan Press.

Farrell, Joseph, and Matthew Rabin. 1996. "Cheap Talk." *Journal of Economic Perspectives* 10(3):103–18.

Feldman, Martha S. 1989. *Order without Design: Information Production and Policy Making.* Palo Alto, CA: Stanford University Press.

Ferejohn, John. 1987. "Incumbent Performance and Electoral Control." *Public Choice* 50:5–25.

Fiorina, Morris. 1981. *Retrospective Voting in American National Elections.* New Haven, CT: Yale University Press.

Fiorina, Morris P., and Kenneth A. Shepsle. 1990. "A Positive Theory of Negative Voting." In *Information and Democratic Processes,* ed. John A. Ferejohn. Urbana: University of Illinois Press.

Fishel, Jeff. 1985. *Presidents and Promises: From Campaign Pledge to Presidential Performance.* Washington, DC: CQ Press.

Flemming, Roy B., B. D. Wood, and J. Bohte. 1999. "Attention to Issues in a System of Separated Powers: The Macrodynamics of American Policy Agendas." *Journal of Politics* 61(1):76–108.

Francis, Wayne L., Lawrence W. Kenny, Rebecca B. Morton, and Amy B. Schmidt. 1994. "Retrospective Voting and Political Mobility." *American Journal of Political Science* 38:999–1024.

Fudenberg, Drew, and Jean Tirole. 1991. *Game Theory.* Cambridge, MA: MIT Press.

Galloway, George B. 1994. *History of the House of Representatives, 1789–1994.* Washington, DC: U.S. Government Printing Office.

Gerber, Elisabeth A., and John E. Jackson. 1993. "Endogenous Preferences and the Study of Institutions." *American Political Science Review* 87:639–56.

Gilligan, Thomas W., and Keith Krehbiel. 1987. "Collective Decision-Making and Standing Committees: An Informational Rationale for Restrictive Amendment Procedures." *Journal of Law, Economics, and Organization* 3:287–335.

Gilmour, Robert S. 1971. "Central Legislative Clearance: A Revised Perspective." *Public Administration Review* 31:150–58.

Ginsburg, Benjamin and Martin Shefter. 1990. *Politics by Other Means: The Declining Importance of Elections in America.* New York: Basic Books.

Goldberger, Arthur S. 1964. *Econometric Theory.* New York: Wiley.

Goldsmith, William M. 1983. *The Growth of Presidential Power.* 3 vols. New York: Chelsea House.

Greene, William. 2003. *Econometric Analysis,* 5th ed. New York: Macmillan Publishing Co.

Gronke, Paul, Jeffrey Koch, and J. Matthew Wilson. 2003. "Presidential Approval, Presidential Support, and Representatives' Electoral Fortunes." *Journal of Politics* 65:785–808.

Groseclose, Tim, and N. McCarty. 2001. "The Politics of Blame: Bargaining Before an Audience." *American Journal of Political Science* 45:100–19.

Hager, Gregory L., and Terry Sullivan. 1994. "President-centered and Presidency-centered Explanations of Presidential Public Activity." *American Journal of Political Science* 38:1079–1103.

Hall, Richard L. 1996. *Participation in Congress.* New Haven, CT: Yale University Press.

Hammond, Thomas H. 1986. "Agenda Control, Organizational Structure, and Bureaucratic Politics." *American Journal of Political Science* 30(2):379–420.

Hansen, J. Mark. 1992. *Gaining Access.* Chicago: University of Chicago Press.

Harsanyi, J. C. 1973. "Games with Incomplete Information Played by 'Bayesian' Players." *Management Science* 14:159–82, 320–34, 486–502.

Hazlett, Thomas W. 1998. "Assigning Property Rights to Radio Spectrum Users: Why Did FCC License Auctions Take 67 Years?" *Journal of Law and Economics* 41:529–37.

Herzel, Leo. 1951. "Public Interest and the Market in Color Television Regulation." *University of Chicago Law Review* 18:802–16.

Hetherington, Marc J. 1996. "The Media's Role in Forming Voters' National Economic Evaluations in 1992." *American Journal of Political Science* 40:372–95.

Himelfarb, Richard. 1995. *Catastrophic Politics: The Rise and Fall of the Medicare Catastrophic Coverage Act of 1988.* State College: Pennsylvania State University Press.

Huntington, Samuel. 1973. "Congressional Responses to the Twentieth Century." In *The Congress and America's Future,* 2d ed., ed. David B. Truman, 6–38. Englewood Cliffs, NJ: Prentice Hall.

Ingberman, Daniel, and Dennis Yao. 1991a. "Circumventing Formal Structure Through Commitment: Presidential Influence and Agenda Control." *Public Choice* 70:151–79.

Ingberman, Daniel, and Dennis Yao. 1991b. "Presidential Commitment and the Veto." *American Journal of Political Science* 35:351–89.

Iyengar, Shanto, and Donald R. Kinder. 1987. *News That Matters: Television and Public Opinion.* Chicago: University of Chicago Press.

Jaccard, James, and Robert Turrisi. 2003. *Interaction Effects in Multiple Regression,* 2d ed. Thousand Oaks, CA: Sage.

Jackson, John E., and David C. King. 1989. "Public Goods, Private Interests, and Representation." *American Political Science Review* 83:1143–64.

Jacobson, Gary, and Samuel Kernell. 1983. *Strategy and Choice in Congressional Elections.* New Haven, CT: Yale University Press.

Johnson, Haynes, and David S. Broder. 1996. *The System: The American Way of Politics at the Breaking Point.* Boston: Little, Brown and Co.

Joint Committee on the Organization of Congress. 1993. *Organization of Congress.* Washington, DC: U.S. Government Printing Office.

Jones, Bryan D. 1994. *Reconceiving Decision-Making in Democratic Politics: Attention, Choice, and Public Policy.* Chicago: University of Chicago Press.

Jones, Bryan D., Frank R. Baumgartner, and Jeffrey C. Talbert. 1993. "The Destruction of

Issue Monopolies in Congress." *American Political Science Review* 87:657–71.

Jones, Charles O. 1994. *The Presidency in a Separated System.* Washington, DC: Brookings Institution Press.

Kelley, Stanley. 1983. *Interpreting Elections.* Princeton, NJ: Princeton University Press.

Kernell, Samuel. 1991. "Facing an Opposition Congress: The President's Strategic Advantage." In *The Politics of Divided Government,* ed. Gary Cox and Samuel Kernell. Boulder, CO: Westview Press.

Kernell, Samuel. 1993. *Going Public: New Strategies of Presidential Leadership.* Washington, DC: CQ Press.

Kessel, John H. 2001. *Presidents, the Presidency, and the Political Environment.* Washington, DC: CQ Press.

Kessler, Daniel, and Keith Krehbiel. 1996. "Dynamics of Cosponsorship." *American Political Science Review* 90:555–66.

King, David C. 1997. *Turf Wars: How Congressional Committees Claim Jurisdiction.* Chicago: University of Chicago Press.

Kingdon, John W. [1984] 1995. *Agendas, Alternatives, and Public Policies.* New York: HarperCollins.

Kline, Rex. 1998. *Principles and Practice of Structural Equation Modeling.* New York: Guilford Press.

Krehbiel, Keith. 1991. *Information and Legislative Organization.* Ann Arbor, MI: University of Michigan Press.

Krehbiel, Keith. 1998. *Pivotal Politics: A Theory of U.S. Lawmaking.* Chicago: University of Chicago Press.

Lacy, Dean. 2001. "Nonseparable Preferences, Measurement Error, and Unstable Survey Responses." *Political Analysis* 9(2):1–21.

Larocca, Roger. 2004. "Strategic Diversion in Political Communication." *Journal of Politics* 66(2):188–207.

Light, Paul C. 1991. *The President's Agenda: Domestic Policy Choice from Kennedy to Reagan,* 3d ed. Baltimore, MD: Johns Hopkins University Press.

Light, Paul C. 1999. *The True Size of Government.* Washington, DC: Brookings Institution Press.

Lodge, Milton, Marco R. Steenbergen, and Shawn Brau. 1995. "The Responsive Voter: Campaign Information and the Dynamics of Candidate Evaluation." *American Political Science Review* 89:309–26.

Longley, Lawrence D., and Walter J. Oleszek. 1989. *Bicameral Politics: Conference Committees in Congress.* New Haven, CT: Yale University Press.

Luce, Robert B. 1926. *Congress: An Explanation.* Cambridge, MA: Harvard University Press.

Lupia, Arthur, and M. McCubbins. 1998. *The Democratic Dilemma: Can Citizens Learn What They Need to Know?* Cambridge: Cambridge University Press.

MacKuen, Michael B., Robert S. Erickson, and James A. Stimson. 1992. "Peasants or Bankers? The American Electorate and the U.S. Economy." *American Political Science Review* 86:597–611.

Matthews, Stephen A. 1989. "Veto Threats: Rhetoric in a Bargaining Game." *The Quarterly Journal of Economics* 104:347–69.

Mayhew, David. 1991. *Divided We Govern: Party Control, Lawmaking, and Investigations 1946–1990.* New Haven, CT: Yale University Press.

McCarty, Nolan, and Lawrence S. Rothenberg. 1996. "Commitment and the Campaign Contribution Contract." *American Journal of Political Science* 40:872–904.

McCombs, Maxwell, and Jian-Hua Zhu. 1995. "Capacity, Diversity, and Volatility of the Public Agenda." *The Public Opinion Quarterly* 59(4): 495–525.

Miller, Gary J. 1993. "Formal Theory and the Presidency." In *Researching the Presidency: Vital Questions, New Approaches,* ed. George C. Edwards III, John Kessel, and Bert Rockman. Pittsburgh, PA: University of Pittsburgh Press.

Miller, George. 1956. "The Magic Number Seven, Plus or Minus Two." *Psychological Review* 63:81–97.

Miller, Jeffrey C. 1994. "The Role of Information in Public Policy Making." *Health Policy on Target,* August 1, 1994.

Mills, Mike. 1990. "Tight Squeeze on Spectrum Tunes Out New Uses." *Congressional Quarterly Weekly Report,* September 8, 1990.

Mills, Mike. 1991a. "Communications: Administration Renews Push for Airwaves Auction." *Congressional Quarterly Weekly Report,* March 2, 1991.

Mills, Mike. 1991b. "Communications: Veto Threat Follows Approval of Spectrum-Transfer Bill." *Congressional Quarterly Weekly Report,* July 13, 1991.

Mills, Mike. 1993. "Telecommunications: Energy and Commerce OKs Bill to Sell Radio Frequencies." *Congressional Quarterly Weekly Report,* May 15, 1993.

Moe, Terry. 1994. "Presidents, Institutions, and Theory." In *Researching the Presidency: Vital Questions, New Approaches,* ed. George C. Edwards III, John Kessel, and Bert Rockman. Pittsburgh, PA: University of Pittsburgh Press.

Moe, Terry, and S. C. Teel. 1970. "Congress and Policy Maker: A Necessary Reappraisal." *Political Science Quarterly* 85:443–70.

Mouw, Calvin, and Michael MacKuen. 1992. "The Strategic Agenda in Legislative Politics." *American Political Science Review* 86:87–105.

Mucciaroni, Gary. 1992. "The Garbage Can Model and the Study of Policy-making: A Critique." *Polity* 24:459–82.

Munger, Michael C., and G. M. Torrent. 1993. "Committee Power and Value in the U.S. Senate: Implications for Policy." *Journal of Public Administration Research and Theory* 3(1):46–65.

National Telecommunications and Information Administration. 1991. "U.S. Spectrum Management Policy: Agenda for the Future." Washington, DC: U.S. Government Printing Office.

Nelson, Michael, ed. 2002. *Guide to the Presidency,* 3d ed. Washington, DC: CQ Press.

Neustadt, Richard. 1954. "Presidency and Legislation: The Growth of Central Clearance." *American Political Science Review* 48:641–71.

Neustadt, Richard. 1990. *Presidential Power and the Modern Presidents.* New York: Macmillan.

Oleszek, Walter J. 2001. *Congressional Procedures and the Policy Process.* Washington, DC: CQ Press.

Peterson, Mark A. 1990. *Legislating Together.* Cambridge, MA: Harvard University Press.

Peterson, Mark A. 1992. "How Health Policy Is Used in Congress." In *Intensive Care: How Congress Shapes Health Policy,* ed. T. E. Mann and N. J. Ornstein. Washington, DC: Brookings Institution Press.

Peterson, Mark A. 1995. "The Presidency and Organized Interests: White House Patterns of Interest Group Liaison." *American Political Science Review* 86:612–25.

Petrocik, John R. 1996. "Issue Ownership in Presidential Elections, with a 1980 Case Study." *American Journal of Political Science* 40:825–50.

Pitkin, Hanna Fenichel. 1967. *The Concept of Representation.* Berkeley: University of California Press.

Ponder, Daniel E. 2000. *Good Advice: Information and Policy Making in the White House.* College Station: Texas A&M University Press.

Poole, Keith T., and Howard Rosenthal. 1997. *Congress: A Political-Economic History of Roll Call Voting.* Oxford: Oxford University Press.

Popkin, Samuel. 1994. *The Reasoning Voter: Communication and Persuasion in Presidential Campaigns.* Chicago: University of Chicago Press.

Ragsdale, Lyn. 1998. *Vital Statistics on the Presidency.* Washington, DC: CQ Press.

Reagan, Ronald. 1981. *Public Papers of the President of the United States: Ronald Reagan, 1981.* Washington, DC: U.S. Government Printing Office.

Riker, William H. 1993. "Rhetorical Interaction in the Ratification Campaigns." In *Agenda Formation,* ed. William H. Riker. Ann Arbor: University of Michigan Press.

Rivers, Douglas, and Nancy Rose. 1985. "Passing the President's Program: Public Opinion and Presidential Influence in Congress." *American Journal of Political Science* 29:397–427.

Rohde, David W. 1991. *Parties and Leaders in the Postreform House.* Chicago: University of Chicago Press.

Romer, Thomas, and Howard Rosenthal. 1978. "Political Resource Allocation, Controlled Agendas, and the Status Quo." *Public Choice* 33:27–44.

Rovner, Julie. 1995. "Congress and Health Care Reform 1993–94." In *Intensive Care: How Congress Shapes Health Policy,* ed. T. E. Mann and N. J. Ornstein. Washington, DC: Brookings Institution Press.

Rubenstine, Ariel. 1998. *Modeling Bounded Rationality.* Cambridge, MA: MIT Press.

Rudalevige, Andrew. 2002. *Managing the President's Program: Presidential Leadership and Legislative Policy Formation.* Princeton, NJ: Princeton University Press.

Schick, Allen. 1995. *The Federal Budget: Politics, Policy, Process.* Washington, DC: Brookings Institution Press.

Shaw, Donald, and Maxwell McCombs. 1977. *The Emergence of American Political Issues: The Agenda-Setting Function of the Press.* St. Paul, MN: West Publishing Co.

Shull, Steven A. 2000. *Presidential-Congressional Relations: Policy and Time Approaches.* Ann Arbor: University of Michigan Press.

Simon, Dennis M., Charles W. Ostrom, and Robin F. Marra. 1991. "The President, Referendum Voting, and Subnational Elections in the United States." *American Political Science Review* 85:1177–92.

Simon, Herbert A. 1955. "A Behavioral Model of Rational Choice." *Quarterly Journal of Economics* 69:99–118.

Simon, Herbert A. 1956. "Rational Choice and the Structure of the Environment." *Psychological Review* 63:129–38.

Simon, Herbert A. 1982. *Models of Bounded Rationality.* Cambridge, MA: MIT Press.

Sinclair, Barbara. 1986. "The Role of Committees in Agenda Setting in the U.S. Congress." *Legislative Studies Quarterly* 11:35–45.

Sinclair, Barbara. 1989. *The Transformation of the U.S. Senate.* Baltimore, MD: Johns Hopkins University Press.

Sinclair, Barbara. 1995. *Legislators, Leaders and Lawmaking: The U.S. House of Representatives in the Postreform Era.* Baltimore, MD: Johns Hopkins University Press.

Sinclair, Barbara. 1997. *Unorthodox Lawmaking: New Legislative Processes in the U.S. Congress.* Washington, DC: CQ Press.

Smith, Steven S. 1989. *Call to Order: Floor Politics in the House and Senate.* Washington, DC: Brookings Institution Press.

Smith, Steven S., and Christopher Deering. 1990. *Committees in Congress.* Washington, DC: CQ Press.

Sniderman, Paul, Richard A. Brody, and Philip E. Tetlock. 1991. *Reasoning and Choice: Explorations in Political Psychology.* Cambridge: Cambridge University Press.

Spitzer, Robert J. 1988. *The Presidential Veto: Touchstone of the American Presidency.* Albany, NY: SUNY Press.

Spitzer, Robert J. 1993. *President and Congress: Executive Hegemony at the Crossroads of American Government.* New York: McGraw Hill.

Steger, Wayne P. 1997. "Presidential Policy Initiation and the Politics of Agenda Control." *Congress and the Presidency* 24:17–36.

Stewart III, Charles H. 1989. *Budget Reform Politics: The Design of the Appropriations Process in the House of Representatives, 1865–1921.* Cambridge: Cambridge University Press.

Stimson, James A. 1990. "A Macro Theory of Information Flow." In *Information and Democratic Processes,* ed. John A. Ferejohn. Urbana: University of Illinois Press.

Stimson, James A., Michael B. Mackuen, and Robert S. Erickson. 1995. "Dynamic Representation." *American Political Science Review* 89:543–65.

Sullivan, Terry. 1988. "Headcounts, Expectations, and Presidential Coalitions in Congress." *American Journal of Political Science* 32:567–89.

Sundquist, James L. 1981. *The Decline and Resurgence of Congress.* Washington, DC: Brookings Institution Press.

Sundquist, James L. 1988. "Needed: A Political Theory for the New Era of Coalition Government in the United States." *Political Science Quarterly* 103:613–35.

Swift, Elaine K. et al. 2004. *Database of Congressional Historical Statistics, 1789–1989.* ICPSR version. Ann Arbor, MI: Inter-University Consortium for Political and Social Research.

Taylor, Andrew J. 1998. "Domestic Agenda Setting: 1947–1994." *Legislative Studies Quarterly* 23:373–97.

Theriault, Sean M. 2002. "Lawmaking and the Modern Congress: Getting on the Legislative Agenda." Paper Presented at the Annual Meeting of the American Political Science Association, Boston, MA.

Thurber, James A., ed. 1996. *Rivals for Power: Presidential-Congressional Relations.* Washington, DC: CQ Press.

Tsebelis, George, and Jeannette Money. 1997. *Bicameralism.* Cambridge: Cambridge University Press.

Tversky, Amos, and D. Kahneman. 1974. "Judgment under Uncertainty: Heuristics and Biases." *Science* 185:1124–31.

Walker, Jack L. 1977. "Setting the Agenda in the U.S. Senate." *British Political Science Review* 7:423–45.

Wayne, Stephen J. 1978. *The Legislative Presidency.* New York: Harper and Row.

Weissert, Carol S., and William G. Weissert. 2002. *Governing Health: The Politics of*

Health Policy, 2d ed. Baltimore, MD: Johns Hopkins University Press.

White, Halbert. 1980. "A Heteroscedasticity-Consistent Covariance Matrix Estimator and a Direct Test for Heteroscedasticity." *Econometrica* 48:817–38.

Wilson, Rick K., and Cheryl D. Young. 1997. "Cosponsorship in the U.S. Congress." *Legislative Studies Quarterly* 22:25–43.

Wooldridge, Jeffrey M. 2003. *Econometric Analysis of Cross Section and Panel Data.* Cambridge, MA: MIT Press.

Zhu, Jian-Hua. 1992. "Issue Competition and Attention Distraction: A Zero-Sum Theory of Agenda-Setting." *Journalism Quarterly* 69:825–36.

Index

Parliaments and Legislatures
Janet M. Box-Steffensmeier and David T. Canon, Series Editors

Parliaments and Legislatures is a series of books on legislative and parliamentary assemblies across the globe, with a focus on the U.S. Congress. We are actively recruiting new work of high quality and innovation for publication in the series and welcome all methodological approaches.